MUSIC IN AMERICAN LIFE

Books in the series:

A Texas-Mexican *Cancionero*

A
Texas-Mexican
Cancionero

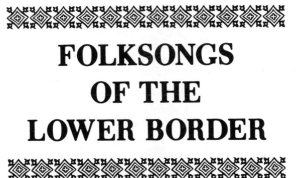

FOLKSONGS
OF THE
LOWER BORDER

Américo Paredes

UNIVERSITY OF ILLINOIS PRESS

Urbana   Chicago   London

© 1976 by the Board of Trustees of the University of Illinois
Manufactured in the United States of America
1 2 3 4 5 P 87 85 83 81

Library of Congress Cataloging in Publication Data
Main entry under title:

A Texas-Mexican *cancionero*.

(Music in American life)
Words in Spanish; includes English translations.
Bibliography: pp. 187-189.
Includes index.
1. Folk-songs, Spanish — Texas. 2. Folk-songs,
Mexican. I. Paredes, Américo.
M1668.4.T49   784.7'5   75-16393
ISBN 0-252-00522-8 (cloth)
ISBN 0-252-00894-4 (paper)

To the memory of my mother,
who could sing a song or two;
and to all the other singers
of the Border,
who left part of themselves
in my keeping.

CONTENTS

The country of the songs. This map locates the major historical events mentioned in the songs of the Lower Rio Grande Border. *Based on a map by Ed Miller*

PREFACE

Although *cancionero* means "songbook," it may also refer to a corpus of folksong. *A Texas-Mexican Cancionero* pretends to be both: a songbook and a representative collection of the folksong corpus of a Texas-Mexican area (the Lower Rio Grande Border) at a particular period in history (1750-1960). While not all-inclusive, it does attempt to give examples of the main forms and the principal themes in Texas-Mexican folksong.

There is only one musical form not represented, the old style of tune used in singing the *décima*. Most *décima* tunes are based on singing styles antedating modern music and present serious difficulties for the average person both in the transcription and in the reading of the music. This book is intended for the average reader rather than for the professional musician; and, as transcriber of tunes, I consider myself somewhat below average. Readers interested in the musical form of the Texas-Mexican *décima* are referred to "The *Décima Cantada* on the Texas-Mexican Border: Four Examples," with musical transcriptions and analysis by George Foss.[1] The *décima* as a poetic form may be found in "El huérfano" (no. 46), which is sung to a *corrido* tune.

The sixty-six songs in this volume were chosen from a Texas-Mexican repertory several times as large. The criterion used in selecting the songs for inclusion was that they be associated with the area or representative of it in some way. Compositions that became current during the 1960s and 1970s are not included. Also excluded are songs that have been universal throughout the Greater Mexican area and that have no particular ties with Lower Border history or attitudes. At least half of the songs included are *corridos*, but the reader will find other folksongs as well. Contrary to popular belief, not all Mexican folksongs are *corridos*. There are several examples of the *danza*, by the way, which has been practically ignored by folklorists as one of the forms of Mexican folksong.

[1] Américo Paredes and George Foss, "The *Décima Cantada* on the Texas-Mexican Border: Four Examples," *Journal of the Folklore Institute* 3:2 (August, 1966), 91-155.

The musicologist and the analyst of folk literature may find little to interest them in the pages to follow. These are songs I have known and sung during the past fifty years or so. I have set down here my own variants of them, my variants as sung at one particular time and place—Austin, Texas, in the early 1970s. I will not imitate some published "folksongers" and claim folkloric status for my repertory because I once was a member of the "folk." I do say, however, that the variants are simple and honest, as I have sung them and heard them sung many times among other Texas-Mexicans. But they are not the minutely faithful transcriptions of specific performances required for scholarly analysis and should not be taken as such.

My main interest has been in the meaning the songs have had for the people who have sung them. From the viewpoint of cultural history, then, the songs and the background materials accompanying them may be of some value. The book speaks to the descendants of the people who made the history in which the songs are embedded. It is their *cancionero*. But it may also serve as an introduction to anyone who is seriously interested in pursuing the study of the folksongs of Greater Mexico. It is with this thought that the Notes to the Songs and the Bibliography are offered. In the Notes to the Songs, I have limited myself to placing each song within the context of Greater Mexican folksong, so only Mexican and Mexican-American references are given. They can serve, along with the Bibliography, as a point of departure for further study. Also given are references to field-recorded performances in the Library of Congress (AAFS) and the University of Texas Folklore Archives at Austin. Very few of these songs have been studied in depth—"Gregorio Cortez," "José Mosqueda," and "Benjamín Argumedo" are among those few. Almost any one of the others is worthy of a paper, a monograph, or a book.

English versions of the song texts are included for the benefit of those readers who may have some difficulty with the original Spanish. These are literal prose translations and not attempts at poetry. Words that are not easily translatable without a great deal of explanation have been left in Spanish and are italicized. Most of such terms are discussed in the Glossary. English words found in the original Spanish are underlined. Besides the Spanish words taken from the translations, the Glossary also contains some definitions of rural and Border dialect terminology from the Spanish texts, terms that could give trouble to the reader of Spanish and that may not be found in most bilingual dictionaries. Terms discussed in the background comments on the songs are not included in the Glossary.

Two terms used throughout the book need to be defined here rather than in the Glossary. I use "Lower Rio Grande Border" (often shortened to "Lower Border" or "Border") for the area along both banks of the Rio Grande from the two Laredos to the Gulf. "Greater Mexico" refers to all the areas inhabited by people of Mexican culture—not only within the present limits of the Republic of Mexico but in the United States as well—in a cultural rather than a political sense.

It is impossible for me to acknowledge all I owe to the singers of the Border, who taught me their songs over a long period of years. Some of them are mentioned elsewhere in this book. There were many more, living and dead, who left part of themselves with me. To young Dottie Jordan I owe a special debt for her patience and good humor in checking out my tune transcriptions, and for her valuable suggestions regarding the mysteries of musical notation. She did not live to see this book in print, but it also contains some part of her.

INTRODUCTION

T he songs collected here are a people's heritage—their unselfconscious
record of themselves, alien for the most part to documents and books.
There are few enough writings about the Border people, who happen to
be my people. The Anglos who came down to us as conquerors saw us as
abysmal savages—benighted by papistry (priest-ridden, as that great Texas
liberal, J. Frank Dobie, used to say) and debased by miscegenation (with
ditchwater instead of blood in our veins, as another great Texas liberal and
scholar, Walter Prescott Webb, once put it). The supercivilized intellectuals of the Mexican plateau were kinder to us; they merely knew us as *los
bárbaros del Norte,* the barbarians of the North.

The whole of a people's past is reflected in these songs, from the days
when they journeyed out into Chichimecaland, mid-eighteenth century
pioneers, traveling north until they reached the Rio Grande, drank of its
waters, and traveled no more. They settled on the river banks long before
there was such a thing as the United States of America, and they struck
roots that would last for centuries. They clustered around the river, for its
waters were life. To these people, during their first century here, the river
was the navel of the world.

Then came the pale-eyed strangers from the north, and the homeland
was divided. The river—once a focus of life—became a barrier, a dividing
line, an international boundary. Families and friends were artificially
divided by it. For a long time, however, life went on very much as it had
before. Officially, the people on one bank of the river were Mexicans;
those on the other side were Americans, albeit an inferior, less-than-
second-class type of American in the eyes of the new rulers of the land.
But the inhabitants on both river banks continued to be the same people,
with the same traditions, preserved in the same legends and the same
songs. Together they entered into a century-long conflict with the English-
speaking occupiers of their homeland. Time has changed things, as the
governments from Washington and Mexico City have made their presence
felt. Even so, the bonds reaching across the river have not been broken,
just stretched out a bit to meet the demands of two forms of officialdom,
originally disparate but growing more like each other day by day.

The songs in this book mean a great deal to me, though I am not by any means alone in treasuring them. There are others of my generation along the Rio Grande who still remember, for whom success in the contemporary marketplace has not been accompanied by a sense of shame in their old ranchero background. For them, as for me, these songs still stir echoes. But the echoes have deeper overtones, reaching beyond those *fronterizos* who still can contemplate or recapture what they have been. These songs should have resonance in all Mexican-Americans, for they are part of the history of all Mexicans in the United States. They record an important aspect of the Mexican-American's long struggle to preserve his identity and affirm his rights as a human being.

It has been a struggle played out in many settings—in isolated villages of New Mexico as well as in Border "gateways" like Brownsville and Laredo, in urban centers like Los Angeles and in little towns like Crystal City. Nowhere was the conflict longer and more sustained than on the Lower Rio Grande Border. The Border was a wild and unruly place, or so they say. To put it another way, it was a focus of intercultural conflict, based on the Borderer's resolve *de no ser dejado*, not to take it lying down. For thousands of young Chicanos today, so intent on maintaining their cultural identity and demanding their rights, the Border *corrido* hero will strike a responsive chord when he risks life, liberty, and material goods *defendiendo su derecho*.

I started "collecting" these songs around 1920, when I first became aware of them on the lips of *guitarreros* and other people of the ranchos and the towns. Few of those singers are alive today. Nacho Montelongo, who taught me the first chords on the guitar, and many of his songs, still farms on the Mexican side of the river. But most of the others are gone. Some were voices stilled in their prime. I shall always remember Miguel Morán, who landed with the first assault wave on Attu in 1943, with his guitar strapped to his pack, and who came home to die, still carrying that guitar; and Matías Serrata, who landed in France in 1944, and who never came back. It is less painful to think of others who did live out their lives—Nicanor Torres, for example, who lived to be a hundred and could still sing *corridos* at that age. There are many others who will not sing again: Alberto Garza, in his time one of the best-known singers on the Texas side; Jesús Flores, blind singer and *decimero;* Ismael Chapa, itinerant merchant and singer, also blind; José Suárez, *el Cieguito*, for half a century the dean of Border *guitarreros*. Those and many more—young and old, relatives and friends—all part of a tradition that has not died but only changed.

Border singers were of many types and had many singing styles, so it is not easy to generalize about them. Women were important in the transmission of songs, though they were not supposed to sing "men's songs" such as *corridos* and rarely did so in public. Usually they sang at home, almost always without accompaniment, not only at their household tasks but when the family gathered in the evening, at which time all family members might sing in turn. It was rare for women to sing very loudly; in fact, all singers in these intimate family gatherings usually sang in soft or medium voices, in keeping with the tone of *respeto* that was expected within the family. The extended family was important in Border social life, in the towns as well as in the rural areas. Large gatherings composed of the families of brothers, sisters, and cousins were frequently held. They usually took place at the house of a parent or uncle of the nuclear families, or failing that at the home of one of the older family heads. Women took active part in these gatherings but were less likely to sing before the whole group, more because they were occupied at other tasks than because of any taboo. Extended family gatherings always involved feeding men and taking care of children on a larger scale than usual, and there was always conversation with female relatives to occupy a woman's time.

Women did sing at weddings, where they often had the role of performing songs of congratulation to the newlyweds, or of sympathy for the parents of bride and groom, who were losing their children to a new life. These wedding songs—often well-known lyric songs given a new function—were known as *enlaces*. But most of the singing done by the average Border woman was related to her role as mother. Her stock of cradle and nursery songs was not large, if one insists on a formal definition of cradle and nursery songs. In practice, though, her repertory was quite large, for she sang all kinds of songs to her children, from narrative *danzas* to romantic love songs. Most of us heard our first folksongs from our mothers. My own mother taught me many songs, including several in this collection. They are children's songs like "Los inditos" (no. 7) or ritual songs like "Los aguinaldos" (no. 42), for the most part.

Border society, however, was not so rigid that it did not allow exceptions. There were women who became well known as singers without losing their status as respected housewives, though they were likely to be viewed as somewhat unconventional. Doña Petra Longoria de Flores of Brownsville was one of these exceptions. She loved to sing *corridos,* something few women of her generation did. But then, she always had a flair for the daring and the unusual. As a young woman in the early years of the century, she decided she was going to ride the train from Brownsville to San Antonio, and she did so all by her unescorted self. Doña Petra retained her youthful outlook until the end of her days. I have a vivid memory of her at the age of eighty-two, bursting into her living room from the kitchen to sing us "Malhaya la cocina" (no. 56), a half-plucked chicken in one hand and a fistful of feathers in the other.

Jovita Cantú of El Tule, Tamaulipas, was even more unconventional. She not only sang all kinds of songs but was an accomplished guitar-player as well, good enough to compete with male *guitarreros* at large rural gatherings. Her father had been a musician, and she had traveled with him in central Texas in the years before World War I. There a Texas-Mexican poet had fallen in love with her and written her passionate verses which she knew by heart and sometimes recited. A romantic and slightly bohemian figure, she was perhaps unique among the women singers of the Border.

Men counted on a wider range of singing situations, varying from the intimate family gathering to the cantina, with the situation affecting the singing style. The amount of instrumental accompaniment and the tendency toward full-voiced singing increased as one moved away from the intimate circle of the family. There were singers who had their own individual styles, which did not vary much in different situations; but some styles of singing were not approved of outside their proper place. Loud, boisterous singing with much instrumental accompaniment was frowned upon in an intimate family situation; and the head of the house was likely to stop the performance with the admonition, "It's beginning to sound like a *parranda.*"

Border singing situations might be divided into two kinds, "organized audience" and "casual audience" situations. In the first, one had a group that came together for amusement or relaxation, with music as part of the program for the evening. In the second, the group was gathered primarily for purposes other than singing, or there might be no "group" at all in the strict sense of the word. What some Anglo-Americans have called a "lonesome" kind of singing was typical of casual audience situations. Such singing was always unaccompanied by instruments, with long pauses between phrases, slow tempo, and free meter. It might be loud or soft, depending on the singer's momentary awareness of space, but it was always performed in that mood of meditative yearning that is well characterized by the word "lonesome."

Women working in the household or men doing chores around the house often sang softly to themselves in the "lonesome" way, with no audience intended but themselves. The same type of singing was common in the fields when small groups worked together hoeing cotton or shucking corn. If women were in the work group, they might also take part in the singing, though they did not predominate as performers in this kind of situation. Singing in the fields was never group singing, done in chorus. It was always individual singing, though there might be brief moments when two or three singers would harmonize. Not everyone in a working group performed. Each group had two or three who were recognized as the most pleasing or the most enthusiastic singers (*los más cantadores*). The others listened as they worked, pacing themselves with the music and making joking comments and criticisms about the singers.

Men working on horseback also sang in much the same style, though with some important differences, perhaps because women did not take part in their activities. Their performance was usually higher pitched and at a slightly faster tempo. It was also much louder, with a few reflective *gritos* here and there. While the singer in the fields sang only loud enough to be heard by his fellow workers, the man on horseback seemed to take in the whole landscape as his potential audience. Men walking or riding along lonely roads at night—whether alone or in groups—used the markedly slow-tempo style used in the fields, but they sang the loudest of all. If there were two or more of them, they would harmonize. Like the men working on horseback, they took everyone within the range of their voices as a likely audience. And it was quite an experience to sit outside on a still, dark night and hear their distant, lonely music.

The songs used in "lonesome" singing were chosen not for their subject matter but because they fitted the tempo of the situation. Most commonly sung were old *danzas,* some *décima* tunes, love songs, and a few *corridos. Corridos* like "Benjamín Argumedo" (no. 32) and "Kiansis I" (no. 12) were often sung in the fields. Most common of the "lonesome" tunes, perhaps, was "Una noche serena y oscura," not included in this collection because it is widespread over the Greater Mexican area rather than being in any sense a song related to the Border. Subject matter did play some part in the selection of songs for different casual audience situations. Romantic *danzas* and canciones like "La tísica" (no. 51) and "Trigueña hermosa" (no. 49) were quite proper for singing among mixed groups in the fields. But the erotic verses of "La pastora" (no. 1) were reserved for singing among men only, on lonely roads where they could be sung at the top of one's voice.

Intimate family performances could be fairly casual in mood, but they took place in a more organized performance situation. Singing was part of the amusements of the evening, alternating with prose narratives, riddles, and games. As has been said, all members of the family—including women and children—might perform in turn. All types of songs would be performed, from *corridos* to children's ditties. Voices were kept low, but the singing was not necessarily in the "lonesome" style. If there was a guitar in the house, and someone to strum it, some of the songs would be accompanied, usually those sung by the men. Songs were often preceded or followed by explanatory prose narratives. The father usually had the role of oral historian in the family, the mother being more likely to specialize in legends and tales of the supernatural. These family performances were important in the socialization of the Border Mexican child.

Singing was also important at extended-family gatherings and at more formal and more widely attended events such as weddings and fiestas celebrating anniversaries. (Up until the 1890s, it was also the custom to sing ritual songs accompanied by guitars and other instruments at the funerals of young children, but the custom did not survive into the twentieth century.) These performances were more or less extensions of the intimate family performance, except that there was a higher degree of specialization in the participants. The *grito* was taboo, classifying the event as *de familia,* in distinction to situations involving men without women, or men with "women of the other kind." Prose narratives were told to explain *corridos* and other songs, as in the family performances. But not everyone took part in the singing and storytelling. In these large "family" gatherings, the men were the performers, while the women and children participated only as audience.

Nor did all male singers and narrators perform. When it came time to narrate parts of the life of a *corrido* hero, only the oldest and wisest men had the privilege of doing so. Similarly, the singers in the highest repute dominated the musical performance; many men who sang at home did not participate except as listeners. Instrumental accompaniment was essential to such fiestas, though some singers of repute preferred to sing without accompaniment. In fact, the large gathering *de familia* included most singing styles found in other Border singing situations: the lone singer without accompaniment, the singer accompanied by others, the lone singer accompanying himself on the guitar, and the harmonizing singers accompanied by two or more instruments in the nature of a *conjunto.*

Other organized audience situations involved men alone, both as performers and listeners. The cantina performance and the *parranda*—an extended, often ambulatory version of the cantina situation—are the most typical, and the opposite extreme from the intimate family situation. The singing is loud and punctuated by *gritos.* Performance may be by a lone singer accompanying himself, but it is often by two singers harmonizing and backed by several instruments. *Corridos* predominate, but there is rarely any commentary on their background, much less true narration of events.

The *parranda* involves not only visiting cantinas but roaming about, drinking and singing. In former times, rural *parrandas* took place on horseback, while in town automobiles were used. A variation or interlude to the *parranda* was the *serenata,* a term for "serenade" more common on the Border than the Greater Mexican *gallo.* Sweethearts, wives, friends, or even the parents of *parranda* members would be serenaded. The *parranda* then assumed, for the moment, some of the characteristics of the *de familia* situation. Ideally, the approach to the house to be serenaded was made in complete silence, the first sounds being those of the instruments preluding the song. There was no extremely loud singing and no *gritos,* both of which would have been violations of the *respeto* due the house being serenaded. The departure of the serenaders also was supposed to be as quiet as possible.

If it was a parent or friend who was being honored, the head of the household might come out and thank the serenaders before they left. Serenaded girls had to devise other ways of expressing their appreciation. They did not come out on their balconies and throw roses at the musicians because balconies and rose gardens were extremely rare on the Border. If they could manage it, they would show themselves briefly at the window as a signal that they had heard and enjoyed.

Motorized *serenatas* in town had special problems. Police departments usually were unsympathetic toward music in the streets during the wee hours, so most serenades had to be performed before midnight. It was difficult to achieve a completely silent approach on board a rattling old Chevy or model A Ford. This problem could be solved by coasting in on a dead engine up to the house to be serenaded. A silent and dignified departure was more difficult to achieve. The car had to be started again before one could leave, scarcely a noiseless job, and there were times when it would not start at all, so that the serenaders would have to exit pushing. Twentieth-century technology did provide one boon to the *serenata* tradition, the electric light. By the 1930s it had become Border custom for a serenaded girl to switch her bedroom light on and off as a signal of acknowledgment. For quick and efficient communication, it beats balconies and roses.

Folklorists have always been concerned about the type of performer supposed to be typical of any folksong tradition. Do all the "folk" sing— all equally well— in the "dancing, singing throng" style of romantic folklore theory? Or does each group include a mass of passive listeners and "a very small number of active bearers of tradition"—the performers and transmitters, as Von Sydow said of the folktale?[1] In the Border folksong tradition, neither of these two extremes is found. Songs are performed by a variety of singers in a variety of performance situations, any one of which is as valid and as "folkloric" as the others, and equally acceptable to the group itself. It is true that a higher degree of technical specialization is required of the performer as one moves away from the intimate family situation, especially as regards instrumental accompaniment, but this is not consistently true.

One may easily identify extremes: a man singing within the circle of his family, accompanying himself with a few tentative guitar chords, versus the multi-instrument *conjunto* in a cantina, accompanying a singer with some local reputation as a good voice. But a singer who normally performs unaccompanied may be welcomed in a cantina singing situation. Jesús Gómez, whom I knew when he was an old man, never learned to play an instrument, though he was well known as a singer during his lifetime. He used to tell that in his youth he would often be invited to sing in cantinas. He would be accompanied by any guitarists present, though he sang best alone. Such examples involve performance techniques, which are not always important to folklorists in determining who is or is not a "true folksinger." A generally accepted yardstick is the singer's memory and repertory. Border performers and audience agreed on this point; they valued the singer who had the largest repertory and who sang the longest variants of the songs they knew. The more specialized the singer, the more likely it was that his repertory would be ample and that his songs would be good and long. But, again, one cannot make this a hard-and-fast rule. Blind singers like José Suárez and Jesús Flores were truly specialists. They had a tremendous repertory of satisfyingly long songs. All doors were open to them; their singing was as welcome in the cantina as at a small family gathering. On the other hand, men like Nacho Montelongo and

---

[1] C. W. von Sydow, "Folktale Studies and Philology," in *Selected Papers on Folklore*, ed. Laurits Bødker (Copenhagen, 1948); reprinted in *The Study of Folklore*, ed. Alan Dundes (Englewood Cliffs, N.J., 1965), 231.

Fidencio Barrientos were primarily farmers, and folksingers in their spare time. They performed in extended family situations rather than in cantinas. But their repertory rivaled that of Suárez and Flores, though they were not considered as technically accomplished on the guitar as the blind singers.

So it is clear that there were many kinds of performers and transmitters of Border folksong, and that to be considered something of a specialist among his peers the Border singer had to be proficient at the guitar. The highest degree of specialization could be expected in the cantina, but cantina singing situations were not the richest in terms of total folklore performance. It was the intimate and extended family situations that were truly complete folklore performances, with folksinging a part of a complex of events including oral history, legends, riddles, games, and material folklore. A distinction may also be made as to the modes of transmission of Border songs. New songs, especially those coming from the outside, were most often introduced to Border audiences in cantina situations. The folksinging specialist was also a songmaker, as well as a traveler and man of the world. But the main body of the folksong tradition was transmitted in family performance situations, along with other forms of folklore.

A word about the music for the songs that follow. Only the melody line is given, and it is a "typical" melody rather than an authoritative one, a guide as to how one may sing the song. But just one word of advice: keep it simple. The most specialized of our Border singers were far from being sophisticated musicians. The chords shown above the melody line are the simplest and most necessary ones for accompaniment. The fewer musical butterflies, the more genuine and honest the performance will be.

Chords are shown for the six-string guitar, the *guitarra sexta*. This is the most common type of instrument on the Border today, but such was not the case in former times. The typical singer fifty years ago used the *bajo sexto* rather than the *guitarra sexta*. The *bajo sexto* (or *bajo*) is a bass guitar, as its name indicates—not quite as large as the *guitarrón* used in the *mariachi* but bigger than the six-string guitar. As its name does not indicate, the *bajo sexto* has twelve strings instead of six; but it is a different instrument from the usual twelve-string guitar popular among folksingers in the United States, and tuned differently. The *bajo* allows for fewer fancy runs and trills and other such *firuletes* that one can produce on the *guitarra sexta*. *Bajos* have been used almost exclusively as rhythmic and harmonic accompaniment to the voice of the singer, especially in the straightforward pattern of the *corrido*. When more "music" has been necessary—at dances, for example—the *bajo* was combined with the fiddle, the *guitarra sexta*, or the accordion. But most of the songs in this volume are meant to be sung to the basic chord accompaniment of the guitar.

PART
I

Old Songs
from Colonial Days

The usual picture of the Spanish-speaking explorers and colonizers of the Southwest, as painted by writers in the United States, is of a bunch of aristocratic Castilian dandies more interested in the lace ruffles on their sleeves than in the job of exploration and settlement. Even Carey McWilliams, who has done much to rectify some misconceptions about Mexican-Americans, cannot resist Bolton's description of the dashing Captain Luis de Velasco, whose peacock wardrobe requires almost a page to detail. Velasco "invaded" the Southwest in 1598 with Juan de Oñate. Three hundred years later, "Spanish-speaking people re-invaded the borderlands," but this time the "invaders" were led by "landless peons who forded across the Rio Grande in the dead of night."[1]

This is an interesting portrayal of the Spanish-speaking presence in the Southwest: first, toward the end of the sixteenth century, a wave of pure-bred Castilian clotheshorses in search of gold and silver; then, three centuries later, a second wave made up of furtive, landless peons in search of bread and a job. And in between—presumably—nothing.

Anglo writers are not the only ones who have bought this pretty legend. It has flattered the egos of dozens of "old families" in California. And, for thousands of "Spanish" in New Mexico and Colorado, it has made existence tolerable in a country that has despised their too-evident Mexican origins. The legend has also been adopted by descendants of post-1890 immigrants, especially in Texas.

The fiction about the "early Spanish" in the Southwest has been pretty well discredited. Carey McWilliams himself has more than done his part in destroying what he calls the "Fantasy Heritage," by publicizing the Indian, African, and mestizo origins of the "old Spanish" founders of Los Angeles.[2] Other factors, however, are involved aside from the genes of the first Spanish-speaking arrivals into what is now the southwestern United States, chiefly the matter of culture. The descendants of the "early Spanish" no longer are said to be racially different from the post-1890 Mexican immigrants into the United States. But fundamental differences in their culture are said to exist, justifying the classification of the former as "Spanish-Americans" and the latter as "Mexican-Americans." The first are said to be inheritors of a "pre-Mexican" or Spanish colonial culture, while the second are products of a Mexican culture that developed after 1821.

This is to confuse politics with culture. Mexico as a political entity did come into existence in 1821, but the cultural entity that is Mexico had its beginnings soon after Cortés and his men landed at Veracruz in 1519. The Plan de Iguala did have important cultural effects, though political independence did not really affect Mexican culture until some half a century after Vicente Guerrero and Agustín Iturbide indulged in their famous

[1]Carey McWilliams, *North from Mexico: The Spanish-Speaking People of the United States* (Philadelphia, 1949; New York, 1968), 162.

[2]Ibid., 36.

abrazo. Then, perhaps, the "Spanish-Americans" of the Southwest represent a stage in Mexican culture that ended with the days of Antonio López de Santa Ana. This would still make them different from all those *braceros* who have been filtering across the Border since the heyday of *porfirismo*.

This, to some extent, could be true if the early frontier colonies were indeed isolated from the rest of New Spain. Isolation is a relative thing, and it becomes even more so when we attempt to measure past events and conditions according to present-day standards, as we most often do. Compared to the average small town in the contemporary United States, the frontier colonies were indeed isolated. But they were not desert-bound Pitcairn Islands. Intercourse with central Mexico, and with other frontier colonies, was a regular feature of early life. From our jet-age point of view, this commerce proceeded at a snail's pace, but it was lively enough for the tempo of the times. There is no reason to believe that the frontier provinces were any more isolated from Mexico City than were many other areas in south and central Mexico.

Immigration and settlement from central Mexico into what is now the southwestern United States went on through the seventeenth and eighteenth centuries and into the nineteenth, until interrupted by the Anglo-American takeover of the region. The colonies of Texas, California, and Nuevo Santander were founded during this period. After American domination was established in the Southwest, migration northward from Mexico was resumed at its old, leisurely pace except when interrupted by acts of violence. The character of the migration did change; Mexicans no longer came north as settlers and explorers, since the land was no longer theirs. But in the 1850-90 period many still came as wandering pioneers of a sort—as mustangers, buffalo hunters, trail drivers, and vaqueros. The migrations beginning in the 1890s were different as to the numbers and economic condition of the migrants. Culturally speaking, however, the *braceros* who came from Mexico after 1890 were part of a continuous process that had begun in the 1590s.

In sum, the Spanish-speaking people in the United States whose ancestors came from what is now the Republic of Mexico are all one people, as far as any people may claim to be a single whole. Their origins, from the very beginning, were anything but pure Castilian. We are descended from the captains from Castile, it is true. But we are also the children of Luis de Carvajal, the Jew; of Estebanico, the Negro; of Xicoténcatl, the Tlaxcalteca, perhaps a wiser and braver "Aztec" than either Moctezuma or Cuauhtémoc; and also of Sancho, the Asturian shopkeeper, not to mention a few Yaquis, Comanches, and Irishmen here and there. Genetically, we are mestizos; culturally, we belong to a generalized Mexican culture. This is not to say that a rural New Mexican and a Chicano from East L.A. think and act exactly alike. But their apparent differences are due more to the North American environment than to the culture they share with each other and the inhabitants of the Republic of Mexico.

In 1749, midway between the 1590s and the 1890s, the colony of Nuevo Santander was founded, with the lower reaches of the Rio Grande as its focal point. The settling of what is now the Lower Rio Grande Border between Texas and Mexico was part of that continuous process of Mexican penetration into the Southwest that we have been discussing. It is in the area that once was Nuevo Santander that all the songs collected in this book have been sung during my lifetime and before—long, long before. Those songs included in Part I were not composed along the Rio Grande, nor did they originate farther south in Mexico. They came to us from Spain.

Perhaps it is no longer necessary to minimize our Spanish heritage in these days of *chicanismo*. Too many Chicanos have gone to the other extreme from their "Spanish-American" elders; they see themselves exclusively as children of Cuauhtémoc, roasted feet and all. But Spain has given us many things besides part of our ancestry. It is well to remember that, whatever the genetic makeup of the settlers who moved into the frontier provinces, what welded them together into one people were the Spanish language and the Spanish culture.

Another thing Spain gave us was her folksongs. When they came to the Rio Grande, our ancestors brought with them many songs of Spanish origin. The versions of the Spanish songs brought into Nuevo Santander were those that people of Mexican culture were singing in the eighteenth century. The songs were already Mexicanized, to be sure, though how much we cannot know. Some came directly with the settlers as they moved north from places like Querétaro and Monterrey. Other versions may have been borrowed from the neighboring colony of Nuevo México, still a neighbor though separated by hundred of miles of hostile territory. What we do know is that those songs of Spanish origin that have come down to us in the Lower Rio Grande Border area are well adapted to the new lands and to the people who settled them. They are at once very old and very new.

A romantic idea related to the "captains from Castile" syndrome is that the *conquistadores* arrived in Mexico singing the old epics about the wars against the Moors, and that ever after down through the centuries the people of New Spain sang about the exploits of El Cid, Fernán González, and all the other heroes of the *romances viejos*. The *conquistadores* probably did sing the old *romances*. But the new people who developed in what was to become Mexico were interested in their own heroes and their own historical events. It was the Spanish ballads with universal themes that struck deep roots among the people of Mexican culture, ballads in which people are simply people rather than historical characters identified with a specific place and time.

In this section are six songs, well known on the Texas-Mexican Border, that came to us from Spain. "LA PASTORA" originally was a Spanish *romance*, known to scholars as "La bella dama y el pastor." Dating from about the fifteenth century, it was carried by exiled Spanish Jews to North Africa, and by Spanish settlers to the New World, where it has been collected by folklorists in Argentina, Chile, and other Spanish-American countries. Mexican folklorists have not found it within the present-day limits of the Republic of Mexico; but it is well known in California, New Mexico, and the Texas-Mexican Border. Our Border versions are thoroughly Mexicanized, both in language and in detail, such as the *sesteadero* where the beautiful lady attempts to seduce the shepherd. This is a song preferred by young adult males. Many generations of young Border *rancheros* have enjoyed a laugh at the expense of the stupid sheepherder, who simply cannot understand what the beautiful lady is driving at.

"LA CIUDAD DE JAUJA" is related to American songs such as "Oleana" and "The Big Rock Candy Mountain." All of them go back to French medieval poems called *fabliaux,* about a wondrous land (Cockayne, Cake-land, Cucaña) where everything is good to eat. In Spain *romances* parodying the Cucaña theme made fun of the stories brought back by missionaries, explorers, and conquerors about the wonders of the New World. The Valley of Xauxa (Jauja) in Peru—advertised as a fabulously rich area—became associated in folksong and legend with the land of Cucaña. Most often Jauja is pictured as an island ("La isla donde hay mucho que comer") or a city located in an unknown land. *Romances* about Jauja were still popular in the mid-eighteenth century, when the province of Nuevo Santander (later the Lower Texas-Mexican Border) was settled. Our "Ciudad de Jauja" probably descends from one of the eighteenth-century *romances.* Words and music, however, are in the form of the Mexican *corrido,* and the language also has been Mexicanized. It is of Mexican good things to eat that Jauja is made. "La ciudad de Jauja" is a comic song, but during hard times on the Border the humor has become a bit pointed. "Jauja" was widely sung during the Depression of the 1930s, for example. For many generations, Border Mexicans have gone north in search of jobs and better living conditions. In a tongue-in-cheek way, they sometimes have described their journeys as a quest for the mythical land of Jauja.

In spite of the claims made by some folklorists in the United States, the tall tale is not a peculiarly North American genre. The outrageous lie as an art form is known in the folklore of many other peoples, who enjoy artistic lying as a source of humor. In Spain tall tales are called *cuentos andaluces,* and they may be told in prose or verse. In the Americas—North, South, and Middle—the tall tale once was used to parody the wild claims made by early explorers and settlers about the richness of the land. According to early writers, everything in the New World from potatoes to sheep grew to gigantic size, putting to shame the puny products of Europe. A tall tale in ballad form is "EL BORREGO GORDO," about a fabulously big ram. It may be compared to ballads in English like "The Darby Ram." In addition, it is related to songs like "La ciudad de Jauja," since it mentions a land where everything is good to eat.

"EL MARRANO GORDO" seems to be a later version of "El borrego gordo." The words of the two songs are quite similar, though their music is different. "El marrano gordo" is much more widely known throughout the Greater Mexican area than is "El borrego gordo." Tall-tale songs about porkers are also known in Anglo-American tradition—"The Sow Took the Measles," for example.

"DELGADINA" is a Spanish *romance* about a cruel king who falls in love with his beautiful and virtuous daughter. Incest is a favorite subject for ballad singers, just as it has been for tragic dramatists and for novelists. In British balladry a handful of songs are devoted to the theme. In Spanish balladry "Delgadina" stands almost alone in this respect, but it is known throughout the Spanish-speaking world. If any Spanish-speaking group in any part of the world is given to the singing of old ballads, the chances are that "Delgadina" will be in their repertory. We could find no better example of the unity within diversity that characterizes the Spanish-speaking world. The Border "Delgadina" belongs to a general Mexican variant of the Spanish *romance,* one that is known throughout the Greater Mexican area. The text is somewhat Mexicanized: the king and his daughter go to church in Morelia, Michoacán.

"ELENA," also known as "La desdichada Elena," is a *corrido* that developed from a *romance* called "La amiga de Bernal Francés," but it has had a long life as a Mexican *corrido.* It is known throughout the Greater Mexican area. The phrase "Abreme la puerta, Elena" has become proverbial among people of Mexican culture. The tune to which "Elena" is sung has been borrowed for other *corridos,* notably "Arnulfo" (see no. 24). One reason for the currency of "Elena" is its subject. In both *romance* and *corrido,* adultery on the part of the wife is a crime almost as horrible as incest and usually punished by death. Adultery committed by the male is less reprehensible, and there are comic songs about it.

1
La pastora

The rhythm is that of the *danza mexicana,* much like that of the Cuban *habanera* ("La paloma," for example). The tempo is slow and somewhat stately. The melody is sung high and loud, literally at the top of one's voice; and it is most often performed out in the open by young men going to and from work or out *de parranda.* According to his mood, the singer may draw out the last note of a musical phrase for several extra beats, with a pause following. This is a characteristic of much Mexican folksinging.

Tiempo de danza ♩ = 52

A‿o‿ri - llas de‿un ses-tea - de - ro u-na‿o - ve - ja me fal - to,́

y‿u - na jo - ven blan-ca‿y be - lla de‿un pas - tor se‿e - na - mo - ró.

O - ye pas - tor a - do - ra - do, a - quí te‿ha-bla‿u - na pa - lo - ma,

a - rrí - ma - te‿a - quí‿a mi la - do sin te - mor de que te co - ma.

A orillas de un sesteadero
una oveja me faltó,
y una joven blanca y bella
de un pastor se enamoró.

—Oye, pastor adorado,
aquí te habla una paloma,
arrímate aquí a mi lado
sin temor de que te coma.

—Yo te doy cuatro mil pesos,
y de pesos cuatro mil,
tan sólo porque te quedes
esta noche aquí a dormir.—

—No quiero cuatro mil pesos,
ni de pesos cuatro mil,
mi ganado está en la sierra
y con él voy a dormir.—

—Mira qué manitas tengo,
buenas para perfilar,
te las doy porque te quedes
esta noche a platicar.—

—Yo también tengo manitas,
buenas para trabajar,
mi ganado está en la sierra
y con él me voy a estar.—

—Mira qué piecito tengo,
para un zapato lucido,

te lo doy porque te quedes
esta noche aquí conmigo.—

—Yo también tengo piecitos
para un huarache lucido,
mi ganado está en la sierra,
ya me voy, pues no lo olvido.—

—Mira qué piernas tan blancas,
con sus venas tan azules,
te las doy porque te quedes
sábado, domingo y lunes.—

—Yo también tengo piernitas
con sus venas tan azules,
mi ganado está en la sierra,
ya me voy y no lo dudes.—

—Anda, pastor arrastrado,
no me quieres escuchar,
anda véte a tu ganado,
bien te puedes retirar.—

—Dispénsame jovencita,
tus palabras no entendí,
mi ganado está en la sierra
pero yo me quedo aquí.—

—No hay perdón para el que yerra,
mucho menos para ti,
tu ganado está en la sierra,
bien te puedes ir de aquí.—

The Shepherdess

Close to where the sheep were resting, I could not find a ewe;
and a fair and pretty maiden fell in love with a shepherd boy.

"Hear me, beloved shepherd, this dove is speaking to you;
come and sit close by my side, do not fear that I will eat you.

"I'll give you four thousand pesos, and of pesos thousands four,
if only you will stay and sleep here tonight with me."

"I don't want four thousand pesos, or of pesos thousands four;
my sheep are on the mountain, and I must go sleep with them."

"Just look at my little hands, so good at making lace;
you can have them if you'll stay and talk to me tonight."

"I also have little hands, so good at doing hard work;
my sheep are on the mountain, and I must go stay with them."

"Just look at my pretty foot, fit for an elegant shoe;
you can have it if you'll stay with me here tonight."

"I also have pretty feet, fit for an elegant huarache;
my sheep are on the mountain; I'm going now for I cannot forget them."

"Did you ever see such white legs, with such veins of blue?
You can have them if you'll stay Saturday, Sunday, and Monday."

"I also have pretty legs with veins of blue;
my sheep are on the mountain; I'm going now and don't you doubt it."

"Get out, you low-down shepherd, you will not listen to me;
go along and join your sheep, it is high time you left."

"I beg your pardon, young lady, I did not understand your words;
my sheep are on the mountain, but as for me I will stay here."

"He who blunders finds no pardon, you may expect less than that;
your sheep are on the mountain, you had better go away."

2

La ciudad de Jauja

"La ciudad de Jauja" should be sung to a steady, jogging tempo, not too fast, but with the basses strongly marked in a *one*-two-three, *one*-two-three rhythm.

A - rro - yos que co - rren le - che,   ja - rros y   ca - zos de a - to - le,

hay ba-rran-cas de pa-no-chas,hay a-zú-car con pi-no-le.

Desde esa ciudad de Jauja
me mandan solicitar,
que me vaya para allá
un tesoro a disfrutar.

¿Qué dices, amigo? vamos
a ver si dicen verdad,
si es verdad de lo que dicen
nos quedaremos allá.

Las iglesias son de azúcar,
de caramelo los frailes,
de melcocha los monaguillos
y de miel los colaterales.

¡Válgame la Cruz de Queso
en sus peñas de tortilla!
Vuelan los patos asados
con su pimienta y su sal.

Levántate, amigo, y vamos
a ver si dicen verdad,

si es verdad de lo que dicen
nos quedaremos allá.

Arroyos que corren leche,
jarros y cazos de atole,
hay barrancas de panochas,
hay azúcar con pinole.

Hay árboles de tortillas
y labores de empanadas,
eso de tamales turcos,
las calles están regadas.

Ese Guadalupe Guerra
tenía unas chivas muy finas,
y se las cambió a Julián
por unos sacos de harina.

Levántate, amigo, y vamos,
vámonos sin vacilar
donde agarran a patadas
al que quiera trabajar.

The City of Jauja

They have sent from that City of Jauja, asking for me;
they want me to go over there, so I may enjoy a treasure.

What do you say, friend? Let us go see if they're speaking the truth;
if all that they say is true, we will remain there.

The churches are made of sugar, the friars of caramel,
the acolytes of molasses candy, and the altars of honey.

May the Cross of Cheese protect me, on its tortilla rocks!
The roasted ducks fly about garnished with pepper and salt.

Get up, my friend, let us go see if they're speaking the truth;
if all that they say is true, we will remain there.

There are creeks that flow with milk, pots and kettles of *atole;*
there are mounds of brown sugar, there is sugar with *pinole.*

There are trees bearing tortillas and fields with crops of turnovers,
and as for *tamales turcos,* the streets are covered with them.

That Guadalupe Guerra used to have some very fine goats,
and he traded them to Julián for some sacks of flour.

Get up, my friend, let us go, let us go without delay
where they kick hell out of you if you try to work.

3

El borrego gordo

"El borrego gordo" is in *danza* rhythm, as is "La pastora," suggesting that it too is a
romance converted into a *danza* in the late eighteenth or early nineteenth century.
"El borrego gordo" is not sung as loud or as high as "La pastora," but it is played just
a bit faster.

Yo tenía un borrego gordo,
que por gordo lo maté,
le saqué cuarenta arrobas
y otra más que le dejé.

La lana se la quité,
la mandé para Dolores,
me salieron dos mil telas
y quinientos cobertores.

El cuero se lo quité
y me puse a correyar,
saqué cincuenta barzones
y cien reatas de lazar.

Los cuernos se los quité,
los mandé hacer peinetas finas,
a cien pesos las pagaban
todititas las catrinas.

El menudo se lo saqué,
lo mandé pa' Guanajuato,
a cinco pesos pagaban
los borrachitos el plato.

La carne la tasajié,
toda la hice chicharrones,
del tamaño de esta casa
salieron treinta montones.

Me fui para Orizaba,
y compré mucho tabaco,
en el camino lo daba
a cuatro arrobas por tlaco.

En el camino encontré
unas torrijas cantando,
y más adelante estaban
unas torres fabricando.

Las torres eran de azúcar,
los chinitos de azúcar cande,
el pan era de panocha
y el cura de un queso grande.

Ya con ésta me despido,
recuerdo del mes de enero,
le pido a Dios me perdone
las mentiras del carnero.

The Fat Ram

I once had a fat ram, so fat I had to slaughter it;
I got forty *arrobas* of meat out of it, plus another *arroba* I let it keep.

I sheared the wool off the ram and sent it to [the city of] Dolores;
it was made into two thousand lengths of cloth, as well as five hundred coverlets.

I took the skin off the ram and cut it into strips;
I made fifty yoke straps and one hundred rawhide lariats.

I took the horns off the ram and had them made into fine *peinetas;*
all the fashionable ladies bought them at a hundred pesos each.

I took out the tripe and sent it to Guanajuato;
all the drunks paid five pesos a plate for it.

I cut up the meat and made it into cracklings;
it all came to thirty piles, each one as big as this house.

I went to Orizaba and bought a lot of tobacco;
on the way back I sold it, one hundred pounds for a penny.

On the road I ran across some singing *torrijas,*
and farther on some towers were being built.

The towers were made of sugar, the Chinese of rock candy;
the bread was of brown sugar, and the priest was a great big cheese.

Now with this I say farewell, remembering the month of January;
I hope God will forgive me the lies about the ram.

4

El marrano gordo

This is a *corrido*, though not the usual triple-time variety (6/8 or 9/8). It takes the duple-time form (2/4) and also varies from the usual Border *corrido* pattern by having a refrain. The rhythm throughout is a lively *one-two, one-*two that matches the playful spirit of the text.

Yo te - nía un ma - rra - no gor - do que por gor - do lo ma - té,

y_uy ay ay, y_uy ay ay, y_uy ay ay; cien a - rro - bas de man - te - ca

yo - tra   más yo le sa - qué,   co - che   co - che chi - no   cui,

chi - no   chi - no chi - no   cui,   cui   cui   cui   cui.

Yo tenía un marrano gordo
que por gordo lo maté,
y uy ay ay, y uy ay ay, y uy ay ay;
cien arrobas de manteca
y otra más yo le saqué,
coche coche chino cui,
chino chino chino cui,
cui cui cui cui.

El cuero se lo quité
y lo mandé para Europa,
y uy ay ay, etc.
y de allá me condujeron
cuarenta trenes de ropa,
coche coche chino cui, etc.

La gordura la saqué
y la hice chicharrones,
y uy ay ay, etc.
y además de la manteca
salieron diez mil montones,
coche coche chino cui, etc.

Las orejas le quité
y las mandé para China,

y uy ay ay, etc.
y de allá me condujeron
un vagón de ropa fina,
coche coche chino cui, etc.

De la cola del marrano
hice un fuete de azotar,
y uy ay ay, etc.
quinientos pesos me daban
pa'l coche del general,
coche coche chino cui, etc.

La lengua se la saqué,
se la di a mi prenda amada,
y uy ay ay, etc.
de tan sabrosa que estaba
hasta yo me saboreaba,
coche coche chino cui, etc.

La cabeza no vendí,
se la mandé a un cirujano,
y uy ay ay, etc.
pa' que Dios me perdonara
las mentiras del marrano,
coche coche chino cui, etc.

The Fat Hog

I once had a fat hog, so fat I had to slaughter it,
y uy, ay, ay, etc.

I got a hundred *arrobas* of lard out of it, plus another *arroba* more.
Here, pig, sooey pig, etc.

I took the skin off the hog, and I sent it off to Europe;
and from there they sent me forty trainloads of clothing.

I took the fat off the hog, and I made it into cracklings;
I got ten thousand piles of them, aside from the lard I rendered.

I took the ears off the hog, and I sent them off to China;
and from there they sent me a boxcar of fine clothing.

Out of the tail of the hog I made a bullwhip;
they offered me five hundred pesos to use it on the general's coach.

I took the tongue out of the hog and gave it to my beloved;
it was so delicious that even I licked my lips.

I did not sell the head, I sent it to a surgeon,
so that God would forgive me the lies about the hog.

5
Delgadina

This is not a typical *corrido* tune. It is sung to a measured *one*-two-three beat by one voice alone, often without guitar accompaniment. As far as I know, it is never sung in two voices (*primera y segunda*), as is common with the *corrido*.

Del - ga - di - na se pa - sea - ba de la sa - la a la co - ci - na, con su man - to hi - lo de o - ro que su pe - cho le i - lu - mi - na.

Delgadina se paseaba
de la sala a la cocina,
con su manto hilo de oro
que su pecho le ilumina.

Delgadina se paseaba
en su gran sala cuadrada,
con su manto hilo de oro
que en su pecho le brillaba.

—Levántate, Delgadina,
ponte vestido de seda,
porque nos vamos a misa
a la ciudad de Morelia.—

Cuando salieron de misa
en su sala la abrazaba:
—Delgadina, hija mía,
yo te quiero para dama.—

—No permitas, madre mía,
ni la Virgen soberana,
que es ofensa para Dios
y la perdición de mi alma.—

—Júntense los once criados
y encierren a Delgadina,
échenle bien los candados—
dijo el rey con mucha muina.

—Remachen bien los candados,
que no se oiga voz ladina,
si les pide de comer
no le den comida fina.

—Si les pide de beber
le darán agua salada,
porque la quiero obligar
a que sea mi prenda amada.—

—Mariquita, hermana mía,
un favor te pediré,
regálame un vaso de agua
porque me muero de sed.—

—Ay, hermana de mi vida,
no te puedo dar el agua,
si lo sabe el rey mi padre
a las dos nos saca el alma.—

—Papacito de mi vida,
tu castigo estoy sufriendo,
regálame un vaso de agua
que de sed me estoy muriendo.—

—Júntense los once criados,
llévenle agua a Delgadina
en vaso sobredorado
y en jarros de losa china.—

Cuando le llevan el agua
Delgadina estaba muerta,
con sus ojitos cerrados
y con su boquita abierta.

La cama de Delgadina
de ángeles está rodeada,
la cama del rey su padre
de diablos está apretada.

Delgadina está en el cielo
dándole cuenta al Creador
y su padre en los infiernos
con el Demonio Mayor.

Ya con ésta me despido
a la sombra de una lima,
aquí se acaba cantando
la historia de Delgadina.

Delgadina

Delgadina walked about from the hall to the kitchen,
in her cloth-of-gold mantle that illuminates her breast.

Delgadina walked about in her great square hall,
in her cloth-of-gold mantle that shone against her breast.

"Arise, Delgadina, put on a silken dress,
for we are going to mass in the city of Morelia."

When they came back from mass, he embraced her in her hall:
"Delgadina, daughter of mine, I want you to be my mistress."

"Don't let it happen, my mother, nor you, all-powerful Virgin,
for it is a sin against God and the perdition of my soul."

"Come together, my eleven servants, and put Delgadina in prison;
see that she is well locked up," said the king in great anger.

"Fasten the padlocks securely so that no shrill voice is heard;
and if she wishes to eat, do not give her any fine foods.

"If she wishes to drink, you will give her salty water,
because I want to force her to become my sweetheart."

"Mariquita, sister of mine, I will ask you a favor:
give me a glass of water for I am dying of thirst."

"Oh, my beloved sister, I cannot give you the water,
for if the king my father knows it, he will tear out both our souls."

"My beloved father, I am suffering from your anger;
give me a glass of water for I am dying of thirst."

"Come together, my eleven servants, take water to Delgadina
in a gilded glass and in jars of fine china."

When they took her the water, Delgadina was dead,
with her little mouth open and her little eyes closed.

Delgadina's bed is surrounded by angels;
the bed of the king her father is crowded with demons.

Delgadina is in Heaven being judged by God;
her father is in Hell, with the Chief Devil.

Now with this I say farewell, under the shade of a lime tree;
here is the end of the singing of the story of Delgadina.

6
Elena

"Elena" is sung to an eight-phrase tune, so its four-line stanzas are grouped in eight-line units. Occasionally, a single four-line stanza is introduced—the second stanza in our text, for example. The first four phrases of the tune are used for a four-line unit like this one. This is a standard *corrido* tune with a *one*-two-three, *one*-two-three, *one*-two-three strum but played at a moderately slow tempo.

Y en ese plan de Durango,
sin saber cómo ni cuando,
se vinieron a encontrar
don Benito y don Fernando.

—Abreme la puerta, Elena,
abre con toda confianza,
que soy Fernando el Francés,
venido desde la Francia.—

Al abrir la puerta Elena
se les apagó el candil,
se agarraron de la mano,
se fueron para el jardín.

 —Oiga, señor don Fernando,
¿por qué no me habla usté a mí?
Tendrá usté amores en Francia
o quiere a otra más que a mí.—
 —No tengo amores en Francia
ni quiero a otra más que a ti,
ni le temo a tu marido
que se halla al lado de ti.—

 —Perdóname, esposo mío,
perdona mis aventuras,
ya no lo hagas por mí,
hazlo por tus dos criaturas.—
 —De mí no alcanzas perdón
ni encuentras ningún placer,

que te perdone Fernando
que fue todo tu querer.—

 Vuela y vuela, palomita,
dale vuelo a tu volido,
anda a ver cómo le fue
a Elena con su marido.
 La pobrecita de Elena
¡con qué lástima murió!
de tres tiros de pistola
que su marido le dio.

 —Agarra, criada, a esos niños,
llévaselos a mis padres,
si te preguntan de Elena
les dices que tú no sabes.—
 Señoras, pongan cuidado,
lo que en la ocasión pasó,
que a Elena por cautelosa
su marido la mató.

Elena

On that plain of Durango, by an accident of fate,
Don Benito and Don Fernando suddenly came face to face.
"Open the door for me, Elena; open the door without fear,
for I am Fernando the Frenchman, come all the way from France."

As Elena opened the door, the lamp that she held went out;
they took each other by the hand, and they went into the garden.

"Hear me, señor Don Fernando, why will you not speak to me?
Do you have other loves in France; do you love someone else more than me?"
"I have no other loves in France, I love no one else more than you;
nor am I afraid of your husband, for he is standing right here beside you."

"Forgive me, husband of mine, forgive me my indiscretions;
don't do it so much for me, do it for your two children."
"You will not attain my pardon, nor indulgence of any kind;
ask Fernando to forgive you, he who was all your love."

Fly, fly, little dove, give impetus to your flight,
go and find out what happened with Elena and her husband.
Poor, poor Elena, how pitiful was her death!
She died of three pistol shots fired by her husband.

"Maidservant, take these children, take them over to my parents;
if they ask about Elena, tell them that you know nothing."
Ladies, give your attention to what happened on this occasion,
how her husband killed Elena because of her artful ways.

PART II

Songs of Border Conflict

Part II, "Songs of Border Conflict," includes thirty-four songs, more than half the number in this book. Intercultural conflict, after all, has been the most important characteristic of the Texas-Mexican Border, even before the Rio Grande became an international boundary line. Things were relatively peaceful for the colony of Nuevo Santander during the first eighty or ninety years of its existence. Those were prosperous times, during which the river-bank villages grew into towns and cities, while the herds that roamed Nuevo Santander's "backyard"—the Nueces-Rio Grande area—increased into the millions. There were, of course, periodic hurricanes, floods, and droughts; and once in a while small bands of Indians came raiding and carried off a horse or two or lifted a scalp. These things were accepted as problems related to daily life that unsettled but did not threaten the existence of the colony. Even Mexico's independence from Spain, which changed Nuevo Santander into the state of Tamaulipas, had relatively little impact on the Rio Grande people.

In the early 1800s, however, a people of different language and different culture settled in Texas, north of the Nueces. In 1836, the English-speaking settlers of Texas threw off Mexican authority. Immediately they began to move in on other areas of what was then northern Mexico, their first target being the northern part of Tamaulipas—the territory between the Nueces and the Rio Grande. Manifest Destiny mounted a sustained assault on the Rio Grande communities, the armed conflict taking three forms: incursions by Anglo-American raiders and cattle thieves; large-scale raids by Plains Indians, especially the Comanches; and civil wars among the Rio Grande people, as new political influences brought by the Anglo-American invaders caused divisions among the Mexicans themselves. The result was the wrecking of the Rio Grande economy and the incorporation into Texas of the Nueces-Rio Grande area. This early period of conflict ended in 1848, with the Treaty of Guadalupe Hidalgo and the establishment of the Rio Grande as an international boundary.

No songs have come down to us narrating such events as the cattle-stealing raids of Texas "cowboys" from north of the Nueces, the defeat of the Texans at Mier, or the guerrilla warfare against Zachary Taylor's troops during the war between Mexico and the United States. In fact, no narrative songs at all have survived from the pre-1848 period of conflict. The only song we have from this period is "LOS INDITOS," a non-narrative piece that refers to the Comanche raids on the Rio Grande settlements. In its present form it is a children's song.

"Los inditos" preserves the *ranchero*'s memory of raiding Indians lurking nearby in the canebrake. They are Plains Indians, bearing the round shield that frontier Mexicans knew by the Náhuatl word *chimal*. This song has been in my own family for several generations. I learned it from my mother, who learned it from my paternal grandfather. At one time, versions of this song must have been widely known throughout the frontier areas, and even down into the interior of Mexico, where the Plains Indians often carried their raids. Very similar versions have been found in New

Mexico, and there are songs from the interior of Mexico that seem to be parodies of "Los inditos." New Mexican versions usually are titled "El comanchito." Plains Indian raids, leaving death and destruction in their wake, seem like a pretty grim subject for children's songs. The Comanches and other raiding tribes would not seem to have earned the apparently affectionate terms of "comanchito" and "indito" applied to them. The Indians in "Los inditos" do partake of the character assumed by ogres and bogeymen in nursery songs, but only to a point. The very real and terrible cry of frontier times, "¡Ahi vienen los indios!" loses its threatening character when transformed into "Ahi vienen los inditos." The child, of course, becomes a little Indian himself, as he is dandled on his parent's knee and told in song to straighten his *chimal.* It is worth noting, however, that we have no songs saying "Ahi vienen los rinchitos" or "Ahi vienen los gringuitos," identifying our children with little Texas Rangers or little Anglo-American invaders of the Southwest. Indian raids were a terrible thing to the frontier Mexican, but they did not create an "ethnic" resentment against Indians, such as was caused by Anglo penetration. Individual raids might be remembered with grief and rage, but the general feeling was that since Indians were "natural" beings it was in their nature to fight and raid. Their depredations were classed with other natural calamities, such as fires and hurricanes. Anglo-Americans, on the other hand, claimed to be *cristianos* and approached you with an overbearing sense of moral superiority. They established a new system of laws that was supposed to protect everyone, and under this system they sometimes acted worse than the Comanches. Anglos were hypocrites. As one old man put it, "Tiran la piedra y esconden la mano." In contrast, when the Comanche "threw a rock" at you, he made no pretense about it.

With the signing of the Treaty of Guadalupe Hidalgo in 1848, conflict along the Rio Grande changed in character. The Mexicans on the left bank of the river were now legally citizens of the United States, with all the rights of citizenship. In actuality, they were not granted those rights. They were cheated out of their property by English-speaking newcomers and suffered all kinds of indignities from the new masters of the land. An oppressed minority had been created; protest on the part of these newly created Mexican-Americans was early and violent. Not all Mexicans along the Rio Grande protested against Anglo exploitation. Some "good" families made common cause with the Anglo fortune-seekers and were accepted as loyal citizens of the United States (and, later, of the Confederacy). In contemporary terms, they were our first "white, middle-class Latin Americans," while those who protested could be called our first "Chicanos." The oldest folksongs that have come down to us from this turbulent period (roughly 1848 to 1930) are about the first man to organize Texas-Mexican protest against abuses on the part of Anglos who controlled the Border power structure after 1848.

Juan Nepomuceno Cortina belonged to one of the old landholding families on the Rio Grande. In 1846 he was among the ranchero irregulars who fought alongside Mexican troops at Palo Alto and Resaca de la Palma. After the war he tried to live like a good American citizen, but he soon became embittered by the actions of Anglo fortune-makers in the area. One day in 1859 he rode into Brownsville and found city marshal Robert Shears pistol-whipping a vaquero who worked for Cortina's mother. Cortina intervened, shot the marshal, and rode out of town, taking the vaquero with him. He rallied a number of rancheros to his cause and outlined his grievances in a *plan* or manifesto. Then he attacked and occupied Brownsville in an effort to punish the men responsible for the abuses suffered by his people. In spite of what has been written about him by most Anglos—and by some Chicanos as well—Cortina did not take up arms to rob the rich and give to the poor. He was no "Robin Hood" of the Joaquín Murrieta type. His motives were basically political; what he was trying to give all Mexicans in Texas was dignity and social justice.

Cortina's war of protest ended when he was defeated and driven out of Texas by the U.S. cavalry. He continued to operate as a guerrilla both before and after the Civil War. During the French occupation of Mexico he was a general on the republican side and took part in the battle of the Cinco de Mayo. He also was an *enganchado* or Union agent working against the Confederates during the American Civil War. In 1876 Cortina was arrested and confined to Mexico City for the rest of his life, on orders of Porfirio Díaz. He was allowed to make one trip to the Border in 1890 and died in 1892.

The *corridos* about Cortina date back to the late 1850s and the early 1860s. Apparently, several *corridos* about Cortina were sung, but only fragments have survived. "EL GENERAL CORTINA" as it appears in this book is made up of three stanzas from three different *corridos* about Cortina. The first stanza pertains to Cortina's gunfight with Marshal Shears; the second makes reference to Cortina's visit to the Border in 1890; the third stanza refers to his death.

Conflict on the Texas-Mexican Border was intensified with the invasion of Mexico by the French in 1862 and the imposition of Archduke Maximilian as emperor of Mexico. President Benito Juárez led the republican resistance until 1867, when after the withdrawal of French support Maximilian's forces were defeated and Maximilian himself captured and executed as a war criminal. The Border people on both sides of the Rio Grande were strongly pro-Juárez. From this period comes "LOS FRANCESES," which was still in the repertory of older people in the Brownsville area in the 1960s. "Los franceses" is not a *corrido;* it is a series of derisive *coplas* or loose stanzas directed at Maximilian and his French troops, using a seven-syllable line rather than the eight-syllable line typical of the *corrido.* The French may take the Border towns, but they cannot hold them. It is one step north and two steps south for them, all the way back to Guadalajara. Maximilian is shown as crying to Carlotta for help before he is executed. The refrain is a salute to Juárez. The tune of "Los franceses" has a gay, chorus-line beat that suggests the theater. It is possible that the tune was borrowed from some popular French song brought to Mexico along with other facets of "imperial" culture.

When the French first invaded Mexico in 1862, their army was soundly defeated at Puebla on May 5 by a hastily assembled Mexican force under the command of Ignacio Zaragoza. Since then, the Mexican victory is celebrated in the Fiestas del Cinco de Mayo by Mexicans and Mexican-Americans alike. Zaragoza, hero of the battle, was born in Goliad, Texas, and educated in Matamoros, on the Rio Grande, where his family sought refuge after being driven out of Goliad as a result of the independence of Texas. The Border people recognized Zaragoza as a native son and were quite proud of his feat at Puebla. On May 5, 1867, the little town of San Ignacio, in Zapata County, celebrated the Cinco de Mayo, as did all other Border towns. Zaragoza was dead by then, a victim of typhoid fever in the year of his triumph over the French. By 1867 Maximilian's dreams of empire were also dead. He and his army were under siege in Querétaro, where they would surrender on May 15. At the Cinco de Mayo festivities in San Ignacio that May 5 of 1867, a local *guitarrero* named Onofre Cárdenas sang his composition "A ZARAGOZA." The song remained in the oral tradition of the area; I learned it in the 1950s from don Mercurio Martínez, a native of Zapata County. Local pride in Zaragoza may be seen in the epithet given him in the second line of the text: "unconquerable general of the Border."

At San Ignacio's Cinco de Mayo festivities, Onofre Cárdenas sang two of his compositions: "A Zaragoza" and another song much like it called "A GRANT." The man honored along with Ignacio Zaragoza on that occasion was Ulysses S. Grant, the leader of the victorious Union armies in the North American Civil War. By 1867 the Civil War in the United States was long over. Grant had retired from public life, to return to it as the eighteenth president soon afterward. But the Civil War was not forgotten on the Border. It had been another cause for raiding and violence during the 1860s. On the Union-Confederacy issue, the Border people had divided along predictable lines. The wealthier families and their retainers espoused the Confederate cause and looked on the imperialists in Mexico as their allies. The general populace, and some prominent figures like Cortina, favored the Union and made common cause with the *juaristas* in Mexico. This song to Grant is strongly pro-Union. It extols Ulysses S. Grant in much the same terms used for Ignacio Zaragoza. The Texas-Mexican's situation as a citizen of the United States but with strong roots in Mexican culture is well expressed in these two songs. There were also songs about pro-Union Borderers other than Cortina who raided against the Confederates during the Civil War, but apparently these songs have not survived into the second half of the twentieth century. Jovita González has published a song, without music, about one Remigio Treviño, collected at Rio Grande City in 1928. Miss González describes Treviño as "a soldier stationed at Camargo, who in the early sixties made up his mind to kill and expel the few Americans living along the border."

Treviño, who was credited with killing ten Americans, was captured and hanged after a raid on Rio Grande City in 1863. Most probably he was a pro-Union guerrilla. The song about him is in garbled *décimas* rather than in *corrido* form.[1]

The cattle drives to Kansas furnished the subject for the oldest complete *corridos* from the Lower Rio Grande Border—among the oldest in Greater Mexican tradition. During the Civil War many Border Mexicans had attempted to better their lot by allying themselves with the distant *yanquis* of the Union against the local *gringo* Confederates, who were the immediate cause of their troubles. But the triumph of the Union brought little relief to the Borderer. The same people dominated things, whether one called them *yanquis, confederados,* or *gringos.* Pro- or anti-Confederate, however, the Border Mexican did share one thing with his Anglo neighbors: the economic depression that followed the war. Texans found a solution to their economic problems in the demand for beef that arose in the cities of the East. So they gathered huge herds of cattle and drove them north to the railheads in Kansas.

Everyone has heard of the famous cattle drives to Kansas, the subject of many a Western. What is not so well known is that it was cattle owned by Mexicans and Texas-Mexicans (some legally obtained from them and some not) that formed the bulk of the herds driven north from the Nueces-Rio Grande area, the so-called cradle of the cattle industry in the United States. Not all cattle that went north were driven by Anglo cowboys. Many of the trail drivers were Mexicans, some taking their own herds, others working for Anglo outfits. The late 1860s and early 1870s was a period when a good many Mexicans still were *dueños* on the Texas side. In this respect they could meet the Anglo on something like equal terms. But the Texas-Mexican possessed something else that gave him a certain status—the tools and the techniques of the vaquero trade, in which the Anglo was merely a beginner. The Mexican with some justice could feel superior to the Anglo when it came to handling horses and cattle, or facing occupational hazards such as flooded rivers. These attitudes are apparent in the *corridos* about the cattle drives to Kansas, pronounced "Kiansis" by Border rancheros. "El corrido de Kiansis" exists in several variants and is the oldest Texas-Mexican *corrido* that we have in complete form. The *corridos* about Cortina are seven or eight years older, but only fragments of them remain in the memories of old men. "Kiansis" is sung to two different tunes, which I have labeled "KIANSIS I" and "KIANSIS II." The stanzas sung with each tune may be used interchangeably with the other tune. "Kiansis I" is sometimes called the "old" tune. In my youth, it was the tune used by old men who had been born in the 1860s. "Kiansis II" was preferred by the younger men. "Kiansis" has been sung in my family (and in other Border families as well) since the 1860s. I first

[1] Jovita González, "Tales and Songs of the Texas-Mexicans," in *Man, Bird, and Beast,* ed. J. Frank Dobie (Austin, 1930), 110-111.

learned a complete version from one of my granduncles, Hilario Cisneros, born in 1867, who learned it from the vaqueros who had made the first trips on the trail to Kansas.

There is intercultural conflict in "Kiansis," but it is expressed in professional rivalries rather than in violence between men. Death lurks on the horns of a wild bull or in the deep currents of a stream, rather than in the muzzle of a forty-four. Anglo accounts of the cattle drives, however, mention incidents of Mexican vaqueros shot out of hand by Anglo trail bosses because the Mexicans misunderstood orders, and of Mexican outfits attacked by Anglos while on the trail in competition for water and grazing space. The "Kiansis" *corridos* make no mention of such incidents, perhaps because armed conflicts between Mexicans and Anglos were part of another kind of situation, already quite familiar to the Mexican, while the cattle drives to the North were something new and exciting.

Less than sixty years after the opening of the Kansas Trail, Mexicans were again traveling north from the Rio Grande to do a job of work. But they no longer went on horseback as vaqueros, proud of their cattle-herding trade. The southern tip of Texas no longer was cattle country. It had been cleared of brush and planted to vegetables and cotton, especially cotton. The grandson of the vaquero was now a stoop laborer in the cotton fields of Texas. Mexicans began to migrate north in greater and greater numbers, in search of better opportunities. Many went to do seasonal labor in the beet fields and fruit orchards of other states. Others, more farsighted perhaps, did not want to spend all their lives picking cotton. They joined work gangs in the railroad camps and the coal and copper mines. Little by little, they moved into the big cities in states other than Texas. An important phase in the history of the urban Chicano was in the making. In the spring of 1923, the steel industry in Bethlehem, Pennsylvania, began importing Mexican labor from Texas to work in the mills, over the protests of Texas farmers, who feared the loss of their cheap agricultural labor. San Antonio was the starting point for the trains carrying hundred of laborers to Pennsylvania, single men for the most part. To the Texas-Mexican, however, Fort Worth (*For West*) was the real jumping-off place into the great areas beyond. "LA PENSILVANIA" chronicles the experiences of the work gangs, or *enganches,* that made the trip to Bethlehem. Other *corridos*—often patterned on "La Pensilvania"—have been composed about other Mexican migrations leaving Texas for various parts of the United States. But none of them has replaced "La Pensilvania" in Texas-Mexican tradition as the song epitomizing Mexican migrant labor.

The Kansas Trail *corridos* may have ignored the armed conflict between Mexicans and Anglos on the Border, but such conflict went on after the demise of the Confederacy and Maximilian's empire in Mexico. After these large-scale conflicts, a relative calm came to the Mexican side of the Border. It was the iron-fisted peace of Porfirio Díaz's dictatorship, much admired by Anglos of the time because it stilled the protests of the Mexican people against exploitation, both in Mexico and across the river in Texas.

Cortina's raid on Brownsville and his subsequent defeat by the U.S. army had set a pattern for other Texas-Mexicans who were forced into violent protest against exploitation and injustice. Inevitably, the weight of American authority was too much for a Texas-Mexican to fight against. If he was not killed or captured, the man who "defended his right" had to seek refuge across the river in Mexican territory. Such refuge was denied to him after Porfirio Díaz became dictator of Mexico. Díaz made an agreement with the United States whereby he would return any Border Mexican who sought refuge in Mexico. In return, Texas officials saw to it that armed opposition against Díaz was not organized in the towns along the Texas side of the river. "RITO GARCIA" relates events taking place a quarter-century after Cortina's raid. Margarito (Rito) García reacted violently to what would now be termed "police brutality": unwarranted search of his home accompanied by violence to members of his family. Rito fought back and then rode across the river into what he considered "my Mexican soil," though he was a Texas-Mexican. But Guadalupe Mainero, the governor of Tamaulipas, had Rito arrested and handed him over to the Texas law, in accordance with Díaz's agreement with the United States. "Rito García" sounds a note of disenchantment with the Mexican government's ability or willingness to defend the rights of Mexicans in the United States. Other Texas-Mexicans are counseled, "Nunca vayan a pedir a México protección." This is a surprising statement for 1885, the date of García's brush with the law. As late as the 1940s, many Mexican-Americans still were looking to the Mexican government, through its consulates in the United States, to defend the rights that belonged to them as American citizens.

Mexican-American dependence on the Mexican government in the matter of civil rights in the United States has not been given due notice in the history of the present Chicano movement, which too often is seen as a sudden awakening of the Mexican minority in the United States to a consciousness of themselves and of their rights as human beings. As a recent advocate of *chicanismo* has put it, "That lazy *bandido* sleeping beneath the big sombrero in the shade of the adobe hut has suddenly awakened. . . . Certainly the age of self-analysis and self-discovery has finally caught up with him."[2]

Mexican-Americans have been awake to their problems since the time of Cortina. They have also been quite preoccupied with questions of self-analysis and identity, ever since the Treaty of Guadalupe. The Chicano "awakening" of the 1960s is the culmination of a long and continuous struggle, spanning more than a century. Not all of this struggle was violent, by any means. There were serious attempts to organize Mexican-Americans into unions and cooperative organizations. Individuals wrote

[2] Edward Simmen, ed., *The Chicano: From Caricature to Self-Portrait* (New York, 1971), 15.

pamphlets and edited newspapers advocating social reform.[3] The changes that became apparent in the 1960s were brought about by a change in attitudes that was not limited to the Mexican-American minority. If there is any group in the United States that has "suddenly awakened into an age of self-analysis," it is the WASP majority. And it is largely because of a change in majority attitudes that minority protest is more viable and more effective than in the past.

But it is also true that Mexican-American protest has undergone some changes in method and strategy since World War II. One change from the past has been the increasing use of English instead of Spanish in verbal and written protest, resulting in an increased visibility of the Mexican-American to the English-speaking majority. Another has been in the greater use of the mechanisms for political and social action offered by existing institutions in the United States. Such changes were not possible in the past because of Mexican-American attitudes that are reflected in *corridos* like "Rito García."

Margarito García lives in Texas, in the United States, but he thinks of the United States as a "foreign nation" (*nación extranjera*) and of Mexico as "my country" (*mi país*). He thinks of himself as a *mexicano* not only in a cultural but in a political sense. This attitude was shared by most Mexican-Americans of the time, and it is central to the *corrido* of cultural conflict. The Mexican-American in the Southwest felt that he was living in a part of Mexico occupied by a foreign country. When he suffered injustice and exploitation, he had two means of protest. He could "defend his right" with force of arms, or he could appeal to the Mexican government to take action in his favor through the Mexican consulates in the United States. The application of American methods of political and social action to *mexicano* problems is indeed something relatively new. But such methods were not available to Rito García, so he uses his rifle to protest Anglo injustice. The officers he shoots happen to have Spanish names, but they are representatives of "Gringo law" as far as he is concerned.

Once he has "defended his right," Rito seeks refuge in Mexico. Alas, the Díaz government does not share his irredentist views. He is handed over to U.S. authorities by Governor Mainero. This, however, does not shake faith in Mexico on the part of the Border people. The bitter "Never go to Mexico asking for protection" in Rito's *corrido* is a rhetorical rather than a declarative utterance. It should be read, "Mexico's duty is to protect us, but Mainero let us down."

In becoming dictator of Mexico, Porfirio Díaz began by organizing a coup in Brownsville, with the support of rancheros from both sides of the Rio Grande. When his government became repressive, it was among

---

[3] See, for example, José E. Limón, "El Primer Congreso Mexicanista de 1911: A Precursor to Contemporary Chicanismo," *Aztlán: Chicano Journal of the Social Sciences and the Arts* 5:1 and 2 (1974), 85-117.

these same rancheros that the first rebellions against Díaz arose. Catarino E. Garza, who lived on a ranch near San Diego, Texas, launched a revolt against Díaz in 1891. Anglo writers commenting on Garza's revolt have treated him as they have done Cortina. His men are said to have been a bunch of bandits, out for nothing but loot. Garza himself is described as a man without any social or political views, seeking to overthrow the Mexican government more or less singlehanded because of some imagined slight done to him by Díaz officials. The whole rebellion is called a ludicrous affair.[4]

A less prejudiced and better documented view gives us a different picture of Garza's rebellion.[5] Catarino Garza was a Border writer and newspaper editor who had been criticizing the Díaz government in his Texas-based newspaper for several years before the rebellion. As a result of his newspaper campaign against Díaz, he had been in danger of assassination from Díaz agents and had also suffered harassment from authorities in Texas. Garza's rebellion received ample support from Mexicans in south Texas, and he also had the support of influential men in Mexico, including some in the Díaz government. His proclamation of rebellion against Díaz demanded free elections, civilian rather than military rule in Mexico, individual freedoms, land for the peasants, and the restoration of the Constitution of 1857—the same goals that the men of the Revolution would espouse twenty years later.

On December 20, 1891, Garza crossed the Rio Grande into Mexico with about 100 men. Waiting to rise at his call in different parts of Mexico were nuclei of men and arms. But at this point in his career, Catarino Garza committed a fatal mistake. After fighting an indecisive battle at a place called Las Tortillas, he decided to cross back into Texas to regroup his forces, rather than pushing into Mexico to establish contact with the sympathizers waiting for his signal to join in the revolt. Waiting for him on the Texas side were the U.S. cavalry and assorted posses of Texas Rangers and deputies. His small force was broken up by the cavalry; individuals were hunted down by soldiers and lawmen and handed over to Díaz firing squads across the river. His rebellion crushed by U.S. rather than Mexican forces, Garza made his way out of the United States and into Central America, where he was killed trying to organize another revolt.

It is usually said that Catarino Garza's rebellion failed because the Mexican people were not ready for revolt against Díaz in 1891. It is more correct to say that it was the American people who were not ready to see Díaz replaced. In the 1890s, American exploitation of Mexican men and resources was barely getting under way, and Díaz was extremely popular in this country. In 1911 Madero would face obstacles in organizing a

---

[4] See, for example, Frank Cushman Pierce, *A Brief History of the Lower Rio Grande Valley* (Menasha, Wis., 1917), 72; and Norman Laird McNeil, "*Corridos* of the Mexican Border," in *Mexican Border Ballads and Other Lore*, ed. Mody C. Boatright (Austin, 1946), 15-16, 19-20.

[5] Gabriel Saldívar, *Documentos de la rebelión de Catarino E. Garza* (Mexico, 1943).

Mexican revolution in the United States, but he did not undergo the determined repression that was the lot of Catarino E. Garza.

"LOS PRONUNCIADOS" and "EL CAPITAN HALL" are *corridos* about the Garza rebellion. "Los pronunciados" has been sung all along the Lower Border. I first heard it from my father, who was one of Catarino Garza's men. It celebrates the Garza attack on Las Tortillas. "El capitán Hall" apparently has been sung only in or near Zapata County. I have it from Mercurio Martínez, whose family owned Los Cristales, mentioned in the ballad as Don Proceso's ranch. After Garza's men were broken up, a group of them hid out close to Los Cristales. A Texas Ranger captain named Hall attempted to disarm and arrest them but was unable to do so. Later, according to Sr. Martínez, a Border sheriff named Robert Haynes succeeded in talking the *pronunciados* into surrendering. "El capitán Hall" makes fun of the Texas Ranger captain.

Not all Border men who shot it out with the law were completely blameless individuals defending their rights. But so keen was the Mexican sense of injustice against Anglo domination, so vivid the pattern of intercultural conflict in the *corrido,* that sometimes an outlaw with no conscience of social or political justice was elevated into a hero of Border conflict. The best example we have of this tendency concerns José María Mosqueda, who earned a niche in Lower Border history by planning and executing the first train robbery in south Texas, back in 1891. At that time, the only rails south of San Antonio were on a narrow-gauge track that ran from Brownsville to Point Isabel (now Port Isabel) on the Gulf. The railroad cut across a high place in the flats known as Loma Trozada, and it was at this point that Mosqueda and his band held up the train and escaped with several thousand dollars worth of Mexican silver pesos. Mosqueda and one of his men later went to prison for the robbery. Most of the money was never recovered, and legends about the holdup and its consequences are still told along the Border.

It happened that the owners of the stolen money were mostly Mexicans, Texas-Mexicans, and Spaniards. The man who solved the case and arrested Mosqueda—Brownsville city marshal Santiago Brito—also was a Texas-Mexican. Nonetheless, "JOSE MOSQUEDA" is sung as though it were a *corrido* of cultural conflict. Mosqueda and his men raid "American soil"; it is "los americanos" who complain about the deed. The patterns of folk literature and the stresses of intercultural conflict triumph over historical fact in "José Mosqueda." Some minor historical data (a train robbery) are superseded by an overriding historical fact (the clash of cultures).

The period from 1900 to 1911 was a time of transition both in Mexico and in the United States. In the United States certain sections of Anglo society were becoming more and more conscious of social and political issues. "Anarchists" were still vigorously persecuted, but there was a feeling of change in the air. In Mexico things were building up toward the Revolution. Ill feeling against the United States was part of the revolutionary mood. The common man in Mexico could get worked up over rumors that North Americans had bought the cathedral in Mexico City and would turn it into a big department store. Reports about lynchings of Mexicans in Texas were the cause of anti-American riots in Mexico City and other urban centers.

On the Texas-Mexican Border, this period is marked by *corridos* such as "GREGORIO CORTEZ." No other Mexican-American *corrido* has been more widely known. It has been reported wherever Mexicans are found in the United States, not only on the Border but on the West Coast and in the Great Lakes areas. Many other *corrido* heroes—such as Cortina and Rito García—had preceded Gregorio Cortez, but in Cortez's life was epitomized the idea of the man who defends his rights *con su pistola en la mano.* In Karnes County on June 12, 1901, Cortez shot and killed Sheriff Brack Morris, who seconds before had shot Cortez's brother. The sheriff was trying to arrest the Cortezes for a crime they had not committed. Cortez fled, knowing that the only justice available to him in Karnes County would be at the end of a rope. In his flight toward the Rio Grande, Cortez walked more than 100 miles and rode at least 400, eluding hundreds of men who were trying to capture him. On the way he killed another Texas sheriff, Robert Glover of Gonzales County; and he was also accused of the death of Constable Henry Schnabel.

Exhausted, on foot, and out of ammunition, Cortez was captured near Laredo. His case united Mexican-Americans in a common cause, and there were concerted efforts for his defense in the courts. The legal battle lasted three years and included reversals of a couple of speedy and unfair convictions. Finally, Cortez was acquitted of murder in the deaths of Sheriff Morris and Constable Schnabel, a significant victory in the long fight that has been waged by the Mexican-American for equal treatment in American courts. Cortez was sentenced to life imprisonment, however, for the death of Sheriff Glover. Governor O. B. Colquitt pardoned Cortez in 1913. Gregorio Cortez and the *corrido* about him are a milestone in the Mexican-American's emerging group consciousness. A number of tentative organizations resulted from the court fight on his behalf.[6] The readiness with which Mexicans in the United States came together in his defense showed that the necessary conditions existed for united effort.

"Gregorio Cortez" is without a doubt the epitome of the Border *corrido,* with the hero betrayed into the hands of his enemies. To my knowledge, the most widespread of the Border *corridos* in which the hero makes a successful escape across the river is "JACINTO TREVIÑO." Few people who sing "Jacinto Treviño" are aware that the present *corrido* is made up from two different ballads—an original "Jacinto Treviño," which so far as I know has been lost, and another *corrido,* "IGNACIO TREVIÑO," about a man who did battle with the *rinches* in a Brownsville saloon.

---

[6] See Limón, pp. 92-93, for an example.

Ignacio Treviño was a Brownsville policeman around 1911, during a time when the Democratic machine was being challenged by an independent party made up mostly of Texas-Mexicans. The county/state Democratic mob regained control of Brownsville politics after José Crixell, the city marshal, was ambushed and rubbed out by a Texas Ranger. Before Crixell's death, a group of Rangers and sheriff's deputies attempted to hit Ignacio Treviño at Crixell's White Elephant saloon, facing the city square. Treviño barricaded himself in the saloon, with the *rinches* outside. A protracted shootout followed, with no casualties—it seems—but the beer barrels and whisky bottles in the saloon. Finally, a truce was arranged between city men and county/state men. Ignacio Treviño walked out of the White Elephant, and—like many other *corrido* heroes—he sought refuge on the Mexican side of the river. "El comandante" mentioned in the *corrido* is Marshal José Crixell. Tito Crixell was his brother Vicente. Others named were members of the police force. They all were pretty formidable men, but the *corrido* maker makes fun of them because they did not come to Ignacio Treviño's aid.

Jacinto Treviño lived near Los Indios, a few miles upriver from Brownsville. Apparently he was just another peaceful, hard-working ranchero until his celebrated fight with the *rinches* in 1911. A brother of Jacinto's was badly beaten by an Anglo for whom the brother worked, so badly that the brother later died. Jacinto sought out the Anglo and killed him; and then he put the river between him and the *rinches*, while the Anglo community of nearby San Benito put up a reward for him. A few months later, a cousin of Jacinto's named Pablo offered to deliver Jacinto to the Texas authorities. Jacinto was to be lured across the river, to a certain spot in the brush where the officers would wait for him. Two parties of Rangers and deputies went to the spot and ran into gunfire from the brush. Apparently Jacinto got there first and ambushed the ambushers. When the smoke cleared away, Pablo Treviño, a Ranger, and a deputy were dead. Another Ranger and a constable were wounded. Jacinto Treviño crossed back into Mexico, where he lived to a ripe old age.

There once must have been a *corrido* detailing Jacinto's exploits in the brush along the river. But by the 1930s the "Jacinto Treviño" and "Ignacio Treviño" ballads had been amalgamated under Jacinto's name. Jacinto is brought in from the brush and into a saloon owned by someone named Baker, where he fights Ignacio's fight against the *rinches*. Ignacio, meanwhile, disappears from the scene entirely. It is not difficult to see why the Border *corrido* tradition has preferred Jacinto over Ignacio. Ignacio was a brave man, but his quarrel with the *rinches* was part of a power struggle between two political machines. Jacinto, on the other hand, fit the pattern of the typical Texas-Mexican *corrido* hero. He was the peaceful man goaded into violence and defending his right with his pistol in his hand.

In 1915, oh but the days were hot! So says the *corrido* "LOS SEDICIOSOS," commemorating the Texas-Mexican uprising of 1915. In contemporary terms, this uprising could be described as an outsized Watts, taking place in the brush country instead of the urban "ghettoes." But it differed from the Watts disturbances in that the *sediciosos* were acting in accordance with a *plan* or declaration of grievances and intentions. "El Plan de San Diego" has been called many things: a Communist or IWW conspiracy, a Japanese plot, a machination of the Kaiser, a devious move on the part of Venustiano Carranza, a wild and improbable scheme. There was a good deal of the improbable about the "Plan"—especially if we look at it with the clarity of hindsight. And it is probable that the participants were aided and encouraged by the *carrancistas*. The very fact of a successful revolution in Mexico must have encouraged *tejanos* to repeat Cortina's attempt to redress their wrongs through a general uprising.

But the whole "seditionist" movement set in motion by the "Plan" answered to deep-seated feelings in a great number of Mexican-Americans, feelings that have recently been expressed in the Chicano movement. The "Plan de San Diego," furthermore, called for a union of Mexicans with Indians, Negroes, and Orientals—an early attempt to enunciate the current "third world" idea.

Bands of Border men under the leadership of Aniceto Pizaña and Luis de la Rosa raided as far north as King Ranch, burning ranches, derailing trains, killing American civilians, and attacking U.S. army detachments. The American government rushed troops by the thousands to the Rio Grande. But the "Plan de San Diego" failed to bring about a general uprising of Mexicans in the Southwest and of Negroes in the South. The bands raiding in south Texas rarely numbered more than forty men. In the end, De la Rosa withdrew from the fray. Pizaña was arrested on the Mexican side by Carranza officials, and he was confined to the Mexico City area as Cortina had been a half-century before. Meanwhile, Texas Rangers and sheriff's deputies took out their frustration at not being able to catch the *sediciosos* by slaughtering as many innocent Mexican farm workers as they could lay their hands on. Hundreds were summarily "executed" without trial, and many hundreds more fled to Mexico to escape the *rinche* terror. The results were that more land in south Texas was cleared of Mexicans so it could be "developed" by Anglo newcomers in the 1920s.

"Los sediciosos" recounts some of the exploits of Aniceto Pizaña and his men. Luis de la Rosa, who was not a Border man and who was accused of selling out toward the end of the uprising, is pictured unfavorably, though there is no reason to believe that he was any less brave than the other raiders. In spite of this bit of pro-Pizaña partisanship, there is a tone of ambivalence in the whole *corrido*. "Los sediciosos" is half epic ballad and half lyrical lament for the victims of Ranger "executions." The Borderers could not help admiring the *sediciosos,* since their acts were directed against the hated *rinches* and their allies. At the same time, the *mexicotejanos* knew they were victims of bloody repression because of the *sedicioso* dream of a Spanish-speaking Republic of the Southwest. Thus, the *corrido* is not all praise of Pizaña and his followers. There is grief expressed for the victims of Ranger "executions," and the *sediciosos* are said to have left the Texas-Mexicans a bloody swath to remember them by.

The Pizaña uprising was the last major armed protest on the part of Texas-Mexicans. Individual acts of violent protest continued for twenty years or so, and they were often celebrated in *corridos* such as "PABLO GONZALEZ." These were acts of men without great prominence in the political or social history of the region, but their deeds were engraved in common memory because they were seen as symbols—men who stood up for their dignity as human beings and suffered death or exile for their actions. According to what oral tradition tells about him, Pablo González was such a man. I have not been able to find out much about him, except that he lived and died in Rio Grande City. According to tradition, he was walking past the Rio Grande City courthouse with his wife one day, when she was insulted by a lawman. Pablo shot the man and took to the brush with his rifle, where he held off the posses sent after him. But a supposed friend betrayed him; he visited Pablo and unloaded Pablo's rifle when he was not looking. The *rinches* then attacked, and Pablo was shot down as he was trying to reload his rifle.

From the Anglo point of view, the Texas-Mexican was a lawless character who used intercultural conflict to excuse his natural bent for violence and disorder; and it must be admitted that the average *mexicotejano* of those days tended to see almost any act of resistance against the law as a protest against Anglo oppression. There is a close similarity between those Border attitudes and the current, so-called ghetto attitudes toward law and order, and for very much the same reasons. If people are not allowed to share in their own destinies, if they feel they are being governed from above by an alien group, then the "law" is not considered their law, and flouting it becomes one more way of protesting against their inferior status. The conflict retains its cultural character even when the man resorting to violence must fight law enforcement officers who speak his own language and bear Spanish names like his own. The minority policeman, compelled by the nature of his job to become an agent of the forces ranged against his own people, may be seen by his people as a *vendido* or sellout. This is the situation in *corridos* ranging from "Rito García" to "Pablo González."

Not all cases in which a Border man "defended his right" arose from actions by U.S. authorities or the *rinches*. Rural police on the Mexican side of the river could also be oppressive. And with the advent of the Revolution, local warlords at times abused their power in exploiting and bullying peaceful citizens. Under such circumstances, the Borderer of the south bank reacted very much like his cousin in Texas. He defended his right, pistol in hand, and died doing so, or he made his way across the river in the opposite direction, into Texas rather than away from it, after having done his deed. "ALONSO" and "ARNULFO" tell about two such men, both scarcely out of their teens—Alonso Flores and Arnulfo González. Though their family names are known, these two are usually referred to by first name alone, as one does of a person who is very well known by everyone.

There are many people in Brownsville who still remember Alonso Flores. They tell how he came to Brownsville, a boy in his early teens, with his mother and younger brother during the first years of the Revolution. His father had been *autoridad* in a small town in Nuevo León, until there came a man remembered only as "el general Margarito," but whose name probably was Ortiz. Margarito invited Alonso's father to a parley and treacherously killed him. Alonso and his mother fled to Brownsville, while Margarito and his men took over the town. After five or six years, Alonso returned and killed Margarito. He made it safely across the Border into Texas, but later he went back to Mexico and became a revolutionary himself.

Arnulfo González's story is told in his *corrido*. He lived in Allende, Coahuila, some twenty miles from the banks of the Rio Grande; and he died at the age of twenty in a gunfight with a *rural,* a member of the Mexican rural police analogous to the Texas Rangers. Arnulfo dies because he feels he has the right to stare at a rural policeman if he wants to. The *rural* is overbearing and brutal, but he redeems himself by dying bravely along with Arnulfo. The *corridista* grows lyrical in praise of both men, who died defending what each of them thought was his right.

"ALEJOS SIERRA" is a somewhat different type of *corrido* from the ones mentioned so far. It is more in the pattern of the *macho* type of contemporary *corrido* that has been used by social scientists to psychologize about the Mexican's Freudian hangups. There is no clear evidence that the protagonist is protesting anything or avenging any injustice done to him or to his kin. We do not know any causes for his resentment, and from the way he goes into action it is probable that his reasons for fighting are based on alcohol and *valentía* rather than on a sense of injustice. Perhaps. It is true that as the Border-conflict period passes there are more *corridos* of the saloon-brawl type. The theme of fighting with pistol in hand is developed in a different type of situation. Still, it is hard to tell whether "Alejos Sierra" definitely belongs to the saloon type of *corrido* or not. We do not know the reasons for Alejos's actions. All we see is his anger. The heroic model persists, however, in the words of Alejos's father after the death of his son. The father weeps but he says, "You have died the way men should, fighting on horseback." Perhaps Alejos had no definable grievance, and then some people would be inclined to blame *machismo* for the violent outburst that ends with his death and that of the policeman Hilario. But *machismo* does not really tell us anything. It does not explain why a young man would mount his horse and gallop out to "kill or be killed," any more than it could explain why in the United States other young men straddle motorcycles and roar out seeking violence and excitement.

Not all *corridos* are composed about well-known men; they may be about celebrated places as well. There is a difference between Mexican and

American folk cultures in the attitudes toward the home town or the area of one's birth. There are many Anglo-American songs praising favorite cities and states, but usually they are stage productions or officially sponsored songs rather than folksongs. Anglo-American folk attitudes toward familiar localities usually express humorous disdain, as for example in "Starving to Death on a Government Claim." Mexican folklore and popular music, on the other hand, abound with songs composed to celebrate states, cities, or well-known areas such as the Bajío or the Huasteca. Even obscure little towns such as Pénjamo may become immortalized in song. In this type of song we can appreciate the feeling that people of Mexican culture have always had for their own little plot of God's earth, their *patria chica.* "LAREDO" is about one of the main cities of the Lower Rio Grande Border. It extols the attractions of the city, its beautiful women, and its brave men. "Laredo" has been sung on the Border since the 1920s, so the "guerra mundial" mentioned is World War I. It is significant that the song demands equal treatment for Mexican-Americans because they fought as equals with Anglos in World War I. After World War II, a similar argument would be used in a more organized fashion by groups such as the G.I. Forum.

A very important factor in the history of cultural conflict along the Lower Rio Grande Border was the Mexican Revolution, which began in 1910 and developed into full-scale civil war in 1913. *Carrancista* encouragement has been noted as a factor in the activities of Aniceto Pizaña and his *sediciosos.* Another factor deserving mention is the mere fact of the Revolution in Mexico. For many decades, Mexicans on both sides of the river had existed under much the same conditions. On the north bank they were exploited by Anglos, whose power was backed by the U.S. army, and whose bullyboys were the Texas Rangers. On the Mexican side they were exploited by a creole élite, backed by the Mexican army, with Díaz's *rurales*—another rural constabulary like the Rangers—as the strong-arm unit. Then, all of a sudden, the people in Mexico had revolted. The *rurales* were swept aside, and the Mexican army proved no match for an armed and aroused populace. Men like Pizaña may well have speculated whether the same thing could not happen on the Texas side. At all events, there is no doubt that the Mexican Revolution stirred the imaginations and profoundly affected the lives of people on both sides of the Rio Grande.

"LA TOMA DE CIUDAD JUAREZ" commemorates the first victory of the Revolution. On May 8, 1911, troops loyal to Francisco I. Madero took Ciudad Juárez, opposite El Paso. On May 23, Porfirio Díaz abdicated and left Mexico for France. This *corrido* must have been composed soon after by a *guitarrero* in Ciudad Juárez or El Paso. At one time, when the events were fresh on everyone's mind, it probably was sung all up and down the Texas-Mexican borderline, from El Paso to Brownsville. Then it was forgotten in some places. It no longer seems to be well known in the Juárez-El Paso area, for example. In 1956-57, during a year's stay in El Paso, I found no one in the area who remembered it. But the Lower Border people, with their tradition of *corridos* about daring events, found a place for it in their corpus. They have preserved it to this day, especially the details about the fighting in the streets and the mocking of the loser, Porfirio Díaz. Variants of "La toma de Ciudad Juárez," sung to a somewhat different tune, have been collected in central and southern Mexico; but the texts also are different from ours. They dwell on minor political details and *macho*-type boasting rather than on the details as eyewitnesses must have seen them, making us suspect that the variants from interior Mexico began as *hojas sueltas* or broadside sheets printed in Mexico City rather than with the singing of *guitarreros*.

The Orozco mentioned in the *corrido* is Pascual Orozco, who with Francisco Villa was among the first to rally to Madero's cause. Orozco and Villa headed the *maderista* forces that took Ciudad Juárez. Later, Orozco turned against Madero and fled into Texas, where he reportedly was killed by Texas Rangers, who as was their custom mistook him for a cattle rustler. The Navarro whose loss Díaz laments was General Juan J. Navarro, commander of the federal forces defeated at Ciudad Juárez.

Porfirio Díaz left for Paris, and Francisco Madero became president of Mexico. But Madero made the mistake of putting his trust in holdovers from the Díaz regime. In 1913 Madero was deposed by Victoriano Huerta, a former Díaz general, who had Madero assassinated and proclaimed himself president. The army, the wealthy, and other elements of the old Díaz power structure were happy over Huerta's coup. But popular leaders throughout the country refused to recognize Huerta and declared war against him. Chief among them were Zapata in the south and Villa and Carranza in the north. Since Carranza was from Coahuila, the Mexican states along the lower Rio Grande were strongly *carrancista*. But Matamoros, the chief Mexican city in the area, became *huertista* when the garrison declared itself in favor of Huerta. So on Tuesday, June 3, 1913, at 10 A.M.—exactly as reported in "LA TOMA DE MATAMOROS"—the city came under attack from *carrancista* forces under the command of General Lucio Blanco.

The Matamoros garrison of regular troops, under the command of Major Esteban Ramos, put up a token resistance and then crossed over to Brownsville, where they were interned. The wealthy and conservative families of Matamoros also crossed into Brownsville. Matamoros citizens, however, have a history of defense of their city against armed attack, for which the city has been dubbed *la Heroica*. Groups of young Matamoros men, some of them fourteen and fifteen years old, volunteered for service under irregular *huertista* officers. They fought stubbornly until early in the morning of June 4. A number of them were captured and executed by Blanco's men. The "Chazarreta" mentioned in the *corrido* was Antonio Echazarreta, one of the *huertista* irregulars who captained the volunteer resistance. "López" probably was Lorenzo López, another of the irregular chieftains on the Huerta side. "Barragán" was Dr. Miguel Barragán, *presidente municipal* or mayor of Matamoros during the short-lived *huertista* ascendancy. No one has been able to tell me who was the "antiguo artillero" mentioned in stanza 18. Legend says it was Felipe Angeles (see no. 33), but Angeles was hundreds of miles away from Matamoros at the time.

There is a story told about Blanco's capture of Matamoros that is reflected in our version of the *corrido,* stanzas 10 and 11. The *carrancistas* had a number of sympathizers within the city who also took part in the battle. According to the story, it had been agreed that Blanco's adherents within Matamoros would ring the church bells when they saw that the tide of battle definitely had turned in favor of the attackers. Blanco was repulsed, however, and the *carrancistas* within the city did not ring the bells. But one of the *huertista* defenders, seeing Blanco's men withdrawing, went and rang the bells as a sign of victory. Blanco heard the bells and thought it was his allies within the city, signaling victory; so he attacked again and took the town. It is doubtful that the accidental ringing of the bells was necessary for a *carrancista* victory, since the odds were overwhelmingly against the defenders. But the story persists in oral tradition.

"La toma de Matamoros" is conceived from the viewpoint of the *huertista* refugees in Brownsville, who are shown as lost souls wandering about in Texas. It was probably composed in Brownsville. It must have been composed—or at least recast—by José Suárez, blind singer and the best-known and most highly regarded *guitarrero* in the area for at least half a century (1890-1940). The tune of "La toma de Matamoros," as well as some of its stanzas, strongly resembles "Los sediciosos," another *corrido* in the repertory of "José el Cieguito," as we all called him.

Villa, Zapata, and Carranza drove Huerta from power and then fell out with each other, Carranza emerging the victor in the struggle. This propelled into prominence a number of Border men who early in the Revolution had joined Carranza's forces. One of them was General Pablo González, born in Lampazos, Nuevo León. In 1915, González was commander of the *carrancista* forces occupying Mexico City. One day some junior officers thrust a paper before him which he supposedly signed without reading. It was a general search order. Soon there were reports of a gang of thieves who were robbing wealthy people in Mexico City, gaining entrance into their homes by showing a military search order and using a gray automobile as a getaway car. The newspapers promptly named them "La banda del automóvil gris." Captured, the band turned out to be officers from General González's staff. The Border ballad "EL AUTO-MOVIL GRIS" claims that the members of the Gray Automobile Band were scions of well-to-do Matamoros families who were officers with Carranza, young men who had enjoyed certain advantages such as trips to Europe. During the time they were members of the band, they made periodic visits to the Border, the ballad claims, going as far as San Antonio to spend the money they stole. The protagonist enjoys himself to the full, all the while proclaiming himself a member of "La banda del Automóvil

Gris." There is none of the fake repentance that one usually finds in ballads about criminals in this song.

Of the chief protagonists in the Revolution, none has a more complex life and character than Francisco (Pancho) Villa, the "Centaur of the North." In Mexican oral tradition there are really three Pancho Villas, each eliciting a different set of attitudes. First, there is Pancho Villa the outlaw, the pre-revolutionary Robin Hood robbing the rich to give to the poor. As such, Villa's appeal was limited; his reputation does not approach that of other Mexican Robin Hoods like, for example, Heraclio Bernal. Then there is Villa the revolutionary leader, commander of the famous División del Norte and the most successful of the generals in the Revolution. All Mexicans recognized and admired Villa's military prowess, but their attitude toward him was determined by their own partisan affiliations. If they were *villistas*, then Villa was a cavalier without fear and without reproach. But if they were *carrancistas*, Villa to them was a cruel and sometimes treacherous enemy.

Finally, there is Villa the Border raider, who defied the power of the United States by attacking Columbus, New Mexico, and then playing hide-and-seek with General John J. Pershing's expeditionary force, sent into Chihuahua to capture him. Villa in this third aspect became a hero to all Mexican people, and most especially to those living along the Border, who had been singing ballads about heroes of intercultural conflict ever since the establishment of an international boundary between the two countries.

Villa's manifold character is well illustrated in two songs sung on the Border—"NO DECIAS, PANCHO VILLA" and "LA PERSECUCION DE VILLA." After Lucio Blanco's capture of Matamoros, the Lower Border remained strongly *carrancista,* with Villa supreme farther upriver in Chihuahua. In March, 1915, *villista* troops attacked Matamoros, defended by *carrancista* troops under General Emiliano Nafarrate. Again the Matamoros citizenry volunteered to help defend the city. Villa's forces were decisively defeated, this being the first major action in the Revolution lost by the *villistas.* "No decías, Pancho Villa" makes fun of the commander of the División del Norte. He may be a winner everywhere else, but in Matamoros he more than met his match. The song is an excellent expression of local and partisan pride. Yet the same people who sing this mocking little ditty and who relate how they participated in the repulse of the *villistas* also tell wonderful stories about Villa's successes against Pershing, in which all their pride and sympathy are focused on Villa. Historically, it was *carrancista* troops who defeated American forces at El Carrizal in June, 1916, when Carranza barred any further movement southward by Pershing. But many old *carrancistas* on the Border believe that it was Villa who defeated the Americans at El Carrizal, and they also believe that Villa entered Pershing's camp in disguise and that he tricked American warplanes into surrendering. Obviously, the Villa who was repulsed at Matamoros and the Villa who made a fool of Pershing are not quite the same figure in their minds.

"No decías, Pancho Villa" is not a *corrido*; it is composed of one *copla* (loose stanza) and a refrain. Satirical *coplas* of this sort exist for all historical periods in Mexico. The so-called *corridos* dating from epochs before the Díaz regime usually are *coplas*. "La persecución de Villa" is a *corrido* but of a special long-line variety. Instead of the eight-syllable line usual in the *corrido*, this song has a basic twelve-syllable line that undergoes a number of free variations. "La persecución de Villa" has been sung throughout Mexico, and its text is pretty well standardized, since it has appeared in print a number of times. The Border versions, however, differ from the standardized text in a number of ways. Some of the differences are especially notable. Pershing's soldiers are called *rinches*, and they are accused of being ham eaters as in "Jacinto Treviño" (no. 20).

According to popular belief, Carranza allowed American troops to pursue Villa, as the *corrido* says, so they too might learn how to die. Knowing how to "die well" was one of the major points of honor for the men of the Revolution. Facing death in the heat of battle required courage, but the greatest test was to die calmly and with some flair when facing a firing squad. This was the fate expected by the losers of a battle, especially if they held high rank. When a prominent chieftain was executed, he attracted a good deal of attention, and an audience took note of the manner in which he faced his death. Many a *corrido* was composed about executions. In the balladry of the Lower Border, two have remained fresh in people's minds, while many others have been forgotten or are sung but rarely. These two are "BENJAMIN ARGUMEDO" and "FELIPE ANGELES."

It would be hard to find two more dissimilar men than Angeles and Argumedo. Felipe Angeles was an urbane, highly educated man, a professional soldier noted for his restraint and his devotion to duty. He was educated in France and at Mexico's Colegio Militar, where he later taught and served as director. After Díaz's abdication, Angeles offered his services to Madero and served him faithfully. The usurper Huerta had Angeles arrested and exiled, but Angeles immediately joined other revolutionary chiefs in the fight against Huerta. Joining Villa's staff, he contributed his knowledge of tactics and the use of artillery to Villa's successes. Legends grew about the accuracy of his artillery fire. Angeles fled Mexico after Villa's forces were dispersed. In 1919 he returned to Mexico with a handful of men, hoping to begin a new fight against Carranza. Taken prisoner in Chihuahua, he was shot by order of Carranza on November 26, 1919.

Benjamín Argumedo was a rough-and-ready *norteño* born in Matamoros, Coahuila. He joined Madero as an irregular cavalryman in 1910. Then he turned against Madero and joined Orozco's rebellion. When Madero was assassinated, Argumedo joined Huerta and was the most successful cavalry general on Huerta's side. His cavalry tactics were said to be brilliant. Once Huerta was overthrown, Argumedo went from the extreme right to the left and joined Zapata. Each shift in allegiance usually brought Argumedo a higher rank, but he consistently picked the losing side. When Zapata lost ground before Carranza, Argumedo fought his way north, seeking his own native region of Coahuila. He fell ill in the mountains of Durango, was captured by Carranza troops on February 4, 1916, and shot on February 29. Argumedo seems to have been a quick-tempered and ambitious man, the antithesis of Felipe Angeles. Yet the two men had important things in common. They were undeniably brave, and they had achieved renown for their skill in the military arm of their choice. They were both controversial figures, deeply hated by the *carrancistas* and their chroniclers. Both were losers to Carranza, became fugitives, were captured and sentenced to die. And both showed that they "knew how to die." Furthermore, they both were victims of measures taken by Carranza against his defeated opponents that were considered cruel and repressive by many neutral observers and certainly were thought to be so by the majority of the common people, especially in the north, where both Angeles and Argumedo had adherents.

The term *mañanitas* is often applied to *corridos* like "Benjamín Argumedo" and "Felipe Angeles," which lament the death of a highly regarded chieftain. "Benjamín Argumedo" is so identified in its text. *Mañanitas* usually have a melancholy tune that is a good part of their appeal. They also contain memorable stanzas in which the hero speaks before he dies. In "Benjamín Argumedo" these are the stanzas describing the meeting between Argumedo and his executioner, General Murguía, with Argumedo's reminiscing about his life as a *guerrillero*. In "Felipe Angeles" it is the stanza containing the lines "la muerte no mata a nadie, la matadora es la suerte." This statement synthesizes the attitude toward life and death expressed in the revolutionary *corridos*. Death cannot kill unless fate wills it so. Therefore, one must live without fear and face death calmly when it comes. It is a philosophy of stoicism that Marcus Aurelius would have recognized and approved of.

Smuggling flourished along the Texas-Mexican Border during its first hundred years or so as an international boundary. One side of the river always had something that was lacking on the other side, and ways were found to get things across without going through the red tape of customs. Smuggling was a thriving and fairly respectable activity even before the U.S.-Mexico war established the Rio Grande as an international boundary. One of the chief items transported illegally in those days was textiles, which were smuggled from the United States into Mexico. In the early days they were brought in all the way from Missouri to Santa Fe—along the famous Santa Fe Trail—and then south into Chihuahua. Later, when Anglos settled in Texas, the Nueces-Rio Grande area became a focus for smuggling. Men who later were highly regarded as Texas patriots are said to have indulged in this traffic. Even today, consumer goods in great quantities are smuggled into Mexico—on a small scale by thousands of people, on a large scale by a few professionals.

"MARIANO RESENDEZ" exemplifies the earlier period of smuggling along the Lower Border and dates from the turn of the century. Mariano Reséndez was no ordinary type of outlaw. He was a member of a well-known and highly respected Border family who were landed gentry in the region. Reséndez carried out large-scale smuggling of textiles. According to oral accounts, he crossed his goods on mule trains guarded by armed men, who often fought running battles with Mexican customs men. The Díaz government finally took an interest in Reséndez and he was appre-hended at his home on the Mexican side. Orders were given to take him to Monterrey, but he was shot to death on the way, supposedly when he tried to escape. Application of the infamous *ley fuga* was a standard prac-tice during the Díaz regime. Reséndez created a niche for himself in Border tradition. The *corridos* about him call him *El Contrabandista*—The Smuggler.

There may have been two or more *corridos* about Reséndez; some singers know two different songs about his exploits. Again, it may be a case of two separate songs being shaped out of fragments from a longer variant. I have set down in this book the longest version of "Mariano Reséndez" that I know. It is one of the longest examples of the Border *corrido,* which usually stays within twenty stanzas. In actual singing, not all of the stanzas recorded here may be sung in one performance. There are some textual resemblances between this Border *corrido* and the out-law *corrido* "Heraclio Bernal," which has been sung throughout the Greater Mexican area.

The enactment of the Prohibition Act of 1919 changed the tempo of smuggling activity along the Border. Now it was Mexico that had some-thing greatly wanted by people on the other side of the river. Americans poured into the Mexican Border towns to quench their thirst. I remember a little place on the Matamoros side of the Brownsville-Matamoros cross-ing, just a few yards from the bridge. On the side facing the thirsty *gringo* crossing the bridge into Mexico, a sign announced it as "The First Chance Saloon." On the opposite side, facing the traveler returning to the United States, another sign identified it as "The Last Chance Saloon." But not all people on the American side were willing to go to Mexico when they wanted a drink; so Mexico came to them. Quantities of hard liquor were smuggled across, for the most part by small, independent operators rather than by large smuggling gangs.

The decade of the 1920s was the age of the *tequilero,* tequila being the most common liquor smuggled over. *Tequileros* used many ingenious ways to bring their goods over: in the spare tires of cars crossing the inter-national bridges, for example. Most often, however, they operated in bands of three of four, crossing the river at night by means of homemade boats, or swimming the river and pushing their cargo ahead of them in galvanized metal tubs or inflated skins. Sometimes they were surprised by U.S. Border patrolmen when they made it to the American side of the river. Many would surrender, ending up in the federal penitentiary at

Hilario Cisneros (p. 26), at Las Comas, Tamaulipas, in 1951. Born in 1867, he taught early *corridos* such as "Kiansis" (no. 12) to younger generations. *Author's collection*

ovita Cantú (p. xix), at El Tule, Tamauli-
as, in 1951, when she was in her fifties. The
oung man with her was her only child.
Author's collection

Gil González Cisneros, 25, at Las Comas, Tamaulipas, in 1951. A great-grandnephew of Hilario Cisneros, he was representative of the singing generation of the 1950s. His repertory emphasized songs like "La pastora" (no. 1), as well as *corridos* of Border conflict. *Author's collection*

Fidencio Barrientos, in his sixties, at La Carrera, Tamaulipas, in 1951. Barrientos (p. xxix) was representative of the accomplished non-specialist, who was highly competent as a singer and guitarist but devoted most of his time to other pursuits, usually farming or ranching. *Author's collection*

Jesús Flores, 62, in front of his dwelling in a Brownsville *barrio*, 1951. Flores (pp. xviii, xxiii, 115) was representative of the blind or otherwise handicapped person who became a folksong specialist within his own group. He composed as well as sang *corridos* and *décimas*. *Author's collection*

Juan N. Cortina (no. 8), during the time Cortina was a general in the Juárez forces fighting the French. *Museo Histórico "Casa Mata," Matamoros, Tamps.*

Gregorio Cortez (no. 18), photographed after his release from prison. According to Cortez's family, the picture was taken as a joke. *Author's collection*

General Lucio Blanco, commander of the Carranza forces that took Matamoros in 1913 (no. 28). *Museo Histórico "Casa Mata," Matamoros, Tamps.*

General Emiliano Nafarrate, commander of Carranza forces at Matamoros during the *sedicioso* period (no. 21) and supposedly sympathetic to the guerrillas fighting on the Texas side. *Museo Histórico "Casa Mata," Matamoros, Tamps.*

Don Pedrito Jaramillo (no. 44); one of the few known photos of the famed *curandero*, copied and recopied by hundreds of the faithful. *Author's collection*

A group of Mexican and Mexican-American migrants in front of a San Antonio *enganchista* office, waiting to take the train north (no. 13). The women are food vendors, the two men with cigars seem to be the crew bosses. Note the variety of physical types, dress, and self-image in this early group of migrants. *University of Texas Humanities Research Center, Summerville collection*

An old goatherd and *curandero,* photographed in the 1920s. A good illustration of the peasant Mexican type of the period, and a fine example of dignified old age, regardless of social class or ethnic identification. *University of Texas Humanities Research Center, Smithers collection*

General Francisco Villa (right), with Colonel Roberto Fierro, at Ojinaga in 1912, a few months after Villa had participated in the capture of Ciudad Juárez (no. 27). *University of Texas Humanities Research Center, Smithers collection*

Border patrolmen waiting in ambush at river's edge on a tip that a crossing would occur there on that particular night. Probably posed, but most likely a part of some real operation. Men are identified as U.S. Border patrolmen, though they are dressed more like Texas Rangers of the period. Taken near Brownsville in 1935. *University of Texas Humanities Research Center, Smithers collection*

Three *tequileros* in the act of surrendering to Border patrolmen; obviously posed after the fact. Taken in 1926 along the upper Texas-Mexican Border. *University of Texas Humanities Research Center, Smithers collection*

Longhorn cattle crossing the river from Mexico into Texas. *University of Texas Humanities Research Center, Smithers collection*

An overnight camp during a cattle drive to Kansas, photographed in 1895 by an itinerant photographer. *University of Texas Humanities Research Center, Smithers collection*

Leavenworth. Others came prepared to fight, and they either shot their way out of ambush or died in the attempt. Out of events like these came "LOS TEQUILEROS," "DIONISIO MALDONADO," and "EL CONTRABANDO DE EL PASO."

The attitude of the Border people toward smugglers was a far from negative one. Smuggling occupied a much higher position than other kinds of activities proscribed by law because, in the traditional scale of values, the smuggler was seen as an extension of the hero of intercultural conflict. To appreciate this, one must keep in mind the average Borderer's attitude toward the Rio Grande as an international boundary. When the river became a dividing line instead of a focus for normal activity, it broke apart an area that had once been a unified homeland. People ended up with friends and relatives living in what had legally become a foreign land, hedged in by all kinds of immigration and customs restrictions.

But the borderline was long, and the river guards were few. In the early days, customs and immigration regulations were almost unenforceable. To the residents of the river banks, such regulations were completely unrealistic as well. Friends and relatives living within shouting distance of each other—just across the river—were not allowed to communicate in the easiest way possible, by crossing the river at their point of residence. They were supposed to travel twenty or thirty miles up- or downstream, cross a bridge, then travel the same distance in the opposite direction—a journey of forty to sixty miles to visit people a few hundred yards away. So you did not travel forty or sixty miles; you just crossed the river where you were. This, in a strict sense, was a violation of the law. Furthermore, people visiting back and forth across the river often took gifts of food and other articles with them; and this, of course, was smuggling in a legal sense. So in those times there were tens of thousands of people living along the river who were technically smugglers. The professional smuggler differed from them mainly in the size of his operations.

The laws that prohibited uninterrupted traffic across the river were mainly those of the United States, and the Borderer's experience had not made him love or respect the Anglo law. Furthermore, many of the men who were Border patrolmen and customs officers in the 1920s had been Texas Rangers or sheriff's deputies during the previous decade. They did not believe in treating Mexicans either fairly or gently. The Borderer's belief was that these men did not really attempt to arrest Mexican smugglers, that their main objective was to ambush them and kill them without warning according to the old Texas Ranger practice of shooting first and asking questions later. The insulting and sometimes brutal treatment accorded law-abiding Mexican citizens and Mexican-Americans by customs and immigration officers at international bridges did nothing to make Border people sympathetic to law and order as conceived by the U.S. Treasury Department. So for many years the Border people looked upon smuggling as an extension of intercultural conflict. That is why in the *corridos* Border patrolmen and immigration officers are called *rinches*.

"El contrabando de El Paso" comes from the other end of the Texas-Mexican Border, the Juárez-El Paso area. It is, however, one of the best-known Texas-Mexican *corridos* and has been in oral currency on the Lower Border since the 1920s. Its theme is more universal than smuggling along the Rio Grande; it is that of the wrongdoer who is caught and repents his past transgressions while he is on his way to prison. "Los tequileros" and "Dionisio Maldonado" are local to the Lower Border area and are typical of the smugglers-versus-*rinches* situation that is the theme of the Lower Border smuggling *corrido*. The smugglers do not surrender, nor are they given a chance to do so. They fight to the death. Fights between smugglers and *rinches* are also mentioned in "Laredo" (no. 26), where Laredo men are said to count smuggling among their many accomplishments.

The smugglers of "Los tequileros" begin their fatal journey from Ciudad Guerrero, Tamaulipas, which used to be opposite Zapata, Texas. Guerrero is now under the waters of the lake formed by Falcón Dam, and a new Ciudad Guerrero has been built some distance away. The "famed San Diego," destination of the *tequileros,* is less than a hundred miles northeast of Zapata. It was this San Diego that gave its name to the "Plan de San Diego," of the *sedicioso* days. The *corrido* emphasizes not smuggling but the battle with the *rinches,* who love to kill Mexicans from ambush. This places "Los tequileros" within the cultural-conflict tradition. It is the best known of the smuggling *corridos* on the Lower Border. "Dionisio Maldonado" again tells us of three *tequileros* who are ambushed and killed by the *rinches.* There are few details given in our variant except for the shooting itself, this time close to Laredo. The date given in the opening stanza—1900—is obviously in error. I have heard prose accounts narrated when the *corrido* has been sung, placing the events in the 1920s.

"El contrabando de El Paso" is sometimes called a prisoner's song because it does have a line about "las penas del prisionero." But it is more of a "last goodnight" type of ballad, in which the culprit tells the world that crime does not pay. The prisoner's song usually shows us the protagonist in his cell, yearning for his sweetheart or his mother, counting the prison bars or listening for the footsteps of the executioner—all the while consoled by an angel or a little bird. While "MANUEL GARZA DE LEON," "LA CANCION DE CARLOS GUILLEN," and "LAS ONCE ACABAN DE DAR" do not have all the characteristics just mentioned, they are much more clearly in the prisoner's song category. They are also typical of the songs of this type that have been enjoyed on the Lower Border.

"Manuel Garza de León," however, is not so much about the "sorrows of the prisoner" as it is about the intercultural conditions that have put the protagonist behind the bars. A man goes to prison under laws he had no part in making, according to concepts of justice he does not understand. He feels that he is in prison not because he committed a crime but because he is a Mexican. I have no historical data on Manuel Garza de

León, whose troubles with the American law are remembered in this ballad. The singer who taught it to me learned it from an older singer in 1915. A good part of the text is in character with the usual prison ballad: the sufferings of the prisoner, his poor parents, the time the prisoner spends counting the links on his chain, and so on. But there are passages of a different sort, such as the second stanza. The first two lines of this stanza contain all the regret, all the remorse, that it might take two or three moralizing stanzas to express. Here there is no self-pity, though; the voice speaks in a reflective, almost detached tone. "Drink got me in trouble," it says, "but no one held the cup to my lips. I blame no one for what I did." Then the next two lines of the same stanza put Garza de León's actions into the context of an ever-present intercultural conflict. It was not a judge who sentenced Manuel to thirty years; it was an "American." And the prison guards who harass him with their dogs are called *rinches* too.

"La canción de Carlos Guillén" is indeed a prisoner's song. It is in fact *the* prisoner's song in Greater Mexican tradition. In variants found in interior Mexico—where it is known as "El prisionero de San Juan de Ulúa" or "La canción del prisionero"—all the characteristics of the type are present: the crime, the repentance, the counting of the prison bars, the sorrowing mother, and the little bird that visits the prisoner. On the Lower Rio Grande Border the ballad has been shortened and localized, and it has been attached to the semi-legendary figure of Carlos Guillén.

Guillén, who died in a gun battle in Brownsville in 1898, was a dandy, ballad singer, poet, journalist, political pamphleteer, and hired gun. He published a little newspaper known as *El Céfiro,* also the title of a well-known *danza* of the period. "La canción de Carlos Guillén" or "El prisionero de San Juan de Ulúa" is a *danza* too. Guillén must have liked the *danza* form, and for this reason perhaps the "Prisionero de San Juan de Ulúa" song became attached to his name. Local legends credit him with the composition of other widely known *danzas,* including "El céfiro." In some versions of the legend, Guillén composes the San Juan de Ulúa song while in prison for killing his mistress, a mulatto. In other versions, Guillén merely recasts the song while in prison.

"Las once acaban de dar" can stand as a fully shaped composition, though it is only part of a much longer Border *corrido* dating from the nineteenth century. Nicanor Torres, who taught me this song, remembered some of the events behind it. Two young men in Matamoros killed a foreigner (perhaps an American) because they had seen large amounts of currency in his house. The victim's supposed wealth turned out to be worthless Confederate paper. The two men were sentenced to death and held in the Matamoros jail while awaiting execution by a firing squad. The longer ballad mentioned by Torres must have given full details about the crime and the penalty suffered in retribution. But with the passing of the years, only an emotional core has remained: two young men lying awake in the dark, waiting for death.

7

Los inditos

Use a *huapango* strum when playing this piece on the guitar, but do not play it too fast. It should have the tempo of a baby bouncing on his parent's knee. If you are singing it to a child, it is best to do so without accompaniment. That is the way it was sung to children among our people.

Ahi vie - nen los in - di - tos por el ca - rri - zal,

ahi vie - nen los in - di - tos por el ca - rri - zal.

¡Ay ma - mi - ta! ¡ay pa - pi - to! me quie - ren ma - tar,

¡ay ma - mi - ta! ¡ay pa - pi - to! me quie - ren ma - tar.

Com - pón - te tu chi - mal y vá - mo - nos a pa - sear.

Me ves que es - toy en - fer - mo y no me pue - do le - van - tar,

me ves que es - toy en - fer - mo y no me pue - do le - van - tar.

Ahi vienen los inditos
por el carrizal,
ahi vienen los inditos
por el carrizal.
　¡Ay mamita! ¡ay papito!
　me quieren matar,
　¡ay mamita! ¡ay papito!
　me quieren matar.
Ahi vienen los inditos
por el carrizal.

Compónte tu chimal
y vámonos a pasear,
compónte tu chimal
y vámonos a pasear.
　Me ves que estoy enfermo
　y no me puedo levantar,
　me ves que estoy enfermo
　y no me puedo levantar.
Compónte tu chimal
y vámonos a pasear.

The Little Indians

The little Indians are coming through the canebrake.
　Oh, mommy! Oh, daddy! They want to kill me.

Straighten up your *chimal*, and let us go for a walk.
　You can see that I am sick, and that I cannot get up.

8

El general Cortina

Use a *corrido* strum (*one*-two-three, *one*-two-three) on the guitar, at a moderate tempo, and a fairly free delivery. The song is most often performed without instrumental accompaniment.

E - se ge - ne - ral Cor - ti - nas es li - bre y muy so - be - ra - no,

han su - bi - do sus ho - no - res por - que sal - vó a un me - xi - ca - no.

Los a - me - ri - ca - nos ha - cí - an huel - ga, bo - rra - che - ras en las can - ti - nas,

de gus - to que ha - bí - a muer - to e - se ge - ne - ral Cor - ti - nas.

Ese general Cortinas
es libre y muy soberano,
han subido sus honores
porque salvó a un mexicano.

Viva el general Cortinas
que de su prisión salió,

vino a ver a sus amigos
que en Tamaulipas dejó.

Los americanos hacían huelga,
borracheras en las cantinas,
de gusto que había muerto
ese general Cortinas.

General Cortina

The famed General Cortinas is quite sovereign and free,
the honor due him is greater, for he saved a Mexican's life.

Long live General Cortinas, who has come out of his prison;
he came to visit his friends that he had left in Tamaulipas.

The Americans made merry, they got drunk in the saloons,
out of joy over the death of the famed General Cortinas.

9

Los franceses

Use a staccato *one*-two, *one*-two strum on the guitar. The melody is lively except for
the refrain, where the "Juárez" is sung louder and with emphasis.

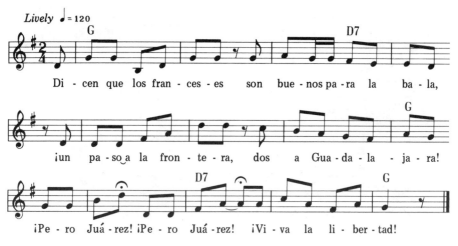

Di - cen que los fran - ces - es   son bue - nos pa - ra la   ba - la,

¡un   pa - so a la fron - te - ra,   dos   a Gua - da - la - ja - ra!

¡Pe - ro   Juá - rez! ¡Pe - ro   Juá - rez!   ¡Vi - va   la   li - ber - tad!

, Dicen que los franceses
son buenos para la bala,
¡un paso a la frontera,
dos a Guadalajara!

> ¡Pero Juárez!
> ¡Pero Juárez!
> ¡Viva la libertad!

Entraron los franceses,
entraron más que al trote,
se les había visto
albur y tecolote.

> ¡Pero Juárez! etc.

Entraron los franceses,
entraron como locos,

pero cuando volvieron
salieron ya muy pocos.

> ¡Pero Juárez! etc.

Maximiliano de Austria
se subió a la picota:
— ¡Jesús! ¡Por Dios! ¡Me matan!
¡Ay, sálvame, Carlota!

> ¡Pero Juárez! etc.

La emperatriz Carlota
se fue para La Habana
porque no pudo ser
libre mexicana.

> ¡Pero Juárez! etc.

The French

They say that the French are good in a fire-fight;
they take one step toward the Border and two back to Guadalajara.
> But Juárez! But Juárez!
> Long live liberty!

The French came in, they came in more than fast;
things looked to them like an easy game of cards.
> But Juárez, etc.

The French came in, they came in like madmen,
but when they went away only a few got out.
> But Juárez, etc.

Maximilian of Austria climbed upon the gibbet:
"Mercy! Heavens! They'll kill me! Oh, save me, Carlotta!"
> But Juárez, etc.

The Empress Carlotta has left for Havana
because she could not be a free Mexican citizen.
> But Juárez, etc.

10
A Zaragoza

The first part of this song has a strong anthem-like beat. It echoes "El himno nacional mexicano," accepted as the Mexican national anthem in 1854, thirteen years before "A Zaragoza" was composed. The second part is lively and mocking, reminding one of "Los franceses" (no. 9).

Martial ♩ = 88

Dios te sal - ve, va - lien - te Za - ra - go - o - za, in - vic - to

ge - ne - ral de la fron - te - e - ra, yo con los

li - bres sa - lu - do tu ban - de - ra que en Pue - bla

tre - mo - ló sin des - can - sar. La ma - ña - na del cin - co de

ma - a - yo que con muy po - cos sol - da - dos me - xi -

ca - a - nos un gol - pe ru - do les dis - te a los ti -

ra - nos que a Pue - bla se a - cer - ca - ban con a - fán.

Lively ♩ = 132

No ol - vi - den, me - xi - ca - nos, que en el cin - co de ma - yo

los zua - vos co - mo un ra - yo co - rrie - ron ¡pa - ra a - trás!

Ti - ran -do cuan -to tra - í - an, los que a Pue - bla ve - ní - an
a - pu - ra - dos de - cí - an: ¡Pe - lear es por de - más!

Dios te salve, valiente Zaragoza,
invicto general de la frontera,
yo con los libres saludo tu bandera
que en Puebla tremoló sin descansar.

Los hijos de la Patria te saludan,
solemnizando tu triunfo en este día,
los venideros también con alegría
bendecirán tu nombre sin cesar.

El pueblito y sus autoridades
tu nombre ensalzan repetidas veces
porque fuiste el terror de los franceses
en Guadalupe, Loreto y en San Juan.

La mañana del cinco de mayo
que con muy pocos soldados mexicanos
un golpe rudo le diste a los tiranos
que a Puebla se acercaban con afán.

No olviden, mexicanos
que en el cinco de mayo
los zuavos como un rayo
corrieron . . . ¡para atrás!
Tirando cuanto traían,
los que a Puebla venían
apurados decían:
— ¡Pelear es por demás!

To Zaragoza

God save thee, brave Zaragoza,
unconquerable general of the Border;
I and all free men salute your flag
that waved unceasingly in Puebla.
The sons of the Fatherland salute you,
celebrating your triumph on this day;
those to come also joyfully
will bless your name unceasingly.

This little town and its authorities
exalt your name on numberless occasions
because you were the terror of the French
at Guadalupe, Loreto, and San Juan.
The morning of the fifth of May,
when with a handful of Mexican soldiers
you dealt a rude blow to the tyrants
who were eagerly approaching Puebla.

Mexicans, don't forget that on the fifth of May
the Zouaves, with lightning speed, ran . . . toward the rear!
Casting off all that they carried, they who were coming to Puebla
exclaimed in their haste, "It is useless to fight."

11
A Grant

This is played and sung very much like the first part of "A Zaragoza" (no. 10).

Martial ♩=88

¡Vi - va Grant! ¡Vi - va Grant! ciu - da - da - nos, que cin - co a - ños la
gue - rra sos - tu - vo, y un e - jér - ci - to e - nor - me man - tu - vo
en de - fen - sa de la li - ber - tad. Y des-
pués de san - grien - tos com - ba - a - tes, do mu - rie - ron va-
lien - tes sol - da - dos, fue - ron li - bres a - que - llos esta - dos que ja - más pre - ten - dían la i - gual - dad.

¡Viva Grant! ¡Viva Grant! ciudadanos,
que cinco años la guerra sostuvo,
y un ejército enorme mantuvo
en defensa de la libertad.

Y después de sangrientos combates,
do murieron valientes soldados,
fueron libres aquellos estados
que jamás pretendían la igualdad.

¡Dios te salve, caudillo del Norte!
Yo saludo tu sacra bandera,
que en el mundo flamea por doquiera,
ofreciendo la paz y la unión.

También México ensalza tu nombre
porque fuiste con él indulgente,
fuiste siempre y serás el valiente
que defiende la Constitución.

To Grant

Long live Grant, citizens, long live Grant,
who sustained the war for five years,
and maintained an enormous army
in defense of liberty.
And after bloody battles
in which brave soldiers died,
those states were free
that had never aspired to equality.

God save thee, chieftain of the North!
I salute your holy flag
that flutters everywhere in the world,
offering peace and unity.
Mexico too exalts your name
because you were kind toward it;
you have always been and shall be the brave one,
the defender of the Constitution.

12
Kiansis

"Kiansis I" is sung in a slow, reflective tempo, most often by one singer alone and
frequently without guitar accompaniment. The rhythm is not the usual one-two-three
strum used for the *corrido*. It is more of a three-*one*-two-three-*one* rhythm similar to
the *colombiana* or *yucateca* strums. "Kiansis II" has a straight *corrido* rhythm. It is
more often sung by two voices, with guitar accompaniment. It is a *canción de grito*,
the type you would expect to hear at cantinas as well as at ranchos.

Cuan-do sa-li-mos pa' Kian-sis con u-na gran-de par-ti-da,

¡ah, qué ca-mi-no tan la-ar-go! no con-ta-ba con mi vi-da.

I

Cuando salimos pa' Kiansis
con una grande partida,
¡ah, qué camino tan largo!
no contaba con mi vida.

Nos decía el caporal,
como queriendo llorar:
—Allá va la novillada,
no me la dejen pasar.—

¡Ah, qué caballo tan bueno!
todo se le iba en correr,
¡iy, ah, qué fuerte aguacerazo!
no contaba yo en volver.

Unos pedían cigarro,
otros pedían que comer,
y el caporal nos decía:
—Sea por Dios, qué hemos de hacer.—

En el charco de Palomas
se cortó un novillo bragado,
y el caporal lo lazó
en su caballo melado.

Avísenle al caporal
que un vaquero se mató,
en las trancas del corral
nomás la cuera dejó.

Llegamos al Río Salado
y nos tiramos a nado,
decía un americano:
—Esos hombres ya se ahogaron.—

Pues qué pensaría ese hombre
que venimos a esp'rimentar,
si somos del Río Grande,
de los buenos pa' nadar.

Y le dimos vista a Kiansis,
y nos dice el caporal:
—Ora sí somos de vida,
ya vamos a hacer corral.—

Y de vuelta en San Antonio
compramos buenos sombreros,
y aquí se acaban cantando
versos de los aventureros.

Kansas, I

When we left for Kansas with a great herd of cattle,
ah, what a long trail it was! I was not sure I would survive.

The *caporal* would tell us, as if he was going to cry,
"Watch out for that bunch of steers; don't let them get past you."

Ah, what a good horse I had! He did nothing but gallop.
And, ah, what a violent cloudburst! I was not sure I would come back.

Some of us asked for cigarettes, others wanted something to eat;
and the *caporal* would tell us, "So be it, it can't be helped."

By the pond at Palomas a vicious steer left the herd,
and the *caporal* lassoed it on his honey-colored horse.

Go tell the *caporal* that a vaquero has been killed;
all he left was his leather jacket hanging on the rails of the corral.

We got to the Salado River, and we swam our horses across;
an American was saying, "Those men are as good as drowned."

I wonder what the man thought, that we came to learn, perhaps;
why, we're from the Rio Grande, where the good swimmers are from.

And then Kansas came in sight, and the *caporal* tells us,
"We have finally made it, we'll soon have them in the corral."

Back again in San Antonio, we all bought ourselves good hats,
and this is the end of the singing of the stanzas about the trail drivers.

Cuan-do sa-li-mos pa' Kian-sis con u-na gran-de co-rri-da,
gri-ta-ba mi ca-po-ra-al: Les en-car-go a mi que-ri-da.

II

Cuando salimos pa' Kiansis
con una grande corrida,
gritaba mi caporal:
—Les encargo a mi querida.—

Contesta otro caporal:
—No tengas cuidado, es sola;
que la mujer que es honrada
aunque viva entre la bola.—

Quinientos novillos eran,
todos grandes y livianos,
y entre treinta americanos
no los podían embalar.

Llegan cinco mexicanos,
todos bien enchivarrados,
y en menos de un cuarto de hora
los tenían encerrados.

Esos cinco mexicanos
al momento los echaron,
y los treinta americanos
se quedaron azorados.

Los novillos eran bravos,
no se podían soportar,
gritaba un americano:
—Que se baje el caporal.—

Pero el caporal no quiso
y un vaquero se arrojó;
a que lo matara el toro,
nomás a eso se bajó.

La mujer de Alberto Flores
le pregunta al caporal:
—Déme usted razón de mi hijo,
que no lo he visto llegar.—

—Señora, yo le diría,
pero se pone a llorar;
lo mató un toro frontino
en las trancas de un corral.—

Ya con ésta me despido
por 'l amor de mi querida,
ya les canté a mis amigos
los versos de la corrida.

Kansas, II

When we left for Kansas on a big cattle drive,
my *caporal* shouted, "Take good care of my beloved."

Another *caporal* replied, "Have no fear, she has no other loves;
for if a woman is virtuous, no matter if she lives among men."

Five hundred steers there were, all big and quick;
thirty American cowboys could not keep them bunched together.

Then five Mexicans arrive, all of them wearing good chaps;
and in less than a quarter-hour, they had the steers penned up.

Those five Mexicans penned up the steers in a moment,
and the thirty Americans were left staring in amazement.

The steers were vicious, it was very hard to hold them;
an American shouted, "Let the *caporal* go into the corral."

But the *caporal* refused, and a vaquero took the dare;
he got himself killed by the bull, that's all he managed to do.

The wife of Alberto Flores asks of the *caporal*,
"Give me word of my son, I have not seen him arrive."

"Lady, I would tell you, but I know that you will cry;
he was killed by a bull with a blazed face against the rails of a corral."

Now with this I say farewell, by my sweetheart's love;
I have now sung for my friends the stanzas about the cattle drive.

13
La Pensilvania

This is one of the few *corridos* I know that attempts to match musical form to content. The tune imitates the tickety-tackety, tickety-tackety rhythm of a car going along the rails at a fast clip. The tempo is too lively for the usual *corrido* strum. The simplest accompaniment is a *one*-two strum, each count taking a whole measure, as if the tune were in 2/4 rather than in 6/8. It may be varied with a rapid *one*-two-three, *one*-two-three strum using the thumb on the bass and the first and second fingers respectively on the second and first strings of the guitar.

El día vein-tio-cho de_a-bril,   a las seis de la ma-ña-na,

sa-li-mos en un en-gan-che pa-ra_el es-ta-do de Pen-sil-va-nia.

El día veintiocho de abril,
a las seis de la mañana,
salimos en un enganche
para el estado de Pensilvania.

Mi chinita me decía:
—Yo me voy en esa agencia,
para lavarle su ropa,
para darle su asistencia.—

Y el enganchista nos dice:
—No se lleven la familia,
para no pasar trabajos
en el estado de West Virginia.—

—Pa' que sepas que te quiero,
me dejas en Foro West;
cuando ya estés trabajando
me escribes de donde estés.

—Cuando ya estés trabajando
me escribes, no seas ingrato;
de contestación te mando,
de recuerdo, mi retrato.—

Al llegar a West Kentockle
cambiamos locomotora,
de allí salimos corriendo
ochenta millas por hora.

Adiós Foro West y Dalas,
pueblos de mucha importancia;
ya me voy pa' Pensilvania
por no andar en la vagancia.

Adiós estado de Texas,
con toda su plantación;
ya me voy pa' Pensilvania
por no pizcar algodón.

Cuando llegamos allá,
que del tren ya nos bajamos,
nos dicen las italianas:
—¿Di'onde vienen, mexicanos?—

Contestan los mexicanos,
los que ya sabían inglés:
—Venimos en un enganche
de la suidad de For West.—

Estos versos son compuestos
cuando ya venía en camino,
poesías de un mexicano
de nombre de Constantino.

Ya con ésta me despido,
con mi sombrero en las manos,
y mis fieles compañeros
son trescientos mexicanos.

Pennsylvania

On the twenty-eighth day of April, at six o'clock in the morning,
we left on a labor contract for the state of Pennsylvania.

My beloved said to me, "I want to go on that job,
so I can wash your clothes, so I can cook your meals."

But the labor contractor told us, "Don't take your families along,
so you won't have any trouble in the state of West Virginia."

"Just to show you that I love you, leave me, then, in Forth Worth;
when you are settled and working, write me, wherever you are."

"When you are settled and working, please write me, don't be mean;
when I answer I will send you my picture to remember me by."

When we got to West Kentucky, we switched locomotives;
we went out of there going at eighty miles per hour.

Farewell, Forth Worth and Dallas, you very important towns,
I'm going to Pennsylvania to avoid a vagrant's life.

Farewell, you state of Texas, with all of your planted fields,
I'm going to Pennsylvania so I won't have to pick cotton.

When we arrived there, once we had got off the train,
the Italian girls asked us, "Mexicans, where are you from?"

And the Mexicans answered, those who already knew English,
"We have come on a labor contract from the city of Fort Worth."

These stanzas were composed while I was still on the way;
they're the verses of a Mexican by the name of Constantino.

Now with this I say farewell, with my hat in my hands,
and my faithful companions are three hundred Mexicans.

14
Rito García

This song is in the standard *corrido* form, though like many other *corridos* the tune is in 9/8 rather than in 6/8. The strum still is the basic *one*-two-three beat, except that there is a strongly accented bass on every third strum instead of on every other one as in *corridos* composed on a 6/8 measure.

A - ño de mil   o - cho-cien-tos   o - chen-ta y cin - co con - tó - o,

voy a em-pe - zar   a can - ta - ar el   ca - so   que   me pa - só - o.

Año de mil ochocientos
ochenta y cinco contó,
voy a empezar a cantar
el caso que me pasó.

Viviendo en El Cenizal
ese año en el primer mes,
don Jacinto fue a catear
mi casa con otros tres.

El dia ocho me salí
con objeto de cazar,
cuando a poco rato oí
a mi familia llorar.

Viendo mi casa ultrajada
sin haber justa razón,
me salí al camino armado
a esperar la comisión.

Luego que los devisé,
traiban a mi hijo amarrado,
al punto les disparé
de donde estaba parado.

La bala salió cual rayo,
era de arma ventajosa,
y vi caer del caballo
a don Jacinto Hinojosa.

Le hirieron a mi hijo un brazo,
sin defensa el infeliz,
y luego le di un balazo
a Uvenceslao Solís.

Conociendo bien las leyes
del país americano,
me pasé a buscar abrigo
a mi suelo mexicano.

Mi suelo muy inhumano,
pues no me dieron abrigo,
que siendo yo mexicano
no tuve ningún amigo.

Al momento me insortaron,
iba con mi hijo el más tierno,
el día once me arrestaron
los empleados del gobierno.

En Nuevo León me arrestaron
después de un camino largo,
los empleados me trajeron
a la cárcel de Camargo.

Tuve que estar siete meses
preso en aquella ciudad,
los jueces me aseguraban
que no me habían de pasar.

Yo nunca hubiera pensado
que mi país tirano fuera,
que Mainero me entregara
a la nación extranjera.

Es verdad que nada valgo,
pero siempre me entregaron,
me pasaron para Hidalgo,
fue donde me sentenciaron.

Allí no alcancé clemencia,
ni me quisieron oir,
pues voy a la penitencia
eternamente a sufrir.

Bien sabe la Providencia
qué es lo que siento en mi pecho,
que voy a la penitencia
por defender mi derecho.

Adiós, mi patria adorada,
adiós, todos mis amigos,
adiós, mi familia amada,
para siempre me despido.

Me voy a la penitencia,
así lo quiso la suerte,
voy a arrastrar la cadena
hasta que venga la muerte.

Mexicanos, no hay que fiar
en nuestra propia nación,
nunca vayan a pedir
a México protección.

Ya con ésta me despido
pues se me llegó este día,
vivan los hombres valientes
como fue Rito García.

Rito García

In the year of eighteen hundred and eighty-five, by the count,
I will begin to sing of the thing that happened to me.

I was living at El Cenizal, in the first month of that year,
when Don Jacinto came and searched my house, along with three other men.

On the eighth day of the month, I had gone out to hunt,
when after a while I heard my family crying.

Seeing my house outraged, for no just reason,
I came out on the road with my weapon to await the posse's return.

When they appeared, I saw that they had my son tied up;
I immediately fired on them from where I was standing.

The bullet flew out lightning, for my weapon was a good one,
and I saw Don Jacinto Hinojosa fall from his horse.

My poor son could not defend himself, they wounded him in the arm;
so then I put a bullet through Uvenceslao Solís.

Knowing well how the law works in the United States,
I went across the river, seeking shelter on my Mexican soil.

My own land was cruel to me, because they gave me no shelter,
and though I was a Mexican I did not find a friend.

They declared me a wanted man, I was with my youngest son;
the officers of the government arrested me on the eleventh.

I was arrested in Nuevo León after having traveled far;
the officers brought me to the jail in Camargo.

I had to remain a prisoner for seven months in that city;
the judges kept assuring me I would never be taken across.

I never would have thought that my country would be so unjust,
that Mainero would hand me over to a foreign nation.

I don't count for much, it's true, but they did hand me over;
they took me across at Hidalgo, and that is where they sentenced me.

I found no clemency there; they would not even listen to me;
so I'm going to the penitentiary, to suffer the rest of my life.

Well does God know what I feel within my breast,
that I am going to the penitentiary for defending my right.

Farewell, my beloved country, farewell, all my friends;
farewell, my dear family, I am leaving you forever.

I go to the penitentiary because such was my fortune;
I go to drag a chain until the day that death comes.

Mexicans, we can put no trust in our own nation;
never go to Mexico asking for protection.

Now with this I say farewell, for my day has come;
long live brave men such as was Rito García.

15
Los pronunciados

This is a regular *corrido* tune. Hold the " ¡ay!" for a slow count of three, or longer if you prefer.

El dí - a diez de di - ciem-bre, ¡que dí - a tan se - ña - la - do!
en el ran-cho 'e Las Tor - ti - llas ¡ay! sie - te muer-tes han cau-sa-do.

El día diez de diciembre,
¡qué día tan señalado!
en el rancho 'e Las Tortillas ¡ay!
siete muertes han causado.

Cuando pasaron el río,
cantando varias canciones,
gritaban los pronunciados ¡ay!
—Vamos buscando rabones.—

El domingo en la mañana,
como por el camposanto,
unos hombres de a caballo ¡ay!
se dieron un cuanto-cuanto.

Partieron en la violencia,
que parecía que volaban:
—Viva Catarino Garza ¡ay!—
a grito abierto gritaban.

Decía el jefe Salinas:
—Hoy tienen que sobrar liachos;
arrímense los primeros ¡ay!
echen pie a tierra muchachos.

—La primera a la derecha,
la segunda por el centro,
la tercera por la izquierda ¡ay!
muchachos, todos adentro.—

Gritaban los pronunciados:
—Ríndanse, jijos de un cuerno.—
—No nos rendimos—decían ¡ay!
—Viva el supremo gobierno.—

Gritaban los pronunciados:
—Ríndanse, no sean porfiados;
le damos fuego al cuartel ¡ay!
y mueren todos quemados.—

Ese jefe Mazarrubia
muy mal herido quedó,
y entre poquitos momentos ¡ay!
del mundo se separó.

El capitán Darío Hernández
al asistente tumbó,
por interés del sombrero ¡ay!
cinco balazos le dio.

El pobre de don Cristóbal
solito se lamentaba,
nomás de ver su asistente ¡ay!
de los clamores que daba.

Gritaba un pronunciado,
a orillas de una barranca:
—Alto al fuego, compañeros ¡ay!
se vio una bandera blanca.—

Se hicieron de los caballos,
de carabinas y sillas;
gritaban los pronunciados ¡ay!
—Esto le cargan a Díaz.—

Gritaban los pronunciados
con demasiado valor:
—Esto le cargan a Díaz ¡ay!
si al cabo es buen pagador.—

The Insurgents

On the tenth day of December, what a memorable day it was!
At the ranch of Las Tortillas, seven men were killed.

When they crossed the river, they were singing various songs;
the insurgents were shouting, "We are looking for bob-tails."

On Sunday morning, somewhere near the cemetery,
a number of men on horseback had themselves a fight.

They charged so violently that it seemed that they were flying;
"Long live Catarino Garza!" they shouted at the top of their voices.

The chieftain Salinas said, "There will be a lot of extra bedrolls today.
Come closer, those of you nearest, and off your horses, boys.

"The first group on the right flank, the second in the center;
the third on the left flank. Boys, everyone forward."

The insurgents shouted, "Surrender, you sons of a cow's horn."
"We won't surrender," they answered; "long live the federal government."

The insurgents shouted, "Surrender, do not be stubborn;
or we'll set the barracks on fire, and you will all burn to death."

That chieftain Mazarrubia was gravely wounded,
and in a very few moments he abandoned this world.

Captain Darío Hernández shot down the adjutant;
he shot him five times, just so he could have his hat.

Poor Don Cristóbal kept his sorrow to himself;
he grieved to see his adjutant and to hear his groans of pain.

An insurgent shouted, as he stood close to a gully,
"Cease firing, comrades, a white flag is in sight."

They made off with the horses, with the rifles and the saddles;
the insurgents shouted, "Charge this to Porfirio Díaz."

The insurgents shouted, with a great deal of audacity,
"Charge this to Porfirio Díaz; we know his credit is good."

16
El capitán Hall

"El capitán Hall" is sung to the same tune as "Los pronunciados."

En el rancho 'e don Proceso	Salieron pa' Los Granjenos,
se dio el primer agarrón . . .	hallando la lumbre ardiendo,
con un costillar de vaca iay!	allí les dijo Landín iay!
le hizo bonito jalón.	—Orita estaban saliendo.—

Cuando el capitán Jol vido:
— ¡Válgame Dios, qué bolón!
no les podemos entrar ¡ay!
porque yo traigo torzón.—

Alejo con prontitud
la carabina sacó,
y no encontrando la funda ¡ay!
en los suaderos la echó.

Margarito Benavides,
que andaba muy bien montado,
dijo: —A los primeros tiros ¡ay!
yo no me quedo parado.—

El capitán Darío Hernández,
cuando los vió desfilar:
—No se vayan, hermanitos ¡ay!
vengan, bueyes, al nopal.—

Captain Hall

At Don Proceso's ranch, he had his first encounter . . .
with a side of beef, and he gave it a pretty hard time.

They went on to Los Granjenos, and they found a fire still burning;
then Landín told them, "They left just a moment ago."

When Captain Hall took a look, "My goodness, what a big bunch of them!
We can't have a go at them because I've got the gripes."

Alejo very quickly drew out his rifle,
and not finding the rifle boot, stuck it between his saddle blankets.

Margarito Benavides, who was riding a very good horse,
said, "As soon as they start shooting, you won't find me standing here."

Captain Darío Hernández said, when he saw them ride away,
"Don't go away, pals; come back and eat your cactus, you oxen."

17
José Mosqueda

"José Mosqueda" is played slightly faster than most other Border *corridos*. There is a
jaunty air to it. Use a staccato strum on the guitar.

El die-ci-nue-ve de e-ne-ro el pue-blo se al-bo-ro-tó-o,

cuan-do fue el pri-mer a-sal-to que Jo-sé Mos-que-da dio-o.

El diecinueve de enero
el pueblo se alborotó,
cuando fue el primer asalto
que José Mosqueda dio.

Decía José Mosqueda
con su pistola en la mano:
—Tumbamos el ferrocarril
y en terreno americano.—

Decían los americanos:
—¡Qué mexicanos tan crueles!
Dejaron el ferrocarril
bailando fuera 'e los rieles.—

En el rancho de La Lata,
donde se vio lo bonito,
en donde hicieron correr
al señor Santiago Brito.

Más allá, en El Calaboz',
donde se vio lo muy fino,
en donde hicieron correr
al diputado Justino.

Decía José Mosqueda
en esa Loma Trozada:
—Pues a correr, compañeros,
porque ahi viene la platiada.—

Decía Simón García
en su caballo melado:
—Vamos a gastar dinero,
todos para el otro lado.—

Decía Fabián García
en una voz y sin sueño:

—Vámonos tirando bien,
con rumbo a El Capitaneño.—

El cobarde de Blas Loya,
que hasta el caballo cansó,
con dos bultos de dinero
hasta que el río cruzó.

Decía don Esteban Salas
como queriendo llorar:
—Por haber hecho los hierros
también me van a llevar.—

Decía don Esteban Salas:
—Esto les voy a decir,
por haber hecho los hierros
dos años voy a sufrir.—

Decían los adoloridos,
debajo de los mesquites:
—Se va a poner en venduta
la fragua de Juan Benítez.—

A Simón no lo aprehendieron,
pues no se dejó arrestar;
al estado de Sonora
se fue para vacilar.

Ya con ésta me despido
al salir a una vereda,
pues el que ha tumbado el tren
se llama José Mosqueda.

Mosqueda, yo ya me voy,
mi compañero se queda,
pues el que ha tumbado el tren
se llama José Mosqueda.

José Mosqueda

On the nineteenth of January, the people were all astir;
that was when José Mosqueda carried out his first assault.

Then said José Mosqueda, with his pistol in his hand,
"We knocked over the railroad train, and right on American soil."

The Americans said, "How cruel these Mexicans are!
They have left the railroad train jigging outside the rails."

It was at La Lata ranch where some pretty things were seen;
it was there that they made Mr. Santiago Brito run away.

Farther on, at El Calaboz', where the finest things were seen,
it was there that they made Deputy Justino run away.

Then said José Mosqueda, at that Broken-Off Hill,
"Comrades, it is time to gallop; that pile of silver is coming."

Then said Simón García, on his honey-colored horse,
"Let us all go spend our money on the Mexican side of the river."

Then said Fabián García, in an even and vigilant voice,
"Let us strike out directly toward El Capitaneño."

That despicable Blas Loya, he even wore out his horse,
carrying two bundles of money, until he had crossed the river.

Then said Don Esteban Salas, as if he was going to cry,
"For having made the iron bars, they are going to take me too."

Then said Don Estaban Salas, "I am going to tell you this;
for having made the iron bars, I shall suffer for two years."

All the aggrieved people said, as they sat beneath the mesquites,
"They are going to auction off Juan Benítez's blacksmith shop."

They did not capture Simón, for he would not be arrested;
he went to the state of Sonora to have himself a good time.

Now with this I say farewell, coming out upon a trail;
for the man who knocked over the train is named José Mosqueda.

Mosqueda, I'm leaving now, my companion stays behind;
for the man who knocked over the train is named José Mosqueda.

18
Gregorio Cortez

"Gregorio Cortez" is sung a bit more slowly than the average *corrido*, with the basses on the guitar strongly accented.

En el con-da-do de El Car-men mi-ren lo que ha su-ce-di-do,
mu-rió el Che-ri-fe Ma-yor, que-dan-do Ro-mán he-ri-do.

En el condado de El Carmen
miren lo que ha sucedido,
murió el Cherife Mayor,
quedando Román herido.

En el condado de El Carmen
tal desgracia sucedió,
murió el Cherife Mayor,
no saben quién lo mató.

Se anduvieron informando
como media hora despúes,
supieron que el malhechor
era Gregorio Cortez.

Ya insortaron a Cortez
por toditito el estado,
que vivo o muerto se aprehenda
porque a varios ha matado.

Decía Gregorio Cortez
con su pistola en la mano:
—No siento haberlo matado,
lo que siento es a mi hermano.—

Decía Gregorio Cortez
con su alma muy encendida:
—No siento haberlo matado,
la defensa es permitida.—

Venían los americanos
más blancos que una amapola,
de miedo que le tenían
a Cortez con su pistola.

Decían los americanos,
decían con timidez:
—Vamos a seguir la huella
que el malhechor es Cortez.—

Soltaron los perros jaunes
pa' que siguieran la huella,
pero alcanzar a Cortez
era seguir a una estrella.

Tiró con rumbo a Gonzales
sin ninguna timidez:
—Síganme, rinches cobardes,
yo soy Gregorio Cortez.—

Se fue de Belmont al rancho,
lo alcanzaron a rodear,
poquitos más de trescientos,
y allí les brincó el corral.

Cuando les brincó el corral,
según lo que aquí se dice,
se agarraron a balazos
y les mató otro cherife.

Decía Gregorio Cortez
con su pistola en la mano:
—No corran, rinches cobardes,
con un solo mexicano.—

Salió Gregorio Cortez,
salió con rumbo a Laredo,
no lo quisieron seguir
porque le tuvieron miedo.

Decía Gregorio Cortez:
—¿Pa' qué se valen de planes?
No me pueden agarrar
ni con esos perros jaunes.—

Decían los americanos:
—Si lo alcanzamos ¿qué hacemos?
Si le entramos por derecho
muy poquitos volveremos.—

Allá por El Encinal,
según lo que aquí se dice,
le formaron un corral
y les mató otro cherife.

Decía Gregorio Cortez
echando muchos balazos:
—Me he escapado de aguaceros,
contimás de nublinazos.—

Ya se encontró a un mexicano,
le dice con altivez:
—Platícame qué hay de nuevo,
yo soy Gregorio Cortez.

—Dicen que por culpa mía
han matado mucha gente,
pues ya me voy a entregar
porque eso no es conveniente.—

Cortez le dice a Jesús:
—Ora sí lo vas a ver,
anda diles a los rinches
que me vengan a aprehender.—

Venían todos los rinches,
venían que hasta volaban,
porque se iban a ganar
diez mil pesos que les daban.

Cuando rodearon la casa
Cortez se les presentó:
—Por la buena sí me llevan
porque de otro modo no.—

Decía el Cherife Mayor
como queriendo llorar:
—Cortez, entrega tus armas,
no te vamos a matar.—

Decía Gregorio Cortez,
les gritaba en alta voz:
—Mis armas no las entrego
hasta estar en caliboz'.—

Decía Gregorio Cortez,
decía en su voz divina:
—Mis armas no las entrego
hasta estar en bartolina.—

Ya agarraron a Cortez,
ya terminó la cuestión,
la pobre de su familia
lo lleva en el corazón.

Ya con ésta me despido
a la sombra de un ciprés,
aquí se acaba el corrido
de don Gregorio Cortez.

Gregorio Cortez

In the county of El Carmen, look what has happened;
the Major Sheriff is dead, leaving Román badly wounded.

In the county of El Carmen such a tragedy took place:
the Major Sheriff is dead; no one knows who killed him.

They went around asking questions about half an hour afterward;
they found out that the wrongdoer had been Gregorio Cortez.

Now they have outlawed Cortez throughout the whole of the state;
let him be taken, dead or alive, for he has killed several men.

Then said Gregorio Cortez, with his pistol in his hand,
"I don't regret having killed him; what I regret is my brother's death."

Then said Gregorio Cortez, with his soul aflame,
"I don't regret having killed him; self-defense is permitted."

The Americans were coming; they were whiter than a poppy
from the fear that they had of Cortez and his pistol.

Then the Americans said, and they said it fearfully,
"Come, let us follow the trail, for the wrongdoer is Cortez."

They let loose the bloodhounds so they could follow the trail,
but trying to overtake Cortez was like following a star.

He struck out for Gonzales, without showing any fear:
"Follow me, cowardly *rinches*; I am Gregorio Cortez."

From Belmont he went to the ranch, where they succeeded in surrounding him,
quite a few more than three hundred, but he jumped out of their corral.

When he jumped out of their corral, according to what is said here,
they got into a gunfight, and he killed them another sheriff.

Then said Gregorio Cortez, with his pistol in his hand,
"Don't run, you cowardly *rinches*, from a single Mexican."

Gregorio Cortez went out, he went out toward Laredo;
they would not follow him because they were afraid of him.

Then said Gregorio Cortez, "What is the use of your scheming?
You cannot catch me, even with those bloodhounds."

Then said the Americans, "If we catch up with him, what shall we do?
If we fight him man to man, very few of us will return."

Way over near El Encinal, according to what is said here,
they made him a corral, and he killed them another sheriff.

Then said Gregorio Cortez, shooting out a lot of bullets,
"I have weathered thunderstorms; this little mist doesn't bother me."

Now he has met a Mexican; he says to him haughtily,
"Tell me the news; I am Gregorio Cortez.

"They say that because of me many people have been killed;
so now I will surrender, because such things are not right."

Cortez says to Jesús, "At last you are going to see it;
go and tell the *rinches* that they can come and arrest me."

All the *rinches* were coming, so fast that they almost flew,
because they were going to get the ten thousand dollars that were offered.

When they surrounded the house, Cortez appeared before them:
"You will take me if I'm willing but not any other way."

Then said the Major Sheriff, as if he was going to cry,
"Cortez, hand over your weapons; we do not want to kill you."

Then said Gregorio Cortez, shouting to them in a loud voice,
"I won't surrender my weapons until I am in a cell."

Then said Gregorio Cortez, speaking in his godlike voice,
"I won't surrender my weapons until I'm inside a jail."

Now they have taken Cortez, and now the matter is ended;
his poor family are keeping him in their hearts.

Now with this I say farewell in the shade of a cypress;
this is the end of the ballad of Don Gregorio Cortez.

19

Ignacio Treviño

El die - ci - séis de di - ciem - bre a - pes - tó a pól - vo - ra un ra - to,
don - de en - con - tra - ron los rin - ches la hor - ma de su za - pa - to.

El dieciséis de diciembre
apestó a pólvora un rato,
donde encontraron los rinches
la horma de su zapato.

Cantina de El Elefante
donde el caso sucedió,
en donde Ignacio Treviño
con los rinches se topó.

Cuando los primeros tiros
la cantina quedó sola,
nomás Ignacio Treviño,
su canana y su pistola.

Decía Ignacio Treviño
con su pistola en la mano:
—No corran, rinches cobardes,
con un solo mexicano.

—Entrenle, rinches cobardes,
que el juego no es con un niño,
soy purito mexicano,
me llamo Ignacio Treviño.—

Decían todos los rinches:
—Esta noche nos quedamos,
les apagamos las luces
y a puro matar nos vamos.—

Cuando los primeros tiros
la policía se acercó
a ese Elefante Blanco
donde el caso sucedió.

Ese señor Willie Krausse
lo tenían por buen gallo,
a l'hora de los balazos
no supo ni del caballo.

Decía Tito Crixell
a l'hora de los balazos:
— ¡Cuánta botella de juíscle,
toditas hechas pedazos!—

Decía Pedro Saldaña,
como queriendo llorar:
—¿Dónde estará el Comandante?
Me quiero desocupar.—

Decía el señor Chon Cuéllar:
—Vamos a ver que pasó.—
Y en la tienda de Fernández
ahi fue donde se metió.

Decía Jimmy Werbiski:
—La cosa está muy caliente,
¿dónde estará el Comandante
pa' que apacigüe su gente?—

Y decía el Comandante,
que ya no hallaba qué hacer:
— ¡Ese es Ignacio Treviño,
lo querían conocer!—

Decía José Calderón,
como queriendo llorar:
—Ignacio, ya no les tires,
no te vayan a matar.—

Decía Ignacio Treviño
con muchisísimo esmero:
—Para que aprendan, muchachos,
como se gana el dinero.—

Ya con ésta van tres veces
que me he lucido bonito,
la primera fue en Mercedes,
en Brownsville y en San Benito.

Ignacio Treviño

On the sixteenth of December, it stank of gunpowder a while;
that was when the *rinches* found the last that would fit their shoe.

At the Elephant Saloon, that's where the events took place;
that's where Ignacio Treviño locked horns with the *rinches*.

At the sound of the first shots, the saloon was deserted;
only Ignacio Treviño remained, with his pistol and cartridge belt.

Then said Ignacio Treviño, with his pistol in his hand,
"Don't run, you cowardly *rinches*, from a single Mexican."

"Come on, you cowardly *rinches*, you're not playing games with a child;
I am a true-born Mexican, my name is Ignacio Treviño."

All the *rinches* were saying, "This night we will stay in town;
we will shoot out their lights, and then we can kill and kill."

At the sound of the first shots, the other policemen drew near
to that well-known White Elephant, where the events took place.

That Mr. William Krausse was considered a real fighter,
but at the time of the shooting, he didn't even know where his horse was.

Then said Tito Crixell, as the shooting was going on,
"So many bottles of whisky, all of them shot to pieces."

Then said Pedro Saldaña, as if he was going to cry,
"Where is the Chief of Police? I want to resign my job."

Then said Mr. Chon Cuéllar, "Let us go see what happened."
But he went only as far as the Fernández store, where he ducked in.

Then said Jimmy Werbiski, "Things are getting very hot.
Where is the Chief of Police? He ought to calm things down."

And the Chief of Police said, not knowing what else to do:
"That is Ignacio Treviño; he has shown you who he is!"

Then said José Calderón, as if he was going to cry,
"Ignacio, stop shooting at them, or else they may kill you."

Then said Ignacio Treviño, speaking in very measured tones,
"Pay attention, boys, and you'll learn how to earn your pay."

With this it will be three times that I've shown what I can do;
the first time was in Mercedes, then in Brownsville and San Benito.

20

Jacinto Treviño

Ya con és - ta van tres ve - ces   que se ha vis - to lo bo - ni - to,

la pri - me - ra fue en Ma - ca - len, en Bróns - vil y en San Be - ni - to.

Ya con ésta van tres veces
que se ha visto lo bonito,
la primera fue en Macalen,
en Brónsvil y en San Benito.

Y en la cantina de Bekar
se agarraron a balazos,
por dondequiera saltaban
botellas hechas pedazos.

Esa cantina de Bekar
al momento quedó sola,
nomás Jacinto Treviño
de carabina y pistola.

—Entrenle, rinches cobardes,
que el pleito no es con un niño,
querían conocer su padre,
¡yo soy Jacinto Treviño!

—Entrenle, rinches cobardes,
validos de la ocasión,
no van a comer pan blanco
con tajadas de jamón.—

Decía el Rinche Mayor,
como era un americano:
—¡Ah, qué Jacinto tan hombre,
no niega el ser mexicano!—

Decía Jacinto Treviño
que se moría de la risa:

—A mí me hacen los ojales,
los puños de la camisa.—

Decía Jacinto Treviño,
abrochándose un zapato:
—Aquí traigo más cartuchos
pa' divertirnos un rato.—

Decía Jacinto Treviño,
con su pistola en la mano:
—No corran, rinches cobardes,
con un solo mexicano.—

Decía Jacinto Treviño:
—Yo ya me vo' a retirar,
me voy para Río Grande
y allá los voy a esperar.—

Decía Jacinto Treviño,
al bajar una bajada:
—¡Ay, qué rinches tan cobardes,
que no me haigan hecho nada!—

Decía Jacinto Treviño,
andando en Nuevo Laredo:
—Yo soy Jacinto Treviño,
nacido en Montemorelos.—

Ya con ésta me despido
aquí a presencia de todos,
yo soy Jacinto Treviño,
vecino de Matamoros.

Jacinto Treviño

With this it will be three times that remarkable things have happened;
the first time was in McAllen, then in Brownsville and San Benito.

They had a shoot-out at Baker's saloon;
broken bottles were popping all over the place.

Baker's saloon was immediately deserted;
only Jacinto Treviño remained, with his rifle and his pistol.

"Come on, you cowardly *rinches,* you're not playing games with a child.
You wanted to meet your father? I am Jacinto Treviño!

"Come on, you cowardly *rinches,* you always like to take the advantage;
this is not like eating white bread with slices of ham."

The chief of the *rinches* said, even though he was an American,
"Ah, what a brave man is Jacinto; you can see he is a Mexican!"

Then said Jacinto Treviño, who was dying of laughter,
"All you're good for is to make the buttonholes and the cuffs on my shirt."

Then said Jacinto Treviño, as he was tying his shoe,
"I have more cartridges here, so we can amuse ourselves a while."

Then said Jacinto Treviño, with his pistol in his hand,
"Don't run, you cowardly *rinches*, from a single Mexican."

Then said Jacinto Treviño, "I am going to retire.
I'm going to Rio Grande City, and I will wait for you there."

Then said Jacinto Treviño, as he came down an incline,
"Ah, what a cowardly bunch of *rinches;* they didn't do anything to me!"

Then said Jacinto Treviño, when he was in Nuevo Laredo,
"I am Jacinto Treviño, born in Montemorelos."

Now with this I say farewell, here in everybody's presence;
I am Jacinto Treviño, a citizen of Matamoros.

21
Los sediciosos

The tune for this *corrido* is in duple time, a fast *one*-two, *one*-two instead of the usual *one*-two-three beat. It is sung to a lively tempo.

En mil no-ve-cien-tos quin-ce, ¡qué dí - as tan ca - lu-ro-sos!

voy a can-tar es-tos ver-sos, ver-sos de los se-di-cio-sos.

En mil novecientos quince,
¡qué días tan calurosos!
voy a cantar estos versos,
versos de los sediciosos.

Ya con ésta van tres veces
que sucede lo bonito,
la primera fue en Mercedes,
en Brónsvil y en San Benito.

En ese punto de Norias
ya merito les ardía,
a esos rinches desgraciados
muchas balas les llovía.

Ya la mecha está encendida
por los puros mexicanos,
y los que van a pagarla
son los mexicotejanos.

Ya la mecha está encendida
con azul y colorado,
y los que van a pagarla
van a ser los de este lado.

Ya la mecha está encendida,
muy bonita y colorada,
y la vamos a pagar
los que no debemos nada.

Decía Aniceto Pizaña,
en su caballo cantando:
—¿Dónde están por ahi los rinches?
que los vengo visitando.

—Esos rinches de la Kineña,
dicen que son muy valientes,
hacen llorar las mujeres,
hacen correr a las gentes.—

Decía Teodoro Fuentes,
abrochándose un zapato:
—A esos rinches de la Kineña
les daremos un mal rato.—

Decía Vicente el Giro
en su chico caballazo:
—Echenme ese gringo grande,
pa' llevármelo de brazo.—

Contesta el americano,
con su sombrero en las manos:
—Yo sí me voy con ustedes,
son muy buenos *maxacanos*.—

Decía Miguel Salinas
en su yegüita almendrada:
— ¡Ay, qué gringos tan ingratos!
que no nos hagan parada.—

En ese punto de Norias
se oía la pelotería,
del señor Luis de la Rosa
nomás el llanto se oía.

El señor Luis de la Rosa
se tenía por hombrecito,
a la hora de los balazos
lloraba como un chiquito.

Decía Teodoro Fuentes,
decía con su risita:

—Echen balazos, muchachos,
¡qué trifulca tan bonita!

—Tiren, tiren, muchachitos,
tiren, tiren de a montón,
que el señor Luis de la Rosa
ha manchado el pabellón.—

Gritaba Teodoro Fuentes:
—Hay que pasar por Mercedes,
para enseñarle a los rinches
que con nosotros no pueden.—

Les dice Luis de la Rosa:
—Muchachos ¿qué van a hacer?
Por Mercedes no pasamos,
y si no lo van a ver.—

Contesta Teodoro Fuentes
con su voz muy natural:
—Vale más que usted no vaya
porque nomás va a llorar.—

Pues pasaron por Mercedes,
y también por San Benito,
iban a tumbar el tren
a ese dipo del Olmito.

Ya se van los sediciosos,
ya se van de retirada,
de recuerdos nos dejaron
una veta colorada.

Ya se van los sediciosos
y quedaron de volver,
pero no dijeron cuando
porque no podían saber.

Despedida no la doy
porque no la traigo aquí,
se la llevó Luis de la Rosa
para San Luis Potosí.

The Seditionists

In nineteen hundred fifteen, oh but the days were hot!
I am going to sing these stanzas, stanzas about the seditionists.

With this it will be three times that remarkable things have happened;
the first time was in Mercedes, then in Brownsville and San Benito.

In that well-known place called Norias, it really got hot for them;
a great many bullets rained down on those cursed *rinches*.

Now the fuse is lit by the true-born Mexicans,
and it will be the Texas-Mexicans who will have to pay the price.

Now the fuse is lit, in blue and red,
and it will be those on this side who will have to pay the price.

Now the fuse is lit, very nice and red,
and it will be those of us who are blameless who will have to pay the price.

Aniceto Pizaña said, singing as he rode along,
"Where can I find the *rinches*? I'm here to pay them a visit.

"Those *rinches* from King Ranch say that they are very brave;
they make the women cry, and they make the people run."

Then said Teodoro Fuentes, as he was tying his shoe,
"We are going to give a hard time to those *rinches* from King Ranch."

Then said Vicente el Giro, sitting on his great big horse,
"Let me at that big Gringo, so we can amble arm-in-arm."

The American replies, holding his hat in his hands,
"I will be glad to go with you; you are very good Maxacans."

Then said Miguel Salinas, on his almond-colored mare,
"Ah, how disagreeable are these Gringos! Why don't they wait for us?"

In that well-known place called Norias, you could hear the sound of firing,
but from Señor Luis de la Rosa, all you could hear was his weeping.

Señor Luis de la Rosa considered himself a brave man,
but at the hour of the shooting, he cried like a baby.

Then said Teodoro Fuentes, smiling his little smile,
"Pour on the bullets, boys; what a beautiful fracas!

"Fire, fire away, my boys; fire, fire all at once,
for Señor Luis de la Rosa has besmirched his colors."

Teodoro Fuentes shouted, "We have to go through Mercedes,
so we can show the *rinches* that we are too much for them."

Luis de la Rosa tells them, "Boys, what are you going to do?
We cannot go through Mercedes, and if you doubt it, you soon will see."

Teodoro Fuentes replies, in a very natural voice,
"It's best that you not go with us, because all you will do is cry."

So they did go through Mercedes, and also through San Benito;
they went to derail the train at the station of Olmito.

The seditionists are leaving, they have gone into retreat;
they have left us a red swath to remember them by.

The seditionists are leaving, they said that they would return;
but they didn't tell us when because they had no way of knowing.

I will not give you my farewell, because I did not bring it with me;
Luis de la Rosa took it with him to San Luis Potosí.

22
Pablo González

This *corrido* is sung slowly. It is a lament for Pablo more than a narrative of his exploits, and it is one of the few Border *corridos* with a refrain. Others, like "El marrano gordo," are humorous in intent. The refrain in "Pablo González" is a kind of dirge, in which the dead man himself speaks.

El dí - a trein - ta de a - bril, co - mo a las tres de la tar - de,
mu - rio Pa - bli - to Gon - zá - lez a ma - nos de un co - bar - de.
¿Qué di - ces, Pa - blo? ¿Qué quie - res que di - ga yo?
Mis dí - as ya se a - ca - ba - ron, mi vi - da ya ter - mi - nó.

El día treinta de abril,
como a las tres de la tarde,
murió Pablito González
a manos de un cobarde.

—¿Qué dices, Pablo?—
—¿Qué quieres que diga yo?
Mis días ya se acabaron,
mi vida ya terminó.—

Estaba don Pablo Cruz,
cuando el difunto cayó,
queriendo arrancar pistola
y el miedo no lo dejó.

—¿Qué dices, Pablo? etc.

Pablo Cruz y Juan González
mancharon el pabellón,
y uno al otro se decían:
—Ya ganamos pa' jabón.—

—¿Qué dices, Pablo? etc.

Decía Victoriano Contreras:
—Yo se los voy a arrestar;
si me tumba del caballo
no me vayan a dejar.—

—¿Qué dices, Pablo? etc.

Decía Federico Max:
—Yo ya traía mi santo;
si le he jerrado a Pablito
me dejo caer al barranco.—

—¿Qué dices, Pablo? etc.

—Adiós, mis queridos hijos,
y adiós mi bella mujer.
'N el rancho 'e Los Villarreales
mi sangre se vió correr.—

—¿Qué dices, Pablo? etc.

Pablo González

On the thirtieth day of April, about three in the afternoon,
Pablito González died at the hands of a coward.

   "What do you say, Pablo?" "What do you expect me to say?
   My days are now finished, my life has come to an end."

When the deceased fell, Don Pablo Cruz was busy
trying to draw his pistol, but his fear would not let him do so.

   "What do you say, Pablo?" etc.

Pablo Cruz and Juan González besmirched their colors,
and they said to each other, "At least we earned enough for soap."

   "What do you say . . ." etc.

Victoriano Contreras said, "I'll go arrest him for you;
if he shoots me off my horse, don't you go leave me behind."

   "What do you say . . ." etc.

Said Federico Max, "I was holding on to my saint.
If I had missed Pablito, I would have jumped into the ditch."

   "What do you say . . ." etc.

"Farewell, my beloved children, farewell, my beautiful wife;
at the Los Villarreales ranch my blood was seen to flow."

   "What do you say . . ." etc.

23
Alonso

"Alonso" is sung in a tense manner, with a tightness at the throat, high and defiant.
The basses are strongly marked.

A - lon-so se va pa' Te - xas en com-pa - ñía de su ma - dre,
y a los quin - ce a - ños vol - vío pa - ra ven - gar a su pa - dre.

Alonso se va pa' Texas
en compañía de su madre,
y a los quince años volvió
para vengar a su padre.

Alonso vino de Texas
de pistola y carrillera:
—A mí me habías de matar,
pelado de tierra afuera.—

El general Margarito
a Alonso mandó llamar
a la cantina 'e Santiago
para allí conferenciar.

—Señor alcalde mayor,
le manda decir Chaguito
que Alonso Flores mató
al general Margarito.—

Luego que ya lo mató
le puso un pie sobre el pecho:
—Así se matan los hombres,
hablándoles por derecho.—

Luego que ya lo mató
se remontó en un ancón,
por los domingos bajaba
muy tranquilo a la estación.

Dice una tía de Alonso:
—Hijo, no andes sobremano;

matastes a Margarito,
cuídate bien de su hermano.—

Y allí le contesta Alonso:
—Tía, no tenga cuidado,
cuando voy a la estación
ando muy bien preparado.—

Pues Alonso no se fue,
y no se fue hasta otro día,
pa' darle pruebas a Félix
que miedo no le tenía.

Margarito se murió,
Alonso está en las espumas:
—Ya les maté el gallo fino,
nomás quedaron las plumas.—

Margarito era valiente
con aquel que le temía,
con una vino pagando
las catorce que debía.

Un domingo en la mañana
Alonso salió pa' Texas:
—Yo ya les tumbé el panal,
ahi les dejo las abejas.

—Pues ora sí, comerciantes,
a trabajar con esmero,
ya les maté a Margarito
que les quitaba el dinero.—

Alonso

Alonso leaves for Texas, accompanied by his mother;
he came back after fifteen years, so he could avenge his father.

Alonso came back from Texas wearing pistol and pistol belt:
"Why don't you try to kill me, you worthless outsider scum."

General Margarito had Alonso called
to Santiago's saloon, so they could confer there.

"Mr. Mayor of the town, Chaguito sends you word
that Alonso Flores has killed General Margarito."

After he had killed him, he placed his foot on his chest:
"This is how men should be killed, meeting them face to face."

After he had killed him, he hid out in a remote place;
on Sundays he would ride down very calmly to the station.

An aunt of Alonso's tells him, "Child, do not be so rash;
you have killed Margarito, but be careful of his brother."

There Alonso answers her, "Aunt, do not be worried;
when I come down to the station, I am always well prepared."

So Alonso did not leave, he did not leave until another day,
so as to give proof to Félix that he was not afraid of him.

Margarito is dead, Alonso is riding high:
"I killed you the fighting cock; nothing was left but his feathers."

Margarito was brave with those who were afraid of him;
he paid with one life the fourteen he had taken.

On a Sunday morning, Alonso left for Texas:
"I knocked down the hive for you, but I'm leaving you the bees."

"So go to it now, you merchants, and take great pains in your work;
I have killed you Margarito, who took the money you made."

24
Arnulfo

The tune for "Arnulfo" is almost identical to the first four phrases of the eight-phrase
tune to which "Elena" (no. 6) is sung. The next to last stanza is six lines instead of
four, so two additional bars are inserted between the second and third bars of the
tune, to allow for the two extra lines. Since this six-line stanza occurs toward the end,
it heightens the effect of the closing stanza or *despedida*.

Vue - la, vue - la pa - lo - mi - ta, pá - ra - te en e - sos tri - ga - les,

an - da a - ví - sa - le a Lu - pi - ta que mu - rió Ar - nul - fo Gon - zá - lez,

se lle - vó u - na ca - be - ci - ta del te - nien - te de ru - ra - les.

De Allende se despidió
a los veinte años cabales,
gratos recuerdos dejó
al pueblo y a los rurales.

    Estaba Arnulfo sentado
y en eso pasa un rural;

le dice: —Oye ¿qué me ves?—
—La vista es muy natural.—

    El rural muy enojado
en la cara le pegó,
con su pistola en la mano
con la muerte le amagó.

Arnulfo se levantó,
llamándole la atención:
—Oiga, amigo, no se vaya,
falta mi contestación.—

Se agarraron a balazos,
se agarraron frente a frente,
Arnulfo con su pistola
tres tiros le dio al teniente.

El teniente era hombrecito,
las pruebas las había dado,
pero se encontró un pollito
y este no estaba jugado.

Pero ¡ay! le dice el teniente,
ya casi pa' agonizar:
—Oiga, amigo, no se vaya,
acábeme de matar.—

Arnulfo se devolvió
a darle un tiro en la frente,
pero en la vuelta que dio
allí le pegó el teniente.

Arnulfo muy mal herido
en un carro iba colando,
cuando llegó al hospital
Arnulfo iba agonizando.

¡Qué bonitos son los hombres
que se matan pecho a pecho,
cada uno con su pistola,
defendiendo su derecho!

En Allende hay buenos gallos,
el que no lo quiera creer
nomás no revuelva el agua
que así se la ha de beber.

Vuela, vuela palomita,
párate en esos trigales,
anda avísale a Lupita
que murió Arnulfo González,
se llevó una cabecita
del teniente de rurales.

Ya con ésta me despido,
pacíficos y fiscales,
aquí se acaba el corrido
del teniente y de González.

Arnulfo

He said farewell to Allende at exactly twenty years of age;
he left pleasant memories with the people and the rural police.

Arnulfo was sitting down, when a rural policeman happens to pass by;
he says to him, "Listen, why are you staring at me?" "Looking is very natural."

The rural policeman was very angry, and he struck him in the face;
with his pistol in his hand, he threatened him with death.

Arnulfo rose to his feet, calling the policeman down:
"Listen, friend, don't go away. My reply is yet to come."

They started shooting at each other, they were fighting face to face;
Arnulfo with his pistol shot the lieutenant three times.

The lieutenant was a brave man, for he had proved it before,
but he encountered a little gamecock that had not been played out.

But, oh, the lieutenant says, almost with his last breath,
"Listen, friend, don't go away. Come back and finish me off."

Arnulfo came back, to put a bullet through his forehead,
but as he turned around, the lieutenant shot him right there.

Arnulfo, very badly wounded, was taken away in a car;
when he got to the hospital, Arnulfo was in his death throes.

How admirable are men who fight to the death face to face,
each one of them with his pistol, defending his right!

In Allende there are good fighters; he who will not believe it,
just let him stir up the waters, and he will have mud to drink.

Fly, fly, little dove, go light on those wheat fields;
go take the news to Lupita that Arnulfo González is dead;
he took a scalp along with him, that of the lieutenant of the *rurales*.

Now with this I say farewell to civilians and to policemen;
this is the end of the ballad of the lieutenant and González.

25
Alejos Sierra

En Pie-dras Ne-gras,Coa-hui-la, se-ño-res, es-to pa-só-o;
el se-ñor A-le-jos Sie-rra co-mo los hom-bres mu-rió-o.

En Piedras Negras, Coahuila,
señores, esto pasó;
el señor Alejos Sierra
como los hombres murió.

El catorce de febrero,
esto pasó en treinta y dos,
cantina del Gato Negro,
pasó una tragedia atroz.

A las cinco de la tarde
hasta temblaba la tierra,
con su pistola en la mano
y a caballo Alejos Sierra.

Tomándose algunas copas
y haciéndolo como ensayo,
se dirigió a la cantina
bien montado en su caballo.

Bien montado en su caballo
decía: —De nadie soy reo,
este día mato o me matan. —
Y se fue hacia el Gato Negro.

Mandaron traer los empleados,
Hilario ya iba a cenar,

lo encontró el cabo Rubén
que lo fuera a acompañar.

Llegaron a la cantina
y lo quisieron sitiar,
y al primero que divisa
le comienza a disparar.

Hilario entró por el frente,
otros por el otro lado,
a los primeros balazos
Hoyos lo tenía abrazado.

Después de algunos minutos
de seguirse disparando,
dos empleados mal heridos
y Alejos agonizando.

Alejos murió al momento,
Hilario murió otro día,
con grande acompañamiento
de los dos se despedían.

—Hijo de mi corazón, —
decía su padre llorando,
—has muerto como los hombres,
en tu caballo peleando.

—Pues yo no guardo rencores
por lo que te haiga pasado,
quiero cubrirte de flores
en tu tumba, hijito amado. —

Ya con ésta me despido
con el cantar de mi tierra,
aquí se acaba el corrido
del señor Alejos Sierra.

Alejos Sierra

In Piedras Negras, Coahuila, gentlemen, this is what happened;
Señor Alejos Sierra died the way that men should die.

On the fourteenth of February, this happened in thirty-two,
at the Black Cat saloon an atrocious tragedy took place.

At five in the afternoon, it seemed that even the earth was shaking;
it was Alejos Sierra on horseback and with his pistol in his hand.

He took a few drinks, doing it by way of preparation;
then he went toward the saloon, well mounted on his horse.

Well mounted on his horse he said, "No one is going to arrest me.
Today I will kill or be killed." And he went toward the Black Cat.

When they sent for the police, Hilario was going out for his supper;
but Corporal Rubén ran into him and asked that he go along.

They arrived at the saloon, and they tried to surround him;
he started firing at the first one he saw.

Hilario went in through the front door, some others the other way;
when the first shots were fired, Hoyos had his arms around him.

After some minutes, during which they kept firing at each other,
two policemen were badly wounded and Alejos was dying.

Alejos died immediately, Hilario died the next day;
a great number of people paid them their last farewells.

"Son of my heart," his father said weeping,
"You have died the way men should, fighting on horseback.

"I do not bear any grudges for what has happened to you;
I want to cover you with flowers in your grave, my beloved son."

Now with this I say farewell, with a song from my native soil;
this is the end of the ballad of Señor Alejos Sierra.

26
Laredo

E - se pue - blo de La - re -do es un pue - blo muy lu - ci - do,

don - de se en - cuen - tra la ma - ta de los hom - bres de - ci - di - dos.

Ese pueblo de Laredo
es un pueblo muy lucido,
donde se encuentra la mata
de los hombres decididos.

Y ese puerto de Laredo
es un puerto muy mentado,
los agentes de la ley
andan siempre con cuidado.

En ese rancho de Lule
varios casos han pasado,
contrabandistas y rinches
sus vidas las han cambiado.

Pero también en el frente,
porque no eran criminal,
¡decir que no se lucieron
en esa guerra mundial!

Debemos de recordar
que muchos jamás volvieron,

por cumplir con su deber
en esa lucha murieron.

No solamente en el frente
demostraron ser humanos,
por eso en Laredo, Texas,
se aprecian los mexicanos.

Y el que le guste pasearse
nunca lo podrá negar,
nomás que cruce el Río Grande,
hay mucho en donde gozar.

Y el que le guste pasearse,
gozar de toda alegría,
que pase a Nuevo Laredo
y gozará noche y día.

Ya con ésta me despido,
tomándome un anisado;
adiós, lindas morenitas
de ese Laredo afamado.

Laredo

That town of Laredo is a very distinguished town,
where is found the cradle of resolute men.

That port of Laredo is a very famous port;
the officers of the law always go about with care.

In that ranch known as Lule, several incidents have taken place;
smugglers and *rinches* have taken each others' lives.

But they have also been at the front, because they were not criminals;
let no one say they did not distinguish themselves in that famed world war.

We should remember that many never came back;
they died in that conflict while doing their duty.

Not only at the front have they demonstrated their humanity;
that is why in Laredo, Texas, Mexicans are held in esteem.

And he who likes to go out—it never can be denied,
let him just cross the Rio Grande, where there is much he can enjoy.

And he who likes to go out and enjoy all kinds of merrymaking,
let him cross over to Nuevo Laredo, and he will enjoy himself night and day.

Now with this I say farewell, while drinking an *anisado;*
farewell, beautiful dark girls of that famed Laredo.

27
La toma de Ciudad Juárez

México está muy contento,
dando gracias a millares,
empezaré por Durango,
Torreón y Ciudad de Juárez,
donde se ha visto correr
sangre de los federales.

Muchachas de Ciudad Juárez
se vieron muy azoradas,
de verse en tantas batidas,
de verse en tantas batallas,
de ver a los maderistas
componiendo sus metrallas.

¡Ah, qué valor de Madero
cuando a ese México entró!
Con sus ametralladoras
Orozco lo acompañó,
haciendo fuego cerrado
hasta que no los venció.

¡Ah, qué valor de Madero,
bonitas son sus acciones!
Que mandó a sus cabecillas

a echar fuera las prisiones,
¡la Virgen de Guadalupe
lo colme de bendiciones!

Porfirio Díaz decía:
—Ya mi gente está volteada,
yo ya no quiero pelear,
ya voy a bajar mi espada;
me agarraron a Navarro,
que era con el que contaba.—

¡Qué bien nos salió, cometa,
lo que venías anunciando!
de ver a los maderistas
en este reino reinando,
Porfirio dado de baja
para Europa caminando.

Porfirio está retratado
con un ramo y un letrero,
y en el letrero decía:
—No pudistes con Madero,
con otros habrás podido
porque eres camandulero.—

The Taking of Ciudad Juárez

Mexico is very happy, people by the thousands are giving thanks;
I will begin with Durango, then Torreón and Ciudad Juárez,
where the blood of government soldiers was seen to flow.

Girls of Ciudad Juárez, you were greatly startled
to find yourselves in so many skirmishes, in so many battles,
to see the *maderistas* setting up their machine guns.

Ah, how brave was Madero when he entered into Mexico!
Orozco and his machine guns accompanied him,
keeping up a steady fire, until he defeated them.

Ah, how brave was Madero, how admirable were his acts!
For he sent his chieftains to empty out the prisons.
May the Virgin of Guadalupe heap benedictions upon him.

Then said Porfirio Díaz, "My men have turned against me.
I don't want to fight any more; I will now lower my sword.
They have made Navarro prisoner, who was the one I could count on."

Comet, how true was the prophecy that you had been announcing!
To see the *maderistas* ruling in this land,
Porfirio out of a job and on his way to Europe.

There's a portrait of Porfirio, with a bouquet of flowers and a lettered sign,
and it says on the sign, "You were no match for Madero;
you were successful against others because you're a tricky rogue."

28

La toma de Matamoros

Voy a cantar estos versos,
pongan mucha atención todos,
voy a cantar la tragedia
de la Heroica Matamoros.

Día martes tres de junio
de mil novecientos trece,
a las diez de la mañana
Lucio Blanco se aparece.

Pues traía miles de hombres,
bien armados y valientes
para tomar esa plaza
y hacer correr a las gentes.

La plaza de Matamoros
estaba fortificada,
con la planta de la luz
estaba bien conectada.

La gente de Matamoros
ya resuelta toda estaba
a defender a su pueblo
aunque la vida costara.

Por hojas sueltas pidieron
la plaza al Mayor Ramos,
diciendo: —Si no la entregan
de todos modos entramos.—

Cuando estas hojas llegaron
a manos del Mayor Ramos,
sonriendo dijo al enviado:
—La plaza no la entregamos.—

Pues decía el Mayor Ramos,
lo mismo que Barragán:
—Lo que es Carranza no gana
y si no ya lo verán.—

Ya la hora se llegó,
pues ya se le cumple el plazo,
por dondequiera se oía
la bala y el cañonazo.

La gente de Matamoros
muy contenta se quedaba
cuando vino la noticia
que Blanco se retiraba.

Pero un repique oportuno,
que no saben quién lo dio,
alentó a los carrancistas
y Blanco se devolvió.

Para las tres de la tarde
había muertos y heridos,
y los soldados de línea
se iban a Estados Unidos.

El empuje fue terrible,
la defensa por demás;
eran pocos los de adentro,
los de afuera muchos más.

Los valientes voluntarios
de López y Chazarreta
se salían de las trincheras
a tirar a la banqueta.

A las diez de la mañana
algunas casas quemaron,
pero éstas fueron venganzas
que llegando consumaron.

Agarraron prisioneros
a unos niños que pelearon,
y otro día en el Parián
a las seis los fusilaron.

Pues lo niños que pelearon
con bastante decisión
al enemigo causaron
bastante admiración.

Pero un antiguo artillero
que era también gobiernista,
a ese no le hicieron nada,
lo defendió un carrancista.

Pero a Antonio Chazarreta
le tocó muy mala suerte,
lo cogieron prisionero
y fue sentenciado a muerte.

Las gentes de Matamoros
perdieron toda esperanza
al oir que por las calles
gritan que viva Carranza.

Las gentes de Matamoros
en Texas aventurando,
dicen que no han de volver
mientras Lucio tenga el mando.

Ya con ésta me despido,
me compadezco de todos,
y con tristeza les digo
que perdimos Matamoros.

The Taking of Matamoros

I am going to sing these stanzas, everyone pay much attention;
I am going to sing the ballad of the Heroic Matamoros.

On Tuesday, the third of June of nineteen hundred thirteen,
at ten o'clock in the morning, Lucio Blanco makes his appearance.

He was bringing with him thousands of men, well armed and brave,
in order to take the city and make the people run.

The city of Matamoros had been fortified;
it was well connected with the power plant.

The people of Matamoros were ready for anything,
determined to defend their town, though it cost them their lives.

In leaflets they demanded the city from Major Ramos,
saying, "If you do not surrender it, we will take it anyway."

When these leaflets came into Major Ramos's hands,
he smiled and told the emissary, "We will not surrender the town."

For Major Ramos said, and Barragán said the same,
"There's no way Carranza can win; if you don't believe it, just wait and see."

Now the hour has arrived, for the time limit has expired;
The sound of bullets and the roar of cannon could be heard everywhere.

The people of Matamoros began to feel very happy
when the news came that Blanco was in retreat.

But an unfortunate ringing of the bells, by no one knows who,
encouraged the *carrancistas,* and Blanco turned back.

By three in the afternoon there were many dead and wounded,
and the regular troops were leaving for the United States.

The pressure was tremendous, the defense was to no avail;
those inside were but a few, those outside were many more.

The valiant volunteers led by López and Chazarreta
were coming out of the trenches and firing from the sidewalks.

At ten o'clock in the morning several houses were burned,
but these were old scores that they settled as they entered.

They took prisoner several young boys who had fought them,
and they executed them in the marketplace next morning at six.

These young boys, who fought with a great deal of resolve,
caused in the enemy a good deal of admiration.

But an old artilleryman, who was also on the side of the government,
he was not harmed, because a *carrancista* defended him.

But for Antonio Chazarreta fortune was very bad;
he was taken prisoner, and he was sentenced to death.

The people of Matamoros abandoned all hope
when in the streets shouts of "Long live Carranza" were heard.

The people of Matamoros are in Texas, suffering misadventures;
they say they will never return as long as Lucio is in command.

Now with this I say farewell; I feel compassion for all,
and with sadness I tell you that we lost Matamoros.

29
El Automóvil Gris

This song is a ballad but not a *corrido*. It has long, irregular lines and is sung to a tune with a heavily marked *one-two-three-four* beat that is reminiscent of the Argentine tango. But "El Automóvil Gris" is not a melancholy song, as are most tangos. On the contrary, there is a rollicking quality to it.

En Ma-ta-mo-ros me ve-rán,   bo-rra-cho, fu-man-do bue-nos pu-ros,

to-man-do co-ñac,   je-rez,   cer-ve-za al son de la a-le-grí-a,

y es-tos pen-dien-tes que ten-go, los ten-go en San An-to-nio,

La-re-do, Te-xas, y a-llá en Be-lén.

Yo soy la ma-no que a-prie-ta,   que a-sal-ta y que ma-ta y ro-ba,

y por don-de-quie-ra que an-do   a to-dos les doy la co-ba;

yo per-te-nez-co a la ban-da   de e-se Au-to-mó-vil Gris,

me lla-mo Hi-gi-nio de An-da   y me he pa-sea-do en Pa-rí-is.

En Matamoros me verán, borracho, fumando buenos puros,
tomando coñac, jerez, cerveza al son de la alegría,
y estos pendientes que tengo, los tengo en San Antonio,
Laredo, Texas, y allá en Belén.

Yo soy la mano que aprieta,
que asalta y que mata y roba,
y por dondequiera que ando
a todos les doy la coba;
yo pertenezco a la banda
de ese Automóvil Gris,
me llamo Higinio de Anda
y me he paseado en París.

En Matamoros me verán, etc.

Y allá en la penitenciaría
donde doce años duré
en compañía de otros hombres
y del Chato Bernabé,
y en esa celda del once
donde murió el Negro Frank,
donde mataron a Udilio,
lo mataron a traición.

En Matamoros me verán, etc.

Y ese don Pablo González,
que la vida nos salvó,
que estando formado el cuadro
su pistola disparó;
yo pertenezco a la banda
de ese Automóvil Gris,
me llamo Higinio de Anda
y me he paseado en París.

En Matamoros me verán, etc.

The Gray Automobile

In Matamoros you may see me, drunk and smoking fine cigars,
drinking cognac, sherry, beer to the sound of merrymaking;
I have things I must do, they'll be done in San Antonio,
Laredo, Texas, and over in Belén.

I am the hand that squeezes, that assaults, that kills and robs,
and everywhere I go, I smooth-talk everyone;
I belong to the famed Gray Automobile band;
my name is Higinio de Anda, and I have enjoyed myself in Paris.

In Matamoros you may see me, etc.

And over there in the penitentiary, where I spent twelve years
in the company of others, including Chato Bernabé,
and in that cell number eleven, where Black Frank died,
where they killed Udilio, he was treacherously killed.

In Matamoros you may see me, etc.

And that Don Pablo González was the one who saved our lives;
the firing squad was at the ready, when he fired his pistol in the air;
I belong to the famed Gray Automobile band;
my name is Higinio de Anda, and I have enjoyed myself in Paris.

In Matamoros you may see me, etc.

30
No decías, Pancho Villa

No decías, Pancho Villa,
que dondequiera eras bueno;
y al llegar a Matamoros,
allí perdistes terreno.

Con mi treinta-treinta me voy a pelear
al camino de la rebelión,
para conquistar libertad, libertad
pa' los habitantes de nuestra nación.

Didn't You Say, Pancho Villa

Didn't you say, Pancho Villa, that you were a good fighter anywhere?
But when you came to Matamoros, there you lost a lot of ground.

With my thirty-thirty I am going to fight on the revolutionary road,
to gain liberty, liberty for the inhabitants of our nation.

31
La persecución de Villa

This is a long-line *corrido*. The tune is in duple time, as are most *corridos* with a basic line longer than eight syllables. Some *corridos* based on eight-syllable quatrains also are in duple time, for example "Los sediciosos" (no. 21).

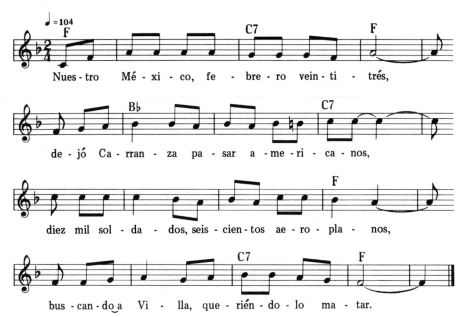

Nues - tro Mé - xi - co, fe - bre - ro vein - ti - trés,
de - jó Ca - rran - za pa - sar a - me - ri - ca - nos,
diez mil sol - da - dos, seis - cien - tos ae - ro - pla - nos,
bus - can - do a Vi - lla, que - rién - do - lo ma - tar.

Nuestro México, febrero veintitrés,
dejó Carranza pasar americanos,
diez mil soldados, seiscientos aeroplanos,
buscando a Villa, queriéndolo matar.

Don Venustiano les dice: —Que
    avancen.
Si son valientes y lo quieren perseguir,
les doy permiso que sigan adelante
pa' que se enseñen también a morir. —

Comenzaron a echar expediciones
y Pancho Villa también se transformó,
muy vestido de soldado americano
en las barbas de Pershing se rio.

Cuando vieron plantar la bandera
y las estrellas que Villa les pintó,
se dejaron caer los aeroplanos
y Pancho Villa prisioneros los tomó.

Cuando llegaron a México estos
    gringos
buscaban pan y galletas con jamón,
y la raza, que estaba muy enojada,
lo que les dieron fueron balas de cañón.

Pobrecitos de los americanos,
pues a sollozos comienzan a llorar,
con dos horas que tenían de combate
a su país se querían regresar.

Los de a caballo ya no se podían sentar
y los de a pie ya no podían caminar,
y Pancho Villa les pasa en su aeroplano
y desde arriba les dice: — ¡Goodbye! —

Ya Pancho Villa no monta a caballo,
pues eso ya no se usa por allá,
Francisco Villa es dueño de aeroplanos
y los arrenda con gran comodidad.

Toda la gente de la Ciudad de Juárez,
toda la gente asombrada se quedó
de ver tanto soldado americano
que Pancho Villa en los postes colgó.

Pues que creían estos rinches tan cobardes,
¿que combatir era un baile de carquís?
Con la cara toda llena de vergüenza
se regresaron otra vez a su país.

Y entonces Pershing recibió el mensaje
que en Carrizales doscientos le mató,
que le agradezca también a Carranza
los prisioneros, él fue el que los salvó.

Pues no sabían estos gringos tan patones,
con Pancho Villa no habían de poder,
Francisco Villa se encuentra en Carrizales,
si acaso gustan, lo pueden ir a ver.

The Pursuit of Villa

Our Mexico, on the twenty-third of February,
Carranza let Americans cross the border,
ten thousand soldiers, six hundred airplanes,
looking for Villa, wanting to kill him.

Don Venustiano tells them, "You may advance.
If you are brave and want to pursue him,
I give you permission to move forward
so that you too will learn how to die."

They began sending out expeditions,
and Pancho Villa then disguised himself;
fully dressed like an American soldier,
he laughed right in Pershing's face.

When they saw the raising of the American flag
and the stars that Villa painted for them,
the airplanes came down to earth,
and Pancho Villa took them prisoner.

When these Gringos arrived in Mexico,
they were looking for bread and crackers with ham;
but *la raza*, who were very angry,
gave them nothing but cannonballs.

Oh, those poor Americans,
they burst out sobbing and crying;
they had only been in battle for two hours,
and they were ready to go back to their country.

Those on horseback no longer could sit down,
and those on foot could no longer walk,
while Pancho Villa flew over them in his airplane,
and from up there he said to them, "<u>Goodbye!</u>"

Pancho Villa no longer rides a horse,
for that is no longer the custom over there;
Francisco Villa is the owner of airplanes,
and he rents them out at very reasonable rates.

All the people in Ciudad Juárez,
all the people were greatly surprised
to see so many American soldiers
that Pancho Villa hanged from telegraph poles.

And then Pershing received the message
that he had lost two hundred dead at Carrizales;
let him also be grateful to Carranza
about the prisoners, for it was Carranza who saved them.

What did these cowardly *rinches* think,
that making war was like a fancy ball?
With their faces all full of shame
they returned once more to their country.

Didn't these bigfooted Gringos know
that they were no match for Pancho Villa?
Francisco Villa is now in Carrizales;
if you so please, you can go see him there.

32
Benjamín Argumedo

"Benjamín Argumedo" is set to a tune of six phrases, allowing for stanzas of four, five, or six lines. In our version most of the stanzas are of four lines, with the first and third lines repeated to fit the six-phrase tune. Occasionally, as in stanzas 2 and 6, an extra line is added after the third line of the normal quatrain. Sing fairly slowly, with dignity.

Para empezar a cantar (bis)
pido permiso primero,
señores son las mañanas (bis)
de Benjamín Argumedo.

Cuando Rodríguez salió, (bis)
que a Sombrerete llegó,
ese general ingrato
dijo que se iba a la sierra
y a Benjamín traicionó.

En esa estancia de El Sauz, (bis)
camino pa' El Paraíso,
estaba Argumedo enfermo, (bis)
enfermo pues Dios lo quiso.

Se los digo en realidad (bis)
que fue el veintiocho de enero
que aprehendieron a Alanís (bis)
y a Benjamín Argumedo.

Como a las tres de la tarde, (bis)
de la tarde de ese día,
aprehendieron a Argumedo (bis)
y a toda su compañía.

En donde estaba Argumedo (bis)
tenían el camino andado,
donde se encontraba enfermo
a orillas de una laguna,
viendo bañar su caballo.

Se fueron todos al punto (bis)
y luego lo sorprendieron,
el pobre se hallaba enfermo (bis)
y por eso lo aprehendieron.

Echaron a Benjamín (bis)
en un carro como flete,
pasaron por San Miguel, (bis)
llegaron a Sombrerete.

Al llegar a la estación (bis)
empieza el tren a silbar,
veinte soldados de escolta (bis)
que lo vayan a bajar.

Otro día por la mañana (bis)
lo fueron a examinar,
le pusieron dos doctores (bis)
que lo pudieran curar.

Cuando Argumedo sanó, (bis)
que se le llegó su día,
lo llevan a presentar (bis)
al tirano de Murguía.

Y ese Francisco Murguía (bis)
le pregunta con esmero:
—¿Qué merced quiere que le haga, (bis)
mi general Argumedo?—

—Oiga usted, mi general, (bis)
yo también fui hombre valiente,
quiero que usted me fusile (bis)
al público de la gente.—

—Mi general Argumedo, (bis)
yo no le hago ese favor,
porque todito lo que hago (bis)
es por orden superior.

—Como a usted le habrá pasado (bis)
en algunas ocasiones,
sabe que he sido nombrado (bis)
general de operaciones.—

Cuando Argumedo ya vio (bis)
que no se le concedía,
él no les mostraba miedo, (bis)
antes mejor sonreía.

—Adiós, montañas y sierras, (bis)
ciudades y poblaciones,
donde me vi entre las balas (bis)
que parecían quemazones.

—Y adiós, reloj de Durango, (bis)
que tanto me atormentaba,
pues clarito me decía (bis)
las horas que me faltaban.

—Adiós el águila de oro (bis)
que en mi sombrero lucía,
¡a dónde vino a parar! (bis)
¡a las manos de Murguía!

—Tanto pelear y pelear, (bis)
con mi mauser en la mano,
para morir fusilado (bis)
en el panteón de Durango.—

Ya se acabó Benjamín, (bis)
ya no lo oímos mentar,
ya está juzgado de Dios, (bis)
ya su alma fue a descansar.

Ya con ésta me despido (bis)
porque cantar ya no puedo,
señores son las mañanas (bis)
de Benjamín Argumedo.

Benjamín Argumedo

I ask your permission before I begin to sing;
gentlemen, this is the ballad of Benjamín Argumedo.

When Rodríguez went out, as far as Sombrerete,
that ingrate of a general said he was going into the mountains,
and he betrayed Benjamín.

At the El Sauz station, on the road to El Paraíso,
Argumedo lay ill, ill for God willed it so.

I truthfully say to you, that it was on the twenty-eighth of January
that they captured Alanís and Benjamín Argumedo.

About three in the afternoon, in the afternoon of that day,
they captured Argumedo and all those who accompanied him.

The road that led to where Argumedo lay was one they had traveled before,
where he was lying ill, by the edge of a lagoon,
watching his horse being bathed.

They went there without delay, and then they surprised him;
the poor man was ill, and that was why they captured him.

They threw Benjamín into a boxcar like a piece of baggage;
they passed through San Miguel and arrived in Sombrerete.

As the train got to the station, the whistle began to blow;
an escort of twenty soldiers was sent to take him off the train.

On the next day in the morning, they went and examined him;
they assigned him two doctors who were supposed to cure him.

When Argumedo got well, when his day of doom arrived,
they take him before that despot of a Murguía.

And that Francisco Murguía asks him with feigned courtesy,
"Is there a request I can grant you, my general Argumedo?"

"Hear me, my general; I also have been a brave man.
I want you to execute me in public, before the people."

"My general Argumedo, I cannot grant you that favor,
because everything that I do is done on superior orders.

"As may have happened to you on certain occasions in the past,
you may know that I have been named field general in charge of this operation."

When Argumedo then saw that his request would not be granted,
he did not show any fear before them, on the contrary he smiled.

"Farewell, mountains and sierras, cities and towns,
where I was once among showers of bullets that were like sheets of fire.

"And farewell, clock of Durango, that tormented me so much,
for it told me very clearly the hours that I had remaining.

"Farewell to the golden eagle that I proudly wore on my hat;
look where it ended up! In the hands of Murguía!

"I fought so long, so long, with my Mauser in my hand;
and all to die by a firing squad in the cemetery of Durango."

Now Benjamín is gone, we no longer hear his name mentioned;
he has been judged by God, and his soul is now at rest.

Now with this I say farewell because I can sing no more;
gentlemen, this is the ballad of Benjamín Argumedo.

33
Felipe Angeles

Like "Benjamín Argumedo," this *corrido* is sung with an air of stateliness and dignity. There is more strength and less melancholy to this tune than to "Benjamín Argumedo."

Se - ño - res, con a - ten - ció - on, les di - ré lo que ha pa - sa - do,

fu - si - la - ron en Chi - hua - hua a un ge - ne - ral a - fa - ma - do.

Señores, con atención,
les diré lo que ha pasado,
fusilaron en Chihuahua
a un general afamado.

Ese dicho general
era un hombre muy valiente
y como buen militar
sabía dirigir su gente.

De artillero comenzó
su carrera militar,
y después de poco tiempo
le tocó ser general.

Como era hombre muy valiente,
y de un valor verdadero,
vengó la horrible traición
que le hicieron a Madero.

Se pasó pa'l extranjero
cuando la guerra mundial,

fue a ayudarles a los gringos
como inspector general.

Luego se vino a su patria
para ver como arreglaba,
abandonar la carrera,
irse a la vida privada.

Pero ya le fue imposible
lo que él deseaba arreglar,
porque los perseguidores
ya no le dieron lugar.

En la Sierra de la Mula
le tocó la mala suerte,
lo agarraron prisionero,
fue sentenciado a la muerte.

Y de allí fue conducido
a la prisión militar
mientras era orden del día
pa' mandarlo fusilar.

Entonces Angeles dijo:
—Mis planes ya son perdidos,
pensaba en cada momento
volver a Estados Unidos.—

Angeles puso un mensaje
al Congreso de la Unión:
—Si he de ser afusilado
soy a su disposición.—

El gobierno constataba
los males que había causado,
la sentencia estaba dada
que había de ser fusilado.

—El reloj marca sus horas,
se acerca mi ejecución;
preparen muy bien sus armas,
apúntenme al corazón.

—Yo no soy de los cobardes
que le temen a la muerte,
la muerte no mata a nadie,
la matadora es la suerte.

—Apúntenme al corazón,
no manifiesten tristeza,
que a los hombres como yo
no se.les da en la cabeza.

—Aquí está mi corazón
para que lo hagan pedazos,
porque me sobra valor
pa' resistir los balazos.—

Ya con ésta me despido
al pie de un verde granado,
fusilaron en Chihuahua
a un general afamado.

Felipe Angeles

Gentlemen, give me your attention, I will tell you what has happened;
a very famous general has been executed in Chihuahua.

This general was a very brave man;
and since he was a good soldier, he knew how to lead his men.

He began his military career as an artilleryman,
and after a short time it was his fortune to become a general.

Since he was a valiant man, a man of real courage,
he avenged the horrible treason that was done to Madero.

During the world war, he went abroad;
he went to help the Gringos as an inspector general.

Then he returned to his country, to see how things could be arranged
so he could abandon his profession and retire to private life.

But it was no longer possible for him to settle things as he wished,
because his pursuers gave him no time to do so.

In the mountains of La Mula he had the misfortune
of being taken prisoner, and he was sentenced to death.

From there he was taken to the military prison,
to await the order of the day requiring his execution.

Then Angeles said, "My plans are all for naught;
I had hoped at any moment to return to the United States."

Angeles sent a message to the Congress of the Union:
"If I must be executed, I am at your disposition."

The government took into account the mischief he had caused;
the sentence was given that he should be executed.

"The clock ticks off the hours, my execution draws near;
prepare well your weapons, and aim at my heart.

"I am not one of those cowards who are afraid of death.
Death does not kill anyone; it is our fortune that kills us.

"Aim at my heart and do not show any sadness;
Remember that men like me should not be shot in the head.

"Here is my heart so you may shoot it to pieces,
for I have more than enough courage to bear the force of your bullets."

Now with this I say farewell at the foot of a green pomegranate;
a famous general has been executed in Chihuahua.

34
Mariano Reséndez

Entre las diez y las doce,
miren lo que se anda hablando,
éste es Mariano Reséndez
pasando su contrabando.

Este es Mariano Reséndez,
el hombre contrabandista,
sesenta empleados mató
y allí los traiba en su lista.

Año de mil novecientos
dejó recuerdos muy grandes,
a don Mariano Reséndez
lo aprehendió Nieves Hernández.

Salía Nieves Hernández
divisando por el llano,
y le pregunta a un ranchero:
—¿No me has visto a don Mariano?—

—Pues sí señor, sí lo vi,
se fue rumbo a La Sierrita,
diciendo que si lo alcanza
quinientas balas le quita. —

Decía Mariano Reséndez,
gritaba de vez en cuando:
— ¡Arrímense, compañeros,
nos quitan el contrabando! —

Decía Mariano Reséndez:
—Muchachos, éntrenle al toro,
vengan a llevar indianas
que son de la Bola de Oro.

—Vengan a llevar indianas
al mismo precio de allá,
que son muy pocos los gastos
y grande la utilidad.

—Eso de pasar indianas
no se me quitan las ganas,
traigo la vida en un hilo
por las malditas indianas. —

Decía Mariano Reséndez
con esa boca de infierno:
—Entrenle, guardas cobardes,
engreídos con el gobierno.

—Traigo una pana muy fina
y un casimir de primera,
y una buena carabina,
éntrenle ora que hay manera. —

Empleados de San Fernando,
no son mas que alburuzeros,
dejan pasar contrabandos
por agarrar maleteros.

Empleados del Encinal
y también de La Sierrita,
que nomás llega Reséndez
y hasta el hambre se les quita.

Empleados de Matamoros,
esos de banda primera,
aquí les traigo licores
dentro de mi cartuchera.

La pólvora es la cerveza,
las balas vino mezcal,
los casquillos son las copas
en que se lo han de tomar.

Avísenle a ese gobierno
que cumpla con sus deberes,
que cuando ponga acordada
no la ponga de mujeres.

Y lástima del destino
que ellos traen entre sus manos,
hasta lástima es que digan
que son puros mexicanos.

De Santa Cruz para abajo,
de Santa Rita pa' arriba,
pelearon fuertes combates
don Mariano y su partida.

De Santa Cruz para abajo
murieron los dos Meléndez,
por defender las indianas
de don Mariano Reséndez.

Decía Mariano Reséndez
con aquella voz divina:
—No me queda más amparo
que Dios y mi carabina. —

Decía Mariano Reséndez
como queriendo llorar:
— ¡Ay, alma mía de mi hermano,
quién lo pudiera salvar! —

Decía Mariano Reséndez
debajo de unos nogales:
—A mí me hacen los mandados,
los puños y los ojales. —

Decía Mariano Reséndez:
—Entrenle, no sean cobardes,
no le teman a las balas
ni se acuerden de sus madres.

—Este es Mariano Reséndez,
que lo querían conocer,
les ha de dar calentura
para poderlo aprehender. —

En su rancho, que era El Charco,
día martes desgraciado,
no pudo el hombre salvarse
porque amaneció sitiado.

Fueron a romper las puertas
cuando llegó el otro hermano,
con ansia le preguntaban:
—¿Dónde se halla don Mariano? —

Don José María Reséndez,
su contestación fue buena:
—Señores, yo no sé nada,
yo vengo de Santa Elena. —

Luego que ya lo aprehendieron
dispuso la autoridad:
—No vayan muy descuidados
que de un tosido se va. —

El carro 'ond' iba Mariano
iba rodeado de lanzas,
decía Mariano Reséndez:
—No pierdo las esperanzas. —

A la Heroica Matamoros,
para allá lo condujeron,
no le valieron influencias
ni dinero que ofrecieron.

En La Bota y San Román
en puro oro lo pesaban,
galantías a la tropa
por ver si lo rescataban.

Pues lo pesaban en oro
y lo evaluaban en plata,
¡quién les ha dicho, señores,
que un hombre bueno se mata!

Las fuerzas de Tamaulipas
a Nuevo León lo entregaron,
luego que lo recibieron
en el acto lo mataron.

Porque le tenían miedo,
que recibiera algún cargo,
lo mataron entre medio
de Agualeguas y Cerralvo.

Empleaditos de Guerrero,
a todos los traigo en lista,
ya no morirán de miedo,
se acabó El Contrabandista.

Empleados de El Encinal,
de San Fernando y de Méndez,
duerman a pierna tendida,
ya mataron a Reséndez.

Quédense con Dios, empleados,
acompañen a Morfeo,
y para que no se asusten
acostumbren el poleo.

Ya con ésta me despido,
cortando una flor de mayo,
aquí se acaban cantando
los versos de don Mariano.

Mariano Reséndez

Between ten and twelve o'clock, look what people are saying;
this is Mariano Reséndez smuggling his contraband goods.

This is Mariano Reséndez, the smuggling man;
he killed sixty officers and carried their names on a list.

The year nineteen hundred left us very vivid memories;
Don Mariano Reséndez was captured by Nieves Hernández.

Nieves Hernández went forth, looking out across the plain,
and he asked of a ranchero, "Have you seen Don Mariano?"

"Well, yes sir, I have seen him; he went toward La Sierrita,
saying that if you catch up with him, you can take his five hundred bullets."

Then said Mariano Reséndez, he would shout now and then,
"Gather round, my companions, or they will take our contraband!"

Then said Mariano Reséndez, "Boys, take the bull by the horns.
Come and get your calicos; they come from the Bola de Oro.

"Come and get your calicos at the same price as on the other side,
for my overhead is low and the profits are great.

"I can never get enough of this business of smuggling calico;
my life hangs on a thread because of these damned calicos."

Then said Mariano Reséndez, in a malevolent voice,
"Come on, you cowardly Border guards, who live off the government's bounty.

"I'm carrying some very fine corduroy, and some first-class cashmere,
and also a good rifle; come try your luck now there's a chance."

The officers at San Fernando are nothing but noisy braggarts;
they let the big contrabands pass, while they catch the small-timers.

You officers of El Encinal, and those of La Sierrita too,
as soon as Reséndez appears, you even lose your appetite.

You officers of Matamoros, who are said to be first-class men,
I am bringing you some liquor inside my ammunition pouch.

The gunpowder is beer, and the bullets are mezcal,
the cartridges are the glasses in which you will drink it up.

Send word to the government that it should meet its obligations,
that when it sets up an *acordada*, it should not staff it with women.

What a pity that such responsibility should be put into their hands,
and it is really a pity that they should call themselves real Mexicans.

Downriver from Santa Cruz and upriver from Santa Rita,
hard battles were fought by Don Mariano and his band.

Downriver from Santa Cruz, the two Meléndezes died
while defending the calicos of Don Mariano Reséndez.

Then said Mariano Reséndez, in that divine voice of his,
"I have no protection left except for God and my rifle."

Then said Mariano Reséndez, as if he was going to cry,
"Oh, brother of my soul, how I wish I could save you!"

Then said Mariano Reséndez, underneath some pecan trees,
"You can run my errands for me, and make my cuffs and buttonholes."

Then said Mariano Reséndez, "Stand and fight, do not be cowards;
don't be afraid of the bullets, and do not think of your mothers.

"This is Mariano Reséndez, you wanted to know him;
you are likely to catch a fever before you can capture me."

In his ranch, which was El Charco, on an unfortunate Tuesday,
the man could not save himself because he woke up surrounded.

They went to break down the doors when his other brother arrived;
they anxiously asked him, "Where can Don Mariano be found?"

Don José María Reséndez's answer was an honest one,
"Gentlemen, I know nothing; I have just come from Santa Elena."

After they had captured him, the authorities decreed,
"Do not be very careless with him, or he'll be gone in a wink."

The cart in which Mariano rode was surrounded by picked men;
Mariano Reséndez said, "I have not lost hope."

To Matamoros, that is where they took him;
his connections were of no avail, and neither was the money that was offered.

At La Bota and San Román they offered his weight in pure gold;
there were courtesies done to the soldiers, to see if they could ransom him.

They offered his weight in gold or the same value in silver.
Who has told you, gentlemen, that a good man like that must be killed!

The soldiers of Tamaulipas handed him over to Nuevo León,
and as soon as they had received him, they killed him out of hand.

Because they were afraid of him, afraid he might be given some office,
they killed him on the road between Agualeguas and Cerralvo.

You policemen of Guerrero, I have you all on my list;
you no longer will die of fright, because The Smuggler is dead.

Police of El Encinal, of San Fernando and Méndez,
now you can sleep soundly, for they have killed Reséndez.

God be with you, you policemen, and may Morpheus accompany you;
and so you won't get fright sickness, make it a custom to drink pennyroyal tea.

Now with this I say farewell, plucking a flower of May;
this is the end of the singing of the stanzas about Don Mariano.

35
Los tequileros

"Los tequileros" is sung vigorously, with strongly accented basses.

El día dos de febrero, ¡que día tan se - ña - la - do!
ma - ta - ron tres te - qui - le - ros los rin - ches del o - tro la - do.

El día dos de febrero,
¡qué día tan señalado!
mataron tres tequileros
los rinches del otro lado.

Llegaron al Río Grande,
se pusieron a pensar:
—Será bueno ver a Leandro
porque somos dos nomás. —

Le echan el envite a Leandro,
Leandro les dice que no:
—Fíjense que estoy enfermo,
así no quisiera yo. —

Al fin de tanto invitarle
Leandro los acompañó,
en las lomas de Almiramba
fue el primero que murió.

La carga que ellos llevaban
era tequila anisado,
el rumbo que ellos llevaban
era San Diego afamado.

Salieron desde Guerrero
con rumbo para el oriente,
allí les tenían sitiado
dos carros con mucha gente.

Cuando cruzaron el río
se fueron por un cañón,
se pusieron a hacer lumbre
sin ninguna precaución.

El capitán de los rinches
platicaba con esmero:
—Es bueno agarrar ventaja
porque estos son de Guerrero. —

Les hicieron un descargue
a mediación del camino,
cayó Gerónimo muerto,
Silvano muy mal herido.

Tumban el caballo a Leandro
y a él lo hirieron de un brazo,
ya no les podía hacer fuego,
tenía varios balazos.

El capitán de los rinches
a Silvano se acercó,
y en unos cuantos segundos
Silvano García murió.

Los rinches serán muy hombres,
no se les puede negar,
nos cazan como venados
para podernos matar.

Si los rinches fueran hombres
y sus caras presentaran,
entonce' a los tequileros
otro gallo nos cantara.

Pues ellos los tres murieron,
los versos aquí se acaban,
se les concedió a los rinches
las muertes que ellos deseaban.

El que compuso estos versos
no se hallaba allí presente,
estos versos son compuestos
por lo que decía la gente.

Aquí va la despedida
en medio de tres floreros,
y aquí se acaba el corrido,
versos de los tequileros.

The Tequila Runners

On the second day of February, what a memorable day!
The *rinches* from the other side of the river killed three tequila runners.

They reached the Rio Grande and then they stopped and thought,
"We had better go see Leandro, because there are only two of us."

They asked Leandro to go with them, and Leandro said he could not:
"I am sorry, but I'm sick. I don't want to go this way."

They kept asking him to go, until Leandro went with them;
in the hills of Almiramba, he was the first one to die.

The contraband they were taking was tequila *anisado;*
the direction they were taking was toward famed San Diego.

They left from Guerrero in an easterly direction;
two cars with many men were waiting for them there.

When they crossed the river, they traveled along a canyon;
then they stopped and built a fire without any regard for danger.

The captain of the *rinches* was saying, speaking in measured tones,
"It is wise to stack the odds because these men are from Guerrero."

They fired a volley at them in the middle of the road;
Gerónimo fell dead, and Silvano fell badly wounded.

They shot Leandro off his horse, wounding him in the arm.
He could no longer fire back at them; he had several bullet wounds.

The captain of the *rinches* came up close to Silvano;
and in a few seconds, Silvano García was dead.

The *rinches* are very brave, there is no doubt of that;
the only way they can kill us is by hunting us like deer.

If the *rinches* were really brave and met us face to face,
then things would be quite different for us tequila runners.

So all three of them died, and these stanzas are at an end;
the *rinches* were able to accomplish the killings they wanted.

He who composed these stanzas was not present when it happened;
these verses have been composed from what people were saying.

Now here is my farewell, in the midst of three flower vases;
this is the end of the ballad, the stanzas of the tequila runners.

36

Dionisio Maldonado

The tune for this *corrido* has been borrowed from an earlier *corrido* known through-out the Greater Mexican area—"Cananea." Each pair of lines is repeated to fit an eight-phrase tune.

Año de mil novecientos,
fecha buena, el día primero,
mataron tres mexicanos
esos rinches de Laredo.

Cuando llegaron a Bruni
las puertas tenían candado,
el que fue a pedir la llave
fue Dionisio Maldonado.

Cuando ya abrieron las puertas
Aguilar ya estaba herido:
—Fuerzas son las que me faltan,
valor siempre lo he tenido. —

Oliveira como era hombre
le dio rienda a su caballo:
—Entrenle, rinches cobardes,
a pelear con este gallo. —

Un rinche que estaba allí,
corazón de una gallina,
salió corriendo pa' fuera
cuando vio una carabina.

Si les preguntan sus nombres
no lo vayan a negar,
fue Dionisio Maldonado,
Oliveira y Aguilar.

Dionisio Maldonado

In the year of nineteen hundred, on a good date, the first of the year,
those *rinches* of Laredo killed three Mexicans.

When they got to Bruni, they found the doors padlocked;
the one who went to ask for the key was Dionisio Maldonado.

By the time they opened the doors, Aguilar was already wounded;
"What I lack is strength to keep fighting, for I have always had the courage."

Oliveira was a brave man, so he gave rein to his horse:
"Come on, you cowardly *rinches,* tangle with this fighting cock."

A *rinche* who was there had the heart of a chicken;
he went running out of there as soon as he saw a rifle.

If they ask you for their names, do not deny who they were;
they were Dionisio Maldonado, Oliveira, and Aguilar.

37
El contrabando de El Paso

The *despedida* or closing stanza refers to this *corrido* as "Las mañanitas del contrabando de El Paso." It is a kind of lament and has the same kind of melancholy tune
as the *corridos* about Angeles and Argumedo.

El día siete de agosto
'stábamos desesperados,
que nos sacaron de El Paso
para Kiansis mancornados.

Nos sacaron de la corte
a las ocho de la noche,
nos llevaron para el dipo,
nos montaron en un coche.

Yo dirijo la mirada
por todita la estación,
a mi madre idolatrada
pedirle su bendición.

Ni mi madre me esperaba,
ni siquiera mi mujer,
adiós todos mis amigos,
¡cuándo los volveré a ver!

Ya se oye silbar el tren,
ya no tardará en llegar,
les digo a mis compañeros
que no vayan a llorar.

Ya comienza a andar el tren,
me encomiendo a un santo fuerte,
ya no vuelvo al contrabando
porque tengo mala suerte.

Ya comienza a andar el tren
y repica su campana,
le pregunto a Míster Hill
que si vamos a Luisiana.

Míster Hill con su risita
me contesta: —No señor,
pasaremos por Luisiana
derechito a Lerinbor. —

Corre, corre maquinita,
suéltale todo el vapor,
anda deja a estos pollitos
derechito a Lerinbor.

Les encargo a mis paisanos
que al brincar el charco seco
no se crean de los amigos,
que son cabezas de puerco.

Yo lo digo con razón
por algunos compañeros
que en la calle son amigos
porque son convenencieros.

Yo cumplí con mi palabra,
amigo de realidad;
cuando uno se halla en la cárcel
se olvidan de la amistad.

Pero de esto no hay cuidado,
ya lo que pasó voló,
algún día se han de encontrar
donde hoy me encuentro yo.

Es bonito el contrabando,
se gana mucho dinero,
pero amigos, nunca olviden
las penas de un prisionero.

El que no lo quiera creer,
que lo quiera exp'rimentar,
que le entren al contrabando,
verán donde van a dar.

Víspera de San Lorenzo,
como a las once del día,
le pisamos los umbrales
a la penitenciaría.

Unos venían por dos años,
otros por un año un día,
y otros por dieciocho meses
a la penitenciaría.

Ahi te dejo, mamacita,
un suspiro y un abrazo,
y éstas son las mañanitas
del contrabando de El Paso.

The El Paso Contraband

On the seventh day of August, we were feeling desperate;
for they took us out of El Paso, chained together, toward Kansas.

They took us out of jail at eight o'clock at night;
they took us to the station, and they put us on a coach.

I direct my gaze over all the station,
seeking my beloved mother, so I may ask for her blessing.

But my mother was not waiting for me, not even my wife was there;
farewell to all my friends, when will I see you again!

Now we can hear the train whistle, it won't be long before it arrives;
I tell my companions to be sure not to weep.

Now the train begins to move, and I commend myself to a powerful saint;
I will not smuggle again, because I have bad luck.

Now the train begins to move, and its bell is ringing;
I ask Mr. Hill if we are going to Louisiana.

Mr. Hill, with his little smile, replies, "No, sir;
we will go through Louisiana, and straight to Leavenworth."

Run, run, little locomotive, with a full head of steam;
go take these young lads straight to Leavenworth.

I advise my countrymen, when you come across the Border,
do not trust your friends, for they are self-serving hypocrites.

I say this with good reason because of some of my acquaintances,
who are your friends in public because it suits their interests.

I lived up to my word, I was truly a friend;
but when you land in jail, they forget all about friendship.

But let us forget what happened, for what is done is done;
may they some day find themselves in the same fix I am in now.

Smuggling is very nice, you can make a lot of money;
but friends, do not forget what a prisoner must suffer.

He who will not believe it, let him try it for himself;
let them have a go at smuggling, and they'll see where they will end.

On the eve of St. Lawrence's day, about eleven in the morning,
we stepped on the threshold of the penitentiary.

Some were coming for two years, others for a year and a day,
and others for eighteen months, to the penitentiary.

Mother of mine, I leave you a sigh and an embrace;
this is the ballad of the contraband of El Paso.

38
Manuel Garza de León

El die-ci-nue-ve de mar-zo, ¡qué fe-cha tan me-mo-ra-ble!

Me le-ye-ron la sen-ten-cia co-mo a las tres de la tar-de.

El diecinueve de marzo,
¡qué fecha tan memorable!
Me leyeron la sentencia
como a las tres de la tarde.

Y cuando yo tomé el vino,
yo lo tomé por mi mano.
—Treinta años vas a sufrir.—
me dijo un americano.

Cuando el tren ya se acercó,
que anunciaba su salida,
me voy a la penitencia
por los días de mi vida.

En la celda donde estaba
yo solo me divertía,
contando los eslabones
que mi cadena tenía.

¡Ay! nos sacan al trabajo
a esos caminos de fierro,
ya faltarían diez minutos
y nos echaban los perros.

Los rinches que nos cuidaban
eran de mal corazón,
no nos dejaban dormir,
validos de la ocasión.

Pobrecitos de mis padres,
eran mi único querer,
por las malas compañías
tarde vine a comprender.

Pobrecitos de mis padres,
ya no se acuerdan de mí,
con dieciocho años de cárcel
creerán que fallecí.

Ya con ésta me despido
sin ofender la nación,
estos son los sufrimientos
de Manuel Garza de León.

Manuel Garza de León

The nineteenth of March, what a memorable date!
They read the sentence to me about three in the afternoon.

Now when I drank the liquor, no one held the glass to my lips.
"You must suffer for thirty years," an American told me.

So then the train approached, and it announced its departure;
I am going to the penitentiary to live out the rest of my days.

In the cell where I was, I amused myself
counting the links that were on my chain.

Ah! They take us out to work on those railroads;
when it was ten minutes till, they would set the dogs on us.

The *rinches* who were guarding us were men of evil hearts;
they took advantage of the situation and would not even let us sleep.

Oh, my poor parents, they were my only love;
because of my bad companions, I came to realize it too late.

Oh, my poor parents, they must have forgotten me;
they must think that I am dead, after eighteen years in jail.

Now with this I say farewell, meaning no offense to the nation;
these are the sufferings of Manuel Garza de León.

39
La canción de Carlos Guillén

(El prisionero de San Juan de Ulúa)

Preso me encuentro tras de la reja,
tras de la reja de mi prisión,
cantar quisiera, cantar no puedo
las tristes quejas del corazón.

De los candados escucho el ruido,
de los cerrojos el resonar,
y luego a poco quedo dormido
pensando siempre en mi libertad.

Preso me encuentro por una ingrata
que se burló de mi buena fe,
pero las horas dijeron: — ¡Mata! —
y yo al momento le disparé.

A veces sueño a mi bella amada,
que yo a su lado me encuentro ya,
pero este sueño se vuelve nada
y vuelvo triste a recordar.

Hace tres días salí al jurado
y en un banquillo se me sentó,
el juez de letras deliberando
como culpable me sentenció.

Así se pasan las horas mías,
siempre en contino sufrir, sufrir,
tristes las noches, tristes los días,
negro es, muy negro, mi porvenir.

Y no es la barca ni la falúa
la que me espera en el alta mar,
es el terrible San Juan de Ulúa
donde mi vida va a terminar.

Cuando haya muerto entre los mares
lleven mis restos a sepultar,
una plegaria pa'l sentenciado
que fue asesino de tanto amar.

Carlos Guillén's Song

A prisoner am I, behind the bars,
behind the bars of my prison;
I would like to sing, but I cannot sing
the sad complaints from my heart.
I hear the noise of the padlocks,
and the clatter of the bolts,
and after a while I fall asleep,
thinking always about freedom.

A prisoner am I, because of a faithless woman
who made a mockery of my good faith;
but then the hours said, "Kill!"
and I immediately fired on her.
At times I dream of my beautiful sweetheart,
that I am finally by her side;
but that dream turns into nothing,
and I sadly wake up again.

Three days ago I went before the jury,
and I was put in the prisoner's dock;
the district judge deliberated
and sentenced me as a guilty man.
And thus I pass these hours of mine,
always in suffering, continual suffering;
sad are my nights, sad are my days,
black, very black, is my future.

And it is neither the barque nor the felucca
that is awaiting me out in the sea;
it is the terrible San Juan de Ulúa,
where my life will come to an end.
When I have died out in the sea,
take my remains to be buried;
and say a prayer for this condemned man
who was a murderer because he loved too much.

40
Las once acaban de dar

Las on - ce a-ca - ban de dar en la pa - rro - quia de en-fren-te,

el cua-dro ya va a for - ma-ar, ya se o-yen pa - sos de gen -te.

—Las once acaban de dar
en la parroquia de enfrente,
el cuadro ya va a formar,
ya se oyen pasos de gente. —

—Ya no llores, Pantaleón,
y ya no esperes clemencia,
ya nos van a fusilar,
ven a escuchar tu sentencia. —

—Yo no esperaba tal suerte
cuando a este crimen llegamos,
pagaremos en la misma
la sangre que derramamos. —

Y así pasó la tragedia,
en fin lo supimos todos,
los fueron a fusilar
'n la cárcel de Matamoros.

The Clock Has Just Struck Eleven

"The clock has just struck eleven in the church across the street;
the firing squad will soon be ready, people are moving about."

"Cease your weeping, Pantaleón, and don't hope any longer for clemency.
They are going to execute us now; come listen to your sentence."

"I never expected such a fate when we embarked on this crime;
we will pay in the same fashion for the blood that we spilled."

And so happened this sad event; in the end we all learned about it.
They were shot by a firing squad in the jail at Matamoros.

PART III

Songs for Special Occasions

Life on the Lower Rio Grande Border was not all conflict, nor was all the singing about the clash of cultures. The comedy and the tragedy of daily life were also themes for songs, some locally composed and some traveling to the Border from other places. There were also songs for rituals and other special occasions, for life was to an extent ritualized, not only in religion but in other affairs. The old Border people have sometimes been called "godless." They had few churches, and they often were impatient of clerical hierarchies and the fine points of dogma; but they were deeply religious. Proof of their devotion were the folk rituals and dramas, the home altars with their folk art, and the singing related to their beliefs—all this taking place during generations when the only representative of the official religion might be the circuit-riding priest, who came by on infrequent visits.

Christmas was the most important season, with the *pastorelas* or shepherds' plays occupying an important place. When the first church was founded in Brownsville, foreign-born priests attempted to suppress the *pastorelas* because they considered them pagan. The plays survived official condemnation, and it is now the churches in the area that try to keep the *pastorelas* alive and have even copyrighted some versions of them. *Pastorelas* were presented in the towns and larger villages, where there were enough resources (human and material) for presenting plays and a large enough population to maintain sizable audiences.

In the smaller villages and *rancherías,* the *posadas* satisfied the desire for dramatic performance in a simpler fashion. The nine nightly performances of the *posadas* could easily be carried out in a village of a dozen houses. Each night, the images of Mary and Joseph were carried in procession from house to house, asking for lodging (*pidiendo posada*). "Lodging" was denied them at each house but the last, the one chosen for that night's festivities. A dialogue was carried on at each house, in song, between those carrying the images and those within the house. The songs used in this dialogue are also called "POSADAS." The one included in this collection is somewhat different in words and melody from the usual, more or less standardized version often seen in print. It is a version that used to be sung in Bagdad, Tamaulipas, on the mouth of the Rio Grande, in the 1880s and 1890s. I learned it from my mother.

The *posadas* were performed during the nine days before December 25. During the period from Christmas until January 6, *aguinaldos* or carols were sung. The boys in the village would go from house to house, singing carols. They would be invited inside and given gifts (*aguinaldos*) and good things to eat and drink. Each house had its *nacimiento* (Nativity scene) adorned with Spanish moss and branches from the Mexican ebony. Melted resin was blown on the moss through a reed, to simulate the snow that few Borderers had ever seen. The "AGUINALDOS" in this collection I also learned from my mother.

Cradle songs have a wider range than do ballads on historical subjects, because the *canción de cuna* pertains to a universal situation, rocking a child to sleep. No *canción de cuna* is better known throughout the Spanish-speaking world than "SEÑORA SANTA ANA." For generations upon generations, children in the Southwest and elsewhere have been rocked to sleep with this song. It changes little in tune and text from country to country. The strong religious background of the song is typical of Spanish-speaking people, as is the candidly secular view of the Holy Family in the last stanza—Mary washing Christ's dirty diapers while Joseph hangs them out to dry.

The *curandero* or healer has occupied an important place in Mexican folk belief. The most famed of the *curanderos* in the Southwest was Don Pedrito Jaramillo. Only El Niño Fidencio, the most renowned of the *curanderos* in the recent history of the Republic of Mexico, surpasses Don Pedrito in widespread acceptance by the Mexican people. Don Pedrito was born in Guadalajara and came to Los Olmos, a ranch close to Falfurrias, Texas, in 1881. He was credited with miraculous cures. People came all the way from interior Mexico to consult him, and he cured a number of Anglos as well. Many considered him a saint and tried unsuccessfully to have him canonized after his death on July 3, 1907. Unofficially, he is still regarded as a saint. People make peregrinations to his grave. Pictures and statuettes of him are to be found on family altars in many homes of south Texas.

These, of course, are customs that follow well-known Mexican cultural patterns. Especially interesting from the viewpoint of intercultural influences is the appearance of Don Pedrito as the central figure in a Mexican-American spiritualist cult. Spiritualism is not native to Mexican folk belief and practice. It is an Anglo middle-class belief, popularized by educated ladies and gentlemen in Victorian times. During the 1950s I talked to members of a Texas-Mexican spiritualist society that claimed several chapters throughout south Texas. They met in regular séances, during which they called on the spirit of Don Pedrito. Curing disease through the agency of Don Pedrito's spirit was the principal reason for calling him.

"DON PEDRITO JARAMILLO," according to my informants, was always sung during the meetings as a song of farewell to Don Pedrito's spirit when the séance ended. It should be noted that in Mexico it is the custom to sing songs of farewell to a saint after a group of pilgrims have ended their visit to his shrine. "Don Pedrito Jaramillo," by the way, has Don Pedrito's death as occurring on July 4, though other sources say he died on July 3. The fact that July 4 is an important holiday may have influenced the change. Informants called this song a *corrido,* and it does have many of the features of the genre. It uses what is basically an octosyllabic quatrain sung to a four-phrase tune, though the fourth line is repeated. There is a typical *corrido* opening: "El día cuatro de julio, presente lo tengo yo." The "Pues ya te vas, hermanito" of the last stanza acts as a *despedida.* But the function of the song is not that of the *corrido.* It is a ritual song, resembling the *alabado* (a song praising God or a saint) or the *despedida* (in the sense of a song saying farewell to a saint after visiting his shrine).

"LA REALIDAD" (also known as "El mundo engañoso") and "EL HUERFANO" belong to the type of song sometimes called *canción de ciego*, on the assumption that most *corrido* singers are "blind beggars." On the Border, at least, this has not been so. The typical *guitarrero* is not a professional but simply a gifted member of the group who may be a farmer, vaquero, carpenter, barber, or clerk when he is not playing. There have always been some *guitarreros,* it is true, who make a good part of their living from singing. The blind and the halt are found among them, since men with physical handicaps find it difficult to make a living at other occupations in the average folk community. Like the professional jongleur, this type of singer depends on his listeners for his livelihood, though the listeners may be his own people and not merely unsympathetic strangers. Sometimes he will stir their sympathies by relating his fall into misfortune. He reminds his listeners that in this deceitful world the wheel of fortune turns and turns, and he who is today on top may find himself at the bottom of the heap tomorrow. For this purpose he has special songs, which he calls upon when the fiesta quietens momentarily or when men get philosophical in their cups. Jesús Flores, for example, a blind *guitarrero* of the Brownsville-Matamoros area, used to sing a song called "La biografía de mi vida," his own composition, in which he told about his own misfortunes.

It is more common for the singer to use traditional songs dealing with the "wheel of fortune" theme. "La realidad" is such a song. The speaker in the ballad tells the story of his life, and in doing so he tells the story of all his listeners as well. He has seen the wheel go up, and he has seen it come down. Life is like that, for the world is evil and friends often prove false. His listeners nod when he has finished, thinking of tomorrow and their own ups and downs in life. And their gift to the singer may be a little larger, perhaps, than it might have been. "La realidad" appeals to the traditional Mexican's feeling for his family and to his ideas about *respeto.* If the singer had only listened to his parents, he would not be in the unfortunate situation he is in now. In "El huérfano," on the other hand, it is the loss of his parents that causes the singer's misfortune. Without family and without friends, a man is worth nothing in this world. Songs like these may be expected of lame and blind singers, but they do not belong to them exclusively. "Wheel of fortune" songs are found in many contexts and are sung by all kinds of singers.

It would be a mistake to paint a full-sized portrait of the Mexican-American's behavior on the basis of songs like "La realidad" and "El huérfano" or the other folklore genres related to them. They are enjoyed because theirs is a standard folk philosophy, similar to the folk wisdom found in proverbs. In fact, proverbs are often worked into this type of song. The last line of "La realidad" is a well-known proverb. "A cada santo se le llega su función" (Every saint has his feast day) may be translated as "Every dog has his day" or "Your chickens will come home to roost," depending on the situation. "Wheel of fortune" songs do not give us the Border Mexican's total world view by any means, but they do portray a significant aspect of it. This is the way the world looks when one is thoughtful or dejected—a long, long avenue of sighs and sorrows.

"La realidad" seems to be native to the Border area. The farthest south it has been reported is Soto la Marina, Tamaulipas, some 150 miles from the Rio Grande. It is a "long" *corrido,* one using a line with more than eight syllables. In this case, the typical line is the twelve-syllable *verso de arte major,* though many lines contain thirteen syllables. The melody is a *corrido* tune of the lively 2/4 variety, eight musical phrases long and fitting two *corrido* quatrains, so that we have what amounts to an eight-line stanza. "El huérfano" is known throughout the Greater Mexican area. It has been reported in central Mexico and in Austin, Texas. The form of "El huérfano" combines two Mexican folksong genres. The text is in the *décima* form, in ten-line octosyllabic stanzas with a characteristic rhyme scheme. The tune, however, is a *corrido* tune in 2/4 time, like that of "La realidad," with ten musical phrases to fit the ten-line *décima* stanza.

People sing songs or listen to them sung because they are entertaining. The main source of entertainment may be found in the song's content, but pleasure may also be derived from the perception of form in a song performance. Some songs, and some stories as well, depend for their main effect on their form. "LA CHIVA" is such a song, depending on the accumulation of a series of details in a progressive chain that conceivably could be stretched out to any length. The progressive chain based on the enumeration of objects is also found in English songs like "The Twelve Days of Christmas." "La chiva" is also reminiscent of "The Song of the Kid," associated with Jewish Passover ritual. Many folktales, especially those told to children, are based on the chain pattern—"The Old Woman and the Pig," for example. But "La chiva," like "The Twelve Days of Christmas" and "The Song of the Kid," is not intended as a children's song or rhyme. It is sung and enjoyed by adults.

"La chiva" was a favorite in the repertory of Juan Guajardo, a legless *guitarrero* from the Border, who belonged in the semiprofessional class of singers referred to when we discussed "La realidad" and "El huérfano." It is worth remembering that the same type of singer who specialized in sad, philosophical songs also liked to sing the comic ones; and the same audiences enjoyed both kinds of songs. The enjoyment of "La chiva" is in the nonsense elements and the strong sense of form. Also important is the ability of the singer to build up the chain without faltering or forgetting, or confusing the sequence of animals and humans involved. If the singer is successful, his virtuosity also gives the listener pleasure.

There is a German cumulative tale that resembles "La chiva" in content. A farmer pays his servant with a hen, then with a cock, then with a goose, then with a goat, and so on until the servant gets a girl and a farm. In our song, however, not one but three women are introduced, representing the three ethnic groups the Border Mexican is most familiar with. Thus, even in a little nonsense song, awareness of cultural differences and cultural conflict is introduced.

"EL CHARAMUSQUERO" is an occupational song of a special sort—the musical cry of the vendor of *charamuscas*, little bars of chewy Mexican candy much like hard caramel. Before the advent of supermarkets in Brownsville and other Border cities, the butcher, the baker, the vegetable man, and the candy vendor all made their rounds and cried out their wares. I learned this song from my mother, who heard it sung by *charamusqueros* in Brownsville some fifty years ago. "El charamusquero" is made up of two *coplas* and a refrain. The second *copla* is found in a number of different songs. The *charamusquero* uses it in his song as a *piropo* or compliment to his women customers. The first stanza identifies the song as belonging to the *charamusquero,* who says he came to Brownsville straight from Mexico, passing through Matamoros along a street on which a well-known store, El Ranchero, was located.

The line "Desde México he venido" is conventional, a formula appearing in many kinds of stanzas. As used on the Border, the "México" in this formula refers to that part of the Republic of Mexico away from the Border areas—what Border people for generations have known as *el interior,* interior or deep-down Mexico. In songs found in central Mexico, "México" most likely will mean Mexico City. The formula is also found in songs criticizing Border mores, with the singer assuming the role of someone just arrived 'from *el interior.* Song no. 61 in this collection belongs in that category.

41
Las posadas

The second stanza is supposed to be two lines only. It is sung to the first two musical phrases of the tune, with a pause at the end.

Muy buenas noches,
aldeanos dichosos,
posada les piden
estos dos esposos.

Serán bandoleros
o querrán robar . . .

Robarte pretendo
pero el corazón,
por eso en tu choza
pedí un rincón.

Vayan más delante,
está una pastoría,
que allí dan posada
de noche y de día.

Vengan, vengan, vengan,
Jesús y María
y su amado esposo
en su compañía.

Abranse esas puertas,
rómpanse esos velos,
que viene a posar
el Rey de los Cielos.

Las Posadas

A very good evening, fortunate villagers,
this husband and wife ask you for lodging.

You may be highwaymen, wishing to rob us . . .

I do want to steal, but only your hearts,
that is why I have asked for a corner in your hut.

Go farther down the road, there's a place where shepherds stay;
there they give lodging by night and by day.

Come, come, come, Jesus and Mary,
and her beloved husband in their company.

Let those doors be opened, let those veils be rent;
the King of Heaven comes to take lodging here.

42
Los aguinaldos

De los aguinaldos
si nos han de dar,
que la noche es corta
y tenemos que andar.

Desde Puente Piedra
venimos andando,

al Niño Chiquito
venimos buscando.

¿Quién cortó el cogollo
de la verde caña?
El Niño Chiquito,
Príncipe de España.

¿Quién cortó el cogollo
del verde limón?
El Niño Chiquito,
rosita en botón.

De los aguinaldos
si nos han de dar,
que la noche es corta
y tenemos que andar.

Los Aguinaldos

Will you give us some New Year's gifts,
for the night is short and we have far to go.

All the way from Puente Piedra we have come walking;
we have come looking for the Little Christ Child.

Who cut off the top of the green sugarcane?
The Little Christ Child, the Prince of Spain.

Who cut the tender shoots off the green lemon tree?
The Little Christ Child, a rose in the bud.

Will you give us some New Year's gifts,
for the night is short and we have far to go.

43
Señora Santa Ana

I have shown guitar chords with the melody for this song, but it is rarely—if ever—
sung to any accompaniment other than the creaking of cradle or rocking chair.

Se - ño - ra San - ta̱ A - na, ¿por qué llo - ra̱ el ni - i - ño?

Por u - na man - za - na que se le̱ ha per - di - i - do.

Señora Santa Ana,
¿por qué llora el niño?
Por una manzana
que se le ha perdido.

Iremos al huerto,
cortaremos dos,
una para el niño
y otra para Dios.

Manzanita de oro,
si yo te encontrara
se la diera al niño
para que callara.

Santa Margarita,
carita de luna,
méceme este niño
que tengo en la cuna.

Duérmase mi niño,	María lavaba,
duérmase mi sol,	San José tendía,
duérmase, pedazo	eran los pañales
de mi corazón.	que el niño tenía.

Lady Saint Anne

Lady Saint Anne, why is my baby crying?
Because of an apple that he has lost.

We will go to the orchard, and will pick two,
one for my baby and the other for God.

Little golden apple, if I could only find you,
I would give it to my baby, so he would hush.

Saint Margaret, little moon-face,
rock for me this baby that I have in the cradle.

Go to sleep my baby, go to sleep my sunshine,
go to sleep, little piece of my heart.

The Virgin Mary was washing, Saint Joseph was hanging out to dry;
these were the diapers that the baby had.

44
Don Pedrito Jaramillo

El día cuatro de julio,
presente lo tengo yo,
que Pedrito Jaramillo
ese día se retiró,
ese día se retiró.

Adiós, hermano Pedrito,
échanos tu bendición
a todos estos hermanos
que estamos en la reunión,
que estamos en la reunión.

Adiós, hermano Pedrito,
de la ciencia espiritual,
aquí nos quedamos tristes,
sabe Dios si volverás,
sabe Dios si volverás.

No se te olvide, Pedrito,
déjanos recomendado
a todos estos hermanos
que se encuentran a tu lado,
que se encuentran a tu lado.

Cuando viene amaneciendo
el corazón nos avisa
del hermanito que era,
el que ya se retiraba,
el que ya se retiraba.

No nos dejes, hermanito,
no nos dejes padecer,
ponnos en el corazón
lo que debemos de hacer,
lo que debemos de hacer.

A las tres de la mañana,
quedándome yo dormido,
oí una voz que decía:
—Adiós, hermanos queridos,
adiós, hermanos queridos. —

Pues ya te vas, hermanito,
a los aires extranjeros,
ya te vas a retirar
a los reinos de los cielos,
a los reinos de los cielos.

Don Pedrito Jaramillo

On the fourth day of July, I remember it well,
Pedrito Jaramillo on that day went away.

Farewell, brother Pedrito, give your blessing
to all these brothers and sisters who are at the meeting.

Farewell, brother Pedrito of the spiritual science;
saddened we remain; God knows if you will return.

Don't you forget, Pedrito, be sure to commend us
to all those brothers and sisters who are by your side.

When the day begins to dawn, our hearts remind us
of the dear brother we had and who has now gone.

Do not leave us, dear brother, do not leave us to suffer;
show us in our hearts the things that we have to do.

At three o'clock in the morning, I happened to fall asleep,
and I heard a voice that said, "Farewell, beloved brothers and sisters."

Now you leave us, dear brother, for other climes;
now you are going away to the Kingdom of Heaven.

45
La realidad

Vengan, jilgueros pajarillos, a estos prados,
entonaremos nuestros cantos de placer,
porque comprendo que el gusto se me ha acabado
y en este mundo sólo encuentro padecer.

    A la edad de catorce años me salí
a navegar con mi triste situación,
si supieran lo que sufro y he sufrido
por no llevar en el mundo dirección.

    Mundo tirano, ¿por qué eres tan engañoso?
¿Por qué te muestras a la vista tan formal?
El desengaño yo lo miro con mis ojos:
en este mundo todo es pura falsedad.

Mundo tirano, ya me tienes fastidiado,
por tus delicias yo me eché a la perdición,
por eso canto en alta voz desesperado:
— ¡Maldito seas y maldita tu ilusión! —

En otro tiempo me encontraba en otra esfera
y a cualesquiera le podía hacer un bien,
hoy los encuentro y me ven como a cualquiera
y no soy digno que los buenos días me den.
    Así es el hombre cuando está posesionado,
todos lo quieren con cariño sin igual,
cambia la suerte y llega a quedar arrancado,
y si lo encuentran ni los buenos días le dan.

Esto lo digo porque en mí mismo ha pasado
con un amigo que era de mi estimación,
llegó hasta el grado de querernos como hermanos
y hoy se burla de mi triste situación.
    Así es el árbol cuando de hojas 'sta copado,
todos se acercan a su sombra a descansar,
viene el invierno y llega a quedar deshojado,
nadie se acuerda que allí vino a veranear.

Viene la muerte y quedaremos igualitos,
en este mundo todo tiene su hasta aquí,
les aseguro que aunque tarde sobra tiempo,
se han de encontrar como yo me encuentro aquí.
    Ya me despido porque vengo de visita,
y les suplico que me otorguen el perdón,
les aseguro que en parroquia o capillita
a cada santo se le llega su función.

Reality

Come, little songbirds, to these meadows,
and together we will join in songs of pleasure;
for I know that I have lost all my contentment,
and I find nothing but trouble in this world.
I went forth when I was fourteen years of age
to wander in my wretched condition;
if you knew what I suffer and have suffered
for not having had guidance in the world.

Tyrannous world, why are you so deceptive?
Why do you appear to be so genuine at first sight?
I have been undeceived by my own experience;
in this world everything is but a falsehood.
Tyrannous world, I have had enough of you;
because of your delights I have been led to my ruin;
that is why I sing desperately and loudly,
"Curse you, and curse your deceit!"

Time was when I moved in other spheres,
and I was able to do good to anyone;
now I meet them, and they treat me with disdain,
and I do not even merit a "Good day" from them.
Thus it is with a man when he is wealthy,
everyone loves him with unequaled affection;
then fortune changes, and he ends up penniless,
and if they meet him, they will not even say "Good day."

I say this because it has happened to me
with a friend whom I held in high esteem
to the point where we loved each other like brothers,
and now he laughs at my wretched condition.
Thus it is with the tree when it is topped with leaves:
everyone comes to it, to rest under its shade;
and then comes winter, and it is bare of leaves:
no one remembers that he spent the summer there.

Death will come, and we will all be the same,
for in this world everything comes to an end;
I assure you that there still is time enough,
and that someday you will be where I am now.
Now I say farewell, for I am just passing through,
and I beg of you to vouchsafe me your pardon;
I assure you that in church or chapel
in due time every saint will have his festival.

46
El huérfano

Pen-san-do es-to me con-fun-do, es muy tris-te y muy no-ta-ble

vi-vir so-lo en es-te mun-do sin te-ner u-no a sus pa-dres,

co-mo u-na plu-ma en el ai-re an-da el hi-jo ya per-di-do,

el huér-fa-no des-va-li-do pier-de l'hon-ra y el de-co-ro:

es - cú - chen - me mis a - mi - gos es - tas lá - gri - mas que llo - ro.

Pensando esto me confundo,
es muy triste y muy notable
vivir solo en este mundo
sin tener uno a sus padres,
como una pluma en el aire
anda el hijo ya perdido,
el huérfano desvalido
pierde l' honra y el decoro:
escúchenme mis amigos
estas lágrimas que lloro.

Cantaba un preso una tarde
una muy triste canción:
—Que si mis padres vivieran
no estuviera en la prisión,
me echaran su bendición,
ya por mí hubieran hablado,
hoy me encuentro aquí encerrado,
sólo un Ser Eterno imploro,
para el preso desgraciado
después de Dios no hay tesoro. —

Unas veces de soldado,
otras veces en prisiones,
y mi padre atribulado,
mi madre con aflicciones,
me llenaba de oraciones
cuando en cuerda yo salía,
¡oh, qué desgracia es la mía!
Todo acaba en un momento,
de dolor y sentimiento,
¿quién de mí se dolerá?

Huérfanos que me han oído
mis carencias y lamentos,
pasaré estos sufrimientos
que mi Dios lo ha permitido,
mis grandes padecimientos
los dirijo en general
a los hijos que ven mal
a sus padres en la vida,
¿dónde estás, madre querida?
ya me canso de llorar.

Para el huérfano no hay sol,
no hay hambre, ni hay frío ni hay nieve,
soportando un cruel rigor
hace todo lo que puede,
ni quién le haga un favor,
todos se muestran tiranos,
tíos, parientes y hermanos
lo avergüenzan en la calle:
apretándose las manos,
¡oh, si viviera mi madre!

Los pasos que voy marcando
yo los llevo muy presentes,
madre mía, soy delincuente,
mira aquí a tu hijo llorando,
mis lágrimas derramando
en tu tumba regaré,
hoy para siempre diré:
—Esta vida es tan amable,
no hay parientes ni hay hermanos,
no hay cosa como la madre. —

The Orphan

Thinking about this I am bewildered; it is very sad and unusual
to live alone in this world without having one's parents;
the lost child wanders like a feather in the wind;
the destitute orphan loses respect and reputation;
give heed, my friends, to these tears I weep.

One afternoon a prisoner was singing a very mournful song:
"If my parents were alive, I would not be in prison;
they would give me their blessing, they would have spoken for me;
now that I am locked up in this place, I can only pray to the Almighty;
for a wretched prisoner, there is no greater treasure than God."

Sometimes I have been a conscript, other times I have been in prison;
and my father was distressed, my mother was afflicted;
she would cover me with prayers when they took me away in shackles.
Oh, what misfortune is mine! Everything lasts but a moment.
Who will have compassion on my pain and my grief?

You orphans who have heard my distress and my laments,
I pass through these sufferings, for my God has so decreed;
as for the story of my afflictions, I address it in general
to those children who treat their parents badly in this life.
Where are you, beloved mother? I can weep no more.

Without recourse, the orphan suffers from the sun, hunger, cold and snow;
he does what he can to endure such cruel harshness;
no one will do him a favor, everyone hardens his heart;
uncles, relatives, and brothers humiliate him in public,
while he wrings his hands, crying, "Oh, if my mother lived!"

The events that I have noted are quite vivid in my memory;
mother of mine, I have transgressed; look at your son weeping here;
I will water your grave with my flowing tears;
and I say now and always, "How delightful is this life;
relatives and brothers count for nothing; there is no one like your mother."

47

La chiva

The basic tune is made up of five musical phrases, corresponding to the five lines of
the first stanza. Beginning with the second stanza, an alternate phrase is inserted
between the third and fourth phrases and repeated to accommodate the introduction
of each new object in the chain.

ten-go el chi - vi - to y mi real y me - dio no se me a - ca - ba.

Con real y medio que yo tenía
compré una chiva,
la chiva tuvo un chivito,
tengo la chiva, tengo el chivito
y mi real y medio no se me acaba.

Con real y medio que yo tenía
compré una burra,
la burra tuvo un burrito,
tengo la burra, tengo el burrito,
tengo la chiva, tengo el chivito
y mi real y medio no se me acaba.

Con real y medio que yo tenía
compré una pava,
la pava tuvo un pavito,
tengo la pava, tengo el pavito,
tengo la burra, tengo el burrito,
tengo la chiva, tengo el chivito
y mi real y medio no se me acaba.

Con real y medio que yo tenía
compré una perra,
la perra tuvo un perrito,
tengo la perra, tengo el perrito,
tengo la pava, tengo el pavito,
tengo la burra, tengo el burrito,
tengo la chiva, tengo el chivito
y mi real y medio no se me acaba.

Con real y medio que yo tenía

compré una gringa,
la gringa tuvo un gringuito,
tengo la gringa, tengo el gringuito,
tengo la perra, tengo el perrito,
tengo la pava, tengo el pavito,
tengo la burra, tengo el burrito,
tengo la chiva, tengo el chivito
y mi real y medio no se me acaba.

Con real y medio que yo tenía
compré una negra,
la negra tuvo un negrito,
tengo la negra, tengo el negrito,
tengo la gringa, tengo el gringuito,
tengo la perra, tengo el perrito,
tengo la pava, tengo el pavito,
tengo la burra, tengo el burrito,
tengo la chiva, tengo el chivito
y mi real y medio no se me acaba.

Con real y medio que yo tenía
compré una china,
la china tuvo un chinito,
tengo la china, tengo el chinito,
tengo la negra, tengo el negrito,
tengo la gringa, tengo el gringuito,
tengo la perra, tengo el perrito,
tengo la pava, tengo el pavito,
tengo la burra, tengo el burrito,
tengo la chiva, tengo el chivito
y mi real y medio no se me acaba.

The Nanny Goat

With a *real* and a half that I had I bought a nanny goat;
the nanny goat had a kid;
I have the nanny goat, I have the kid,
and my *real* and a half still is not spent.

. . . .

With a *real* and a half that I had I bought a Chinese woman;
the Chinese woman had a little Chinese;
I have the Chinese woman, I have the little Chinese;
I have the Negro woman, I have the little Negro;
I have the Gringo woman, I have the little Gringo;
I have the bitch, I have the pup;

I have the turkey hen, I have the turkey chick;
I have the she-ass, I have the little burro;
I have the nanny goat, I have the kid,
and my *real* and a half still is not spent.

48
El charamusquero

Des - de Mé - xi - co he ve - ni - do   por   la   ca - lle de El Ran-che - ro,

y   les   di - go a las mu-cha -chas: A - quí va el cha - ra - mus-que - ro.

Cua-tro por me -dio, nue-ve por real, por-que el tiem-po es-tá fa - tal.

Desde México he venido
por la calle de El Ranchero,
y les digo a las muchachas:
—Aquí va el charamusquero. —

    Cuatro por medio,
    nueve por real,
    porque el tiempo
    está fatal.

Eres como pimientita,
chiquita pero picosa,
y hasta los andados tienes
de mujer escandalosa.

    Cuatro por medio,
    nueve por real,
    porque el tiempo
    está fatal.

The Charamusca Vendor

I have come all the way from Mexico, down by the street of El Ranchero,
and I say to the girls, "Here goes the *charamusca* vendor."

    Four for a *medio*, nine for a *real*,
    because business is very bad.

You are like a little peppercorn, small but biting to the tongue,
and even your way of walking is that of a boisterous woman.

    Four for a *medio*, etc.

PART
IV
Romantic
and Comic Songs

B order folksongs that speak of historical events are usually localized, dealing for the most part with Border history, or with happenings of a broader scope that in some way affected the Border. Non-narrative songs may range widely through the Spanish-speaking world, as we saw with "Señora Santa Ana." This is especially true of the lyric stanza or *copla,* dealing with universal themes like love, death, and laughter. Some *coplas* can be found in Spain, Mexico, and Central and South America in almost identical form—a strong reminder of the cultural unity of all Spanish-speaking peoples. In Part IV, however, I do not include any of the well-known songs belonging to all the Hispanic world, or even to all of Greater Mexico: "Cielito lindo" or "El venadito," for example. The songs in this part are closely identified with the Border in some way, though not all of them are exclusively Border songs.

I learned "TRIGUEÑA HERMOSA" from one of my uncles, who was a labor organizer and member of the IWW before World War I, back in those days when all Mexicans in the United States were asleep, according to some of our chroniclers. My uncle learned the song in his wanderings through the Southwest, where "Trigueña hermosa" has been known for several generations. In 1912 the Mexican composer Manuel M. Ponce—well known for "Estrellita"—discovered "Trigueña hermosa" in Chihuahua and published it in a Mexico City periodical.[1] The Texas-Mexican folklorist Jovita González published a version from the Border in 1929, remarking that it has been among us "one of the most popular of folksongs . . . long before its music was written down by the composer Ponce."[2]

Trigueño (*a*) means "brown," the golden-brown color of wheat. Mexican poets and intellectuals have referred to themselves as *la raza de bronce*, using "bronze" as a poetic equivalent of "brown." Some Chicano writers use the word *café,* a literal and awkward translation from the English. Our own folk speech offers us *trigueño,* which evokes the rich golden-brown color of the mestizo.

"Trigueña hermosa" is textually quite simple and direct, without the usual ornamentation of the Hispanic *copla.* And, since social scientists have made so much of what they call Mexican *machismo,* it is worth noting that in this song—a true folksong rather than a product from a middle-class movie—the male "voice" is neither overbearing nor abject in his address to the woman he loves. What is expressed is love for a woman, a love that will conquer all obstacles with hope, patience, and God's help rather than with belligerence and a forty-five automatic.

As a Lower Border song, "LA NEGRITA" is something of a puzzle. *Negra* and *negrita* are terms of endearment in Mexican folksong, without any reference to skin color or ethnic origins. In this song, however, the *negra* is a Negro woman who has fallen in love with a white man, in a society that frowns on interracial marriages. In Mexican folksong, the

[1] Suplemento de Navidad, *Revista de Revistas,* December 21, 1912.

[2] Jovita González, "Tales and Songs of the Texas-Mexicans," in *Man, Bird, and Beast,* ed. J. Frank Dobie (Austin, 1930), 115-116.

most common obstacles to love are differences in wealth and social status. Skin color may appear, but if it does it plays a minor role. At times a dark skin is idealized:"Yo a las morenas quiero, desde que supe que morena es la Virgen de Guadalupe." Or a person may be told that beauty is more than skin deep and one should not take skin color into account: "No te fijes en color, mira que la vista engaña." But in "La negrita" the focus is not on color of skin as such but on "race," with miscegenation as the basic theme. The "voice" seems to be a black man, who tells black women in general: "The moral of this song is, 'Never trust a white man.' They don't want colored people to mix with them."

I learned "La negrita" from Border people of the generation preceding mine, who had learned it in their youth; so its presence on the Border goes back to the 1870s or 1880s at the very least. The question is how the song came to be part of the Border repertory. Is it a local composition, reflecting Anglo mores as seen by Borderers? Is it a song that goes back to colonial times, when the black man in Mexico was a slave? Did the song wander north from some strongly Afroid Mexican area where it had immediate referents in local behavior?

I have not been able to find any parallels to "La negrita" in other parts of the Greater Mexican area. Still, it is likely that the song came to the Border from some other part of Greater Mexico sometime in the past. The fact that it is in *danza* form suggests that it may be a nineteenth-century recasting of an older song. On the Border, however, Anglo attitudes toward color must have reinforced the theme of "La negrita" in the average Borderer's mind, so that it persisted after the song may have been forgotten in other parts of Mexico.

"LA TISICA" and "A LAS TRES DE LA MAÑANA" are not *corridos,* but they are narrative folksongs; and in some ways they resemble British ballads such as "Edward" and "Lord Randal." Like these British ballads, they tell a story entirely through a dialogue between a mother and her son or daughter. As in "Lord Randal," ·the son or daughter is dying as the story unfolds. "La tísica" uses a plot that was exploited by nineteenth-century sentimental fiction: the bride-to-be who dies of tuberculosis and is buried in her wedding gown, a bride to death rather than to her human lover. But "La tísica" is realistic enough to escape sentimentality because of the dying girl's attitude toward her rival and her groom-that-would-have-been. She is jealous and unforgiving to the last.

"La tísica" portrays what was a grim reality for the people who sang the song in times past. Tuberculosis was especially deadly to women because of customs related to mourning the dead. When a near relative died, the women of the family had to wear completely black clothing for at least a year, and they were supposed to stay indoors as much as possible. Often, another family member would die before the year was up, so that some women wore black a good part of their adult lives. Lack of sunshine and fresh air aggravated the disease among women of afflicted families. There were cases in which all the female members of a family would die.

In "A las tres de la mañana" it is a young man who is dying, and his last hours are haunted by a woman. Border singers associate these two ballads; as one female singer once told me, "It is *la tísica,* she came for him." The songs are patterned one upon the other, and to Border singers "A las tres de la mañana" is a *contestación* ("answer" or sequel) to "La tísica." The attitudes toward the two songs give us a glimpse into another aspect of the feminine world in the river-bank settlements during the latter part of the nineteenth and the early part of the twentieth centuries. During this time, a number of the villages and *rancherías* began to stagnate, if not to die. Total population at best remained constant, or it decreased, with the young men of each generation leaving for the cities. Left behind was a surplus of young women, who competed for the few remaining men. Many of the girls ended as old maids, "aunties" to the children of their more fortunate sisters. Under such conditions, there would be a powerful attraction in a pair of songs about a jilted bride who returns from the grave to wreak vengeance on her faithless lover. So "La tísica" and "A las tres de la mañana" may not be about tuberculosis after all.

The next five songs are of a type common in Mexican tradition, though not exclusive to it. They belong to a broad and universal category, the courtship song; but instead of the tender affection of love songs such as "Trigueña hermosa," these songs express a joking attitude toward relations between the sexes. In "ANDANDOME YO PASEANDO" the singer portrays himself as a dashing young blade, irresistible to women. Comic intent is clearly shown in the title of the song, which also serves as the first line in stanzas 1 and 2. "Andándome yo paseando" (quite similar in intention and content to the "As I was out walking" of Anglo-American ballads) is also the first line in "La esposa infiel," a comic ballad about a man who is making love to a woman when her husband comes home. In our song, however, the story about the unfaithful wife is absent. The protagonist goes along from woman to woman, blithely making love to all of them. The song is full of the supposed symbols of *machismo:* the pistol, the horse, the cowboy chaps, and the big hat. But the attitudes commonly associated with *machismo* are absent; the protagonist is neither a weeping *abandonado* nor a bully. Freudians should love this song, since the pistol and the knife are especially important as phallic symbols. People who sing this song, however, are quite conscious of these objects as symbols. Stanzas 3 and 4 are floating stanzas and are found in other Mexican songs. The last stanza localizes the song in the Border area, however.

In "EL COLUMPICO" we hear a rejected suitor speak. He has courted a girl who in the end chose another man; so he got drunk trying to forget and landed in jail, where the judge lectured him. Again, the whole complex of attitudes that in recent decades has been given the label of *machismo* is satirized. The use of the *esdrújulo* line endings also is a comic device, well known in Hispanic folk poetry, as is the coining of nonsense words in *esdrújulos: colúmpico* for *columpio, enamorétique* for *enamoré, boquítica* for *boquita, sítico* and *nótico* for *sí* and *no.* There is a hint of a later linguistic tendency among Chicanos, in "pachuco" talk, such as the use of *sintarazos* for *sí* and *nones* for *no.* As far as one can tell, "El colúmpico" is a song from the Border area and goes back to the 1860s. During the French occupation of Mexico, Border men joined the guerrillas fighting the occupation forces. They were known to the people of interior Mexico as *tagarnos*. When "El colúmpico" has been reported in interior Mexico, it is identified as "La canción del tagarno"; so it seems that it was one of the favorite songs of the Border guerrillas of that period.

"LA BORREGA PRIETA" and "MALHAYA LA COCINA" are in the "courting dialogue" pattern of folksong. In Mexican tradition this type of song is often called *canción de desprecio* (song of disdain). In "La borrega prieta" a young man directs all kinds of insults at a girl. At the same time he complains of her fickleness, calls her his "beautiful star," and invites her to elope with him. In "Malhaya la cocina" a woman finds all men worthy of censure. A girl is crazy to believe any of them, and if she marries she will spend her life in a smoky kitchen. She curses all men except one, the man she loves.

It is clear that the talk about hating the opposite sex is not to be taken seriously. Rather, it is a means to bring out into the open the singer's attraction for a certain person. In the traditional Border society, where open communication between young men and women was difficult, such songs were used to establish relationships in the early stages of courtship, or to express dissatisfaction with the loved one's behavior when obstacles arose between them. The fact that the songs are of comic intent gives their performance a good deal of permissiveness, as long as they are not openly directed at a specific person during singing.

Songs like "La borrega prieta" are sometimes called lyric *corridos.* They are not narrative, being made up of loose stanzas that may occur in other songs. But they have the *corrido* form, including the *despedida.* The tune of "La güera Chabela," a narrative *corrido* known throughout Greater Mexico, is used for "La borrega prieta." The song is strong on ranchero imagery and rustic humor; it is probably native to the Border country.

"Malhaya la cocina" is not a local composition. It is a widely traveled piece belonging to a type of song known on the Border as *canción de tiple*, because it was sung by *tiples* or popular sopranos who visited the Border with traveling shows. The shows were known as *carpas*, after the canvas tents in which they were housed. They were like small circuses, with acrobats and sideshows. The singing of the *tiple*—who usually went under an "Andalusian" name like Maruja or Carmelita—was a high spot in the main show. Her songs were often picked up by the local people and made part of their oral repertory. Traveling variety shows and *carpas*, in fact, were quite important in the dissemination of folksongs. "Malhaya la cocina" is known throughout Spanish America and has been collected elsewhere in the Southwest, notably in New Mexico. In some countries of South America, it belongs to a type of song called the *caramba*, because of its use of that word.

In "DIME SI, SI, SI" and "CARTA ESCRITA SOBRE UN CAJON" the Border ranchero has a laugh on himself. "Dime sí, sí, sí" reflects the attitudes of most Border people, who were farmers or vaqueros and who looked on sheepherders as a little odd. It is the *pastorón* or stupid sheepherder who speaks in this song, as he does in "La pastora" (no. 1); so the Borderer is not so much laughing at himself as at one particular type of person in his community. The *pastorón* (city people use the term as equivalent to the English "hick") takes a cartful of goatskins to his lady love as a romantic gift. He is drunk besides but cannot offer her any liquor because he drank it all. Aside from the fun made of the sheepherder, the song is appreciated for its nonsense elements, its repetition of *sí* and *no*, and its pleasing rhythm. It probably is a parody of some popular dance piece of the nineteenth century. The melody is that of a schottische, a European dance that—like the polka, the mazurka, and the redowa—became "folklorized" in northern Mexico and the southwestern United States. This song is often taught to children, perhaps because of the bouncy rhythm.

"Carta escrita sobre un cajón" is an example of the way folk groups can adopt parodies made of themselves by outsiders, though in this case the parody is good-natured enough. The text of "Carta escrita sobre un cajón" sounds very much like the comic ranchero verses printed in humorous weeklies such as *El Vacilón* in San Antonio, Texas, during the latter part of the nineteenth and the early decades of the twentieth centuries. Very often these comic verses were in epistolary form, the ranchero and his *compadre* exchanging letters from one week to the next. "Carta escrita sobre un cajón" pokes gentle fun at the simplicity of life in the *ranchos*, where one's problems may include the loss of a burro or the near drowning of a pup during a heavy rain—all of it set down in a letter laboriously written on a box substituting for a desk. From an urban viewpoint, there is a good deal of condescension in the picture painted of the ranchero in this song. But the rancheros on the Border have not noticed the condescension, or they have chosen to ignore it. They have found an engaging and natural figure—albeit a comic one—in don Simón's letter-writing *compadre*. "Carta escrita sobre un cajón" is widely known and greatly enjoyed on the Border.

A *cruda* is a hangover, so "EL CRUDO"—the hero of this song—is a man in that unhappy condition. Like other people of Mexican culture, Borderers did not use the term *machismo* until social scientists invented it, but they recognized the characteristics imputed to *machismo*: exaggerated emphasis on sexual prowess, ability to drink to excess, and pugnaciousness. Until the advent of the singing *charro* of the movies, however, there were more songs satirizing these characteristics than compositions idealizing them. "El crudo" is a comic portrait of *el muchacho alegre* on the morning after. He has been an *espléndido* with his friends the night before, spending his last cent on a night of tequila, music, and *gritos*. Now he wishes he had a few coins to buy a drink as a hangover cure. The bar girl will give him no credit, so he has only the Virgin of Guadalupe to fall back upon. This song has been sung in the Border area for a century. It has also been reported in Jalisco as of 1901 (see notes), so it must have been widely diffused throughout Greater Mexico in earlier times.

49
Trigueña hermosa

This is a song that is best performed in two voices, *primera y segunda.*

Tri-gue-ña her-mo - sa, mi co-ra-zón se en-cuen-tra tris-te,

por-que no sa - be si en al-gún tiem-po le co-rres-pon-des;

lo que te ju-ro es **que** en es-te mun-do no ha-llas o-tro hom-bre

que te quie-ra, tri-gue-ñi-ta, co-mo yo.

Con la es-pe-ran - za, tri-gue-ña her-mo-sa, yo te he que-ri-do,

con la es-pe-ran - za, tri-gue-ña her-mo-sa, yo te he a-do-ra-do;

es-tos tra-ba-jos que en-tre tú y yo he-mos pa-sa-do,

con la es-pe-ran - za de que Dios nos pre-mia-rá.

Trigueña hermosa, mi corazón
se encuentra triste,
porque no sabe si en algún tiempo
le correspondes;
lo que te juro es que en este mundo
no hallas otro hombre
que te quiera, trigueñita, como yo.

Con la esperanza, trigueña hermosa,
yo te he querido,
con la esperanza, trigueña hermosa,
yo te he adorado;
estos trabajos que entre tú y yo
hemos pasado,
con la esperanza de que Dios nos
premiará.

Beautiful Brown Girl

Beautiful brown girl, my heart is sad
because it does not know if you ever will return its love;
but I do swear to you that you will not find another man in this world
who will love you, little brown girl, the way I do.

With that hope, beautiful brown girl, I have loved you;
with that hope, beautiful grown girl, I have adored you;
all the troubles that you and I have shared,
with the hope that God will reward us.

50
La negrita

U - na ne - gri - ta   se e - na - mo - ró   de un jo - ven blan - co

que la mi - ró,   y la ne - gri - ta   pron - to en - fer - mó

por - que su a - man - te la a - ban - do - nó, por - que su a - man - te la a - ban - do - nó.

Pe - ro ¡ay! llo - ran - do de - cía la ne - gra: Voy a mo - rir

con el al - ma en - fer - ma   de tan - to su - frir.

Y la ne - gri - ta   pron - to en-fer - mó   por - que su a-
man - te la a - ban - do - nó,   por - que su a - man - te la a - ban - do - nó.

Una negrita se enamoró
de un joven blanco que la miró,
y la negrita pronto enfermó
porque su amante la abandonó,
porque su amante la abandonó.

   Pero ¡ay!
llorando decía la negra:
—Voy a morir

con el alma enferma de tanto sufrir. —
Y la negrita pronto enfermó
porque su amante la abandonó,
porque su amante la abandonó.

   Toma este ejemplo, negra, por Dios,
jamás a un blanco le des tu amor
porque los blancos no quieren, no,
que se revuelvan los de color,
que se revuelvan los de color.

The Black Girl

A little black girl fell in love
with a young white man who took notice of her,
and the little black girl soon languished away
because her lover abandoned her.

"But, oh!" the black girl would weep and say, "I am going to die;
my soul is sickened from so much suffering."
And the little black girl soon languished away
because her lover abandoned her.

Black woman, for God's sake, take this example to heart;
never give your love to a white man,
because the whites will never allow
those of color to mix with them.

51
La tísica

¡Qué ne - gra es - tá   la no - che!   ¡Cuán - tas es - tre - llas!

A - bre la ven - ta - na, ma - dre, yo quie - ro ver - las.

No, hi - ja de mi vi - da, tú es - tás en - fer - ma

y el se - re - no de la no - che ma - tar - te pue - da.

— ¡Qué negra está la noche!
¡Cuántas estrellas!
Abre la ventana, madre,
yo quiero verlas. —
—No, hija de mi vida,
tú estás enferma
y el sereno de la noche
matarte pueda. —

—Al toque de la una,
madre, yo muero,
y debajo de mi cama
aúlla el perro. —
—No, hija de mi vida,
no digas eso,
tú estás muy mejorada,
ven, dame un beso. —

—Si viene Jorge a verme
no dejen que entre
porque él a mí me ha dicho
quo no me quiere,
porque él a mí me ha dicho,
'Quiero a Dolores'
y sólo a mí me basta
que tú me llores.

—Yo de mortaja quiero
mi ropa blanca,
la ropa que tenía
para mis bodas,
que vengan mis amigas,
me traigan flores,
que vengan todititas,
menos Dolores. —

The Consumptive Girl

"How dark is the night! How many stars!
Open the window, mother, I want to see them."
"No, my darling daughter, you are ill,
and the night dew might kill you."

"When the clock sounds one, mother, I will die,
and the dog is howling under my bed."
"No, my darling daughter, do not say that;
you are much better now; come, give me a kiss."

"If Jorge comes to see me, do not let him come in,
for he has said to me that he does not love me,
for he has said to me, 'I love Dolores,'
and I do not need anyone to weep for me but you.

"I want my white clothes to be my winding sheet,
the clothes that I had for my wedding;
let my girl friends come, let them bring me flowers;
let them all come, except Dolores."

52
A las tres de la mañana

A las tres de la ma-ña - na,   ma - má,   yo mue - ro;

y de - ba - jo de mi ca - ma   a - ú - lla un pe - rro.

Pe - ro hi - ji - to de mi vi - da,   no di - gas e - so;

si ya es-tás muy me - jo - ra - do,   ven, da - me un be - so.

—A las tres de la mañana,
mamá, yo muero;
y debajo de mi cama
aúlla un perro. —
—Pero hijito de mi vida,
no digas eso;
si ya estás muy mejorado,
ven, dame un beso. —

   —En la cruz de mi ventana
brilla una estrella,
y parece que me miran
los ojos de ella. —

—Pero hijito de mi vida,
es un lucero. —
—A las tres de la mañana,
mamá, yo muero.

   —Muy juntito de mi cama
siempre la siento,
y parece que me toca
su dulce aliento. —
—Pero hijito de mi vida,
si ella se ha muerto. —
—A las tres de la mañana
siempre despierto. —

At Three O'Clock in the Morning

"At three o'clock in the morning, mother, I will die;
and a dog is howling under my bed."
"But my beloved son, do not say that;
you are much better now; come, give me a kiss."

"In the cross made by my window a star is shining,
and it seems as if her eyes are looking at me."
"But my beloved son, it is only a bright star."
"At three o'clock in the morning, mother, I will die.

"Very close to my bed, I always feel her,
and it seems as if her sweet breath is touching me."
"But my beloved son, she is dead now."
"At three o'clock in the morning, I always wake."

53
Andándome yo paseando

Andándome yo paseando
me encontré una mujer sola,
me dijo: — ¡Cómo me gustan
los tiros de tu pistola! —
Y es porque me gusta el gusto
y el gusto es andar la bola.

Andándome yo paseando
me encontré otra más muchacha,
me dijo: —¿Qué es del cuchillo? —

Nomás le enseñé la cacha.
Me dijo: —Me voy contigo
a darle vuelo a la hilacha. —

En la barranca te espero,
detrás de aquellos nopales,
como que te chiflo y sales,
como que te hago una seña,
como que vas a la leña,
¡chinita, tú bien lo sabes!

Y en la barranca te espero,
en medio de las veredas,
ensillaré mi caballo,
me pongo mis chaparreras
y mi sombrero grandote,
¡y ora nos vamos de veras!

De Monterrey la chamarra,
de Zacatecas la gorra,
y en Matamoros compré
los tiros de mi pistola,
y es porque me gusta el gusto
y el gusto es andar la bola.

As I Was Out Walking

As I was out walking, I met an unescorted woman.
She said to me, "Oh, how I like the bullets in your pistol!"
And that's because I like my pleasure, and my pleasure is to carouse.

As I was out walking, I met another, younger one.
She said to me, "Where's your knife?" I only showed her the handle.
She said, "I will go with you, and we'll have ourselves a fling."

I'll wait for you in the gully, behind those clumps of cactus.
Suppose I whistle and you come out, and suppose I give you a sign;
suppose you go looking for wood—Baby, you know what I mean!

I'll wait for you in the gully, in the space between the paths.
I will saddle my horse, I will put on my chaps
and my great big hat. And this time we'll really go away!

My jacket is from Monterrey, my cap is from Zacatecas,
and it was in Matamoros that I bought the bullets for my pistol;
and that's because I like my pleasure, and my pleasure is to carouse.

54
El colúmpico

♩ = 108

Cuan-do yo me_e-na-mo-ré - ti-que quién a mí me lo di-

jé - ri - ca que_ha-bía de com-prar co-lúm-pi - co pa - ra que_o-tro

se me - cié - ri - ca. Por lo que sí - ti - co, por lo que nó - ti - co,

por lo que el juéz - ti - co me pre - gun - tó - ti - co, por tu bo - quí - ti - ca,

por tus o - jí - ti - cos, a tus pie - cí - ti - cos me mue - ro yo.

Cuando yo me enamorétique
quién a mí me lo dijérica
que había de comprar colúmpico
para que otro se meciérica.

   Por lo que sítico, por lo que nótico,
   por lo que el juéztico me preguntótico,
   por tu boquítica, por tus ojíticos,
   a tus piecíticos me muero yo.

En un montón de zacátique
me encontré una viborítica,
ella quería picarmítique,
yo quería matarlítica.

Por lo que sítico, etc.

Frente de una ventanitica,
estaba una señorítica,
componiéndose el vestídico
y meneándose todítica.

   Por lo que sítico, etc.

Poderoso San Fernándico,
solíviame estas cadénicas,
porque me ando emborrachándico
por las muchachas ajénicas.

   Por lo que sítico, etc.

The Swing

When I fell in love, I never thought
that I had bought a swing so another guy could ride.

   By saying yes, by saying no,
   by what the judge was asking me,
   by your lips and by your eyes,
   and at your feet I wish to die.

In a pile of hay I found a snake;
it tried to sting me, I tried to kill it.

   By saying yes, etc.

In front of a window there was a maiden
straightening her dress and wiggling all over.

   By saying yes, etc.

Powerful Saint Ferdinand, relieve me of these chains,
for I am getting drunk over other fellows' girls.

   By saying yes, etc.

55

La borrega prieta

Co - mo que que - ría   llo - ve - er, co - mo que que -ría ha - cer ai - re,

co - mo que que - ría   llo - ra - ar e - se co - ra - zón co - bar - de.

Como que quería llover,
como que quería hacer aire,
como que quería llorar
ese corazón cobarde.

Mañana se va tu amante,
ya tiene el pie en el estribo,
¿qué dice ese corazón?
¿Se queda o se va conmigo?

Ayer me dijiste que hoy,
y hoy me dices que mañana,
y así me traes vuelta y vuelta
como pájaro en la rama.

Como que quería llover,
como que caiban gotitas,
yo soy el que me desvelo
por las muchachas bonitas.

Ayer pasé por tu casa
tirando flores al viento,
me alegro que hayas hallado
amores a tu contento.

Me alegro que hayas hallado
amores a tu contento,

así me los hallo yo,
ni agravio ni sentimiento.

Aunque tu mamá me dé
los bueyes y la carreta
yo no me caso contigo,
ojos de borrega prieta.

Y aunque tu papá me dé
la mula y el carretón
no vuelvo a tratar contigo,
ojos de perro pelón.

Y aunque tu papá me dé
la carreta con los bueyes
tú te quedarás buscando
guayabas en los magueyes.

Adiós, mi linda Lucía,
adiós, hermoso lucero,
aguarda correspondencias
por teléfono extranjero.

Despedida no la doy
porque no la traigo aquí,
se la dejé a mi negrita
pa' que se acuerde de mí.

The Black Sheep

It looked as if it would rain, it looked as if the wind would blow;
it looked as if you would weep, my timid sweetheart.

Your lover will leave tomorrow; his foot is now in the stirrup.
What do you say, my heart? Will you stay or will you go with me?

Yesterday you said it would be today, today you tell me tomorrow;
and so you have me turning this way and that, like a bird upon a bough.

It looked as if it would rain, it looked as if it would sprinkle;
I am he who loses sleep over pretty girls.

I passed by your house yesterday, tossing flowers into the air;
I am happy you have found a love that is to your liking.

I am happy you have found a love that is to your liking;
I have been doing the same, no harm done and no hard feelings.

Even if your mother gave me both the oxen and the cart,
I would not marry you, Black-Sheep Eyes.

And even if your father gave me both the mule and the wagon,
I would have nothing to do with you, Hairless-Dog Eyes.

And even if your father gave me the cart and the oxen both,
you would be left looking for guavas on the maguey plants.

Farewell, my dearest Lucia, farewell, beautiful bright star;
you will hear from me by long-distance phone from abroad.

I will not give you my farewell because I did not bring it with me;
I left it with my darling dark one, so she will remember me.

56
Malhaya la cocina

Malhaya la cocina,
malhaya el humo,
malhaya quien se cree
de hombre alguno.
Porque los hombres,
porque los hombres
cuando se sienten queridos
¡caramba!
no corresponden.

Yo comparo a los hombres
con el mosquito,
que dan el picotazo,
luego el brinquito.
Yo los maldigo,
yo los maldigo,
de éste que traigo en el alma,
¡caramba!
de éste no digo.

Curses on the Kitchen

Curses on the kitchen, curses on the smoke,
curses on the woman who will believe any man.
Because men, because men, when they know they're loved,
caramba!
They won't love you back.

I compare men with the mosquito,
for they will sting you and then fly away.
I curse them, I curse them,
except this one that is in my heart, caramba!
Of him I do not speak.

57
Dime sí, sí, sí

A - ca - bo de lle - gar de la ma - ja - da,

de cue - ros trai - go lle - no un ca - rre - tón,

se los trai - go a - re - ga - lar a mi Li - bra - da,

la due - ña de mi co - ra - zón. Di - me sí, sí, sí,

di - me no, no, no, a - guar - dien - te tra - í - a pe - ro
ya se me a - ca - bó; di - me sí, sí, sí, di - me no, no, no,
a - guar - dien - te tra - í - a pe - ro ya se me a - ca - bó.

Acabo de llegar de la majada,
de cueros traigo lleno un carretón,
se los traigo a regalar a mi Librada,
la dueña de mi corazón.

Dime sí, sí, sí, dime no, no, no,
aguardiente traía pero ya se me acabó;
dime sí, sí, sí, dime no, no, no,
aguardiente traía pero ya se me acabó;

Tell Me Yes, Yes, Yes

I have just arrived from the sheep pens,
I am bringing in a wagon full of hides;
I have brought them as a gift to my Librada,
the mistress of my heart.
Tell me yes, yes, yes; tell me no, no, no;
I brought some spirits with me, but now they are all gone.

58
Carta escrita sobre un cajón

Por a - quí to - di - tos bue - nos sin te - ner na - da de nue - vo,

por a - quí to - di - tos bue - nos sin te - ner na - da de nue - vo,

mu - chas me - mo - rias le man - da su com - pa - dre Ge - no - ve - vo.

Mi compadre don Simón,
el dueño de La Lagarta,
ha de dispensar la carta
escrita sobre un cajón.

Por aquí toditos buenos
sin tener nada de nuevo,
muchas memorias le manda
su compadre Genovevo.

La agua aquí estuvo muy buena,
subió una cuarta en la tierra,
que a su comadrita Elena
ya se le ahogaba la perra.

Ya apareció el burro prieto
que se nos perdió en enero,
se hallaron el esqueleto
en el fondo del estero.

Salí a campear con el perro
que todo el tiempo me ayuda,

y me encontré su remuda
pero ya no trae cencerro.

La vaca pinta gateada
andaba bramando sola,
trae estarjada la cola
y una pezuña rajada.

La yegua pinta tordilla
tuvo un potrillo canelo,
le gusta para la silla
al muchacho de Marcelo.

Y ora que tiene lugar
me compone la carreta,
pues ya se muere mi Ancheta
por irse en ella a pasear.

Ya con ésta me despido,
ahi le mando el corazón,
ha de dispensar la carta
escrita sobre un cajón.

Letter Written on a Wooden Box

My *compadre* Don Simón, owner of La Lagarta,
please excuse this letter written on a wooden box.

Everyone here is fine, and with nothing new to tell;
your *compadre* Genovevo sends you his kindest regards.

We had a very good rain; it stood a span on the ground,
so that your *comadre* Elena almost lost her bitch by drowning.

The black burro that we lost in January finally turned up;
they found his skeleton at the bottom of the lake.

I went out to ride the range with the dog that always helps me,
and I found your *remuda*, but the lead horse is no longer belled.

The striped piebald cow was lowing away from the herd;
she has a bruised tail, and one of her hooves is split open.

The gray piebald mare had a cinnamon-colored colt;
Marcelo's boy thinks it will make a good saddle horse.

Now that you have the time, please fix the oxcart for me,
because my Ancheta is dying to go out for a ride in it.

Now with this I say farewell, I send you my heart herewith;
please excuse the letter written on a wooden box.

59
El crudo

♩ = 56

Al pie de un ver-de no-pal yo me a-cos-té,
al rui-do de u-nas gui-ta-rras yo me dor-mí,
al gri-to de u-nos bo-rra-chos yo des-per-té,
¡qué cru-do es-toy! quie-ro cu-rar-me y no hay con qué.

Pe-ro ¡ay, Dios mí-o! quí-ta-me es-ta cru-da,
por-que es-ta cru-da me va a ma-tar.

La Vir-gen de Gua-da-lu-pe me ha de sal-var, ¡qué
cru-do es-toy! la can-ti-ne-ra no quie-re fiar.

Al pie de un verde nopal
yo me acosté,
al ruido de unas guitarras
yo me dormí,
al grito de unos borrachos
yo desperté,
¡qué crudo estoy!
quiero curame y no hay con qué.

Pero ¡ay, Dios mío!
quítame esta cruda,
porque esta cruda
me va a matar.
La Virgen de Guadalupe me ha de salvar,
¡qué crudo estoy!
la cantinera no quiere fiar.

The Man with a Hangover

I lay down at the foot of a green cactus;
I fell asleep to the sound of some guitars;
I woke up to the yelling of some drunks.
What a hangover!
I'd like to cure it, but I lack the wherewithal.

But, oh my Lord! Take this hangover away,
for this hangover is going to kill me.
The Virgin of Guadalupe will surely save me.
What a hangover!
The barmaid will not trust me [for the price of a drink].

PART
V

The *Pocho* Appears

The Treaty of Guadalupe Hidalgo created a new type of social and political being in the United States, the American citizen of Mexican ancestry or Mexican-American; but it did not immediately create the *pocho*—the Americanized or semi-Americanized Mexican so harshly criticized by Mexican intellectuals in recent times. The first forty years or so of Anglo-American occupation in the Southwest saw little change in the culture of the new U.S. citizens of Mexican descent. The majority of them remained very much as they had been before 1848, except for having to cope with an alien authority and an alien tongue. Great numbers of them had no direct contact with Anglo-Americans, and those who did managed with a minimum of English. They communicated for the most part through go-betweens—foremen, special deputy sheriffs, and ward bosses—who were either Mexicans with a smattering of English or Anglos with a similar knowledge of Spanish. In general, the Mexican inhabitants of the Southwest sought to defend their way of life by isolating themselves as much as possible from Anglo influences. Nevertheless, the impact of Anglo culture was felt, even in the Spanish language. By the 1880s and 1890s, Mexicans in the Southwest were using such terms as *dipo* (depot), *marqueta* (market), and *revólver* (revolver), often without knowing these were Anglicisms that had worked into their language.

Around the turn of the century, Mexican migration into the United States began on a large scale. These migrants were more open to Anglo influences than were the older Mexican residents of the Southwest. They came from areas in Mexico where Anglos at that time were practically unknown; consequently, they were not imbued with a tradition of cultural conflict as were the Southwest Mexicans. The migrants, furthermore, came with great illusions about the abundance of the United States and therefore with greater receptivity toward Anglo-American culture. Finally, they came expressly to work for American farmers and ranchers. Consequently, they were much more open to acculturation, especially in their contact with American employers. The migrants gave a Hispanic touch to the cities they visited. Fort Worth became *Foro West,* Sinton was *El Cinto,* and Lubbock was turned into *Lóbica.* But they also made part of their Spanish vocabulary such Anglicisms as *calavera* (cultivator), *escrepa* (scraper), *troca* (truck), *pricula* (precooler), and *madama* (madame, the Anglo boss's wife).

The *pocho,* however, does not really appear until the time of the Revolution in Mexico, when great numbers of Mexican refugees of all social classes settled in cities like Los Angeles and San Antonio. During this period the "Mexiquitos" in the larger cities of the Southwest exhibited two contrasting states of mind. One was a truly refugee state of mind, cultivated especially by the middle-class Mexican but adopted by all older Mexicans, according to which the Mexican's life in the United States was to be insulated from Anglo influences and activities and devoted to the dream of returning to Mexico. Another state of mind was found among the younger people in the *barrios,* who were being forced to adapt to the environment of Anglo cities and who found acculturation an inevitable product of their fight for survival. It was the *barrios* that produced the *pocho,* the early version of the Chicano. And it was in contemptuous reference to the young Mexican-Americans of East Los Angeles, children of migrant workers and middle-class revolutionary refugees alike, that José Vasconcelos is said to have first used the term *pocho.* But, whatever his degree of Americanization, the average Mexican-American of this period continued to think of himself as possessing a "pure" Mexican culture. It was always the other fellow who was an *agringado,* not him. This viewpoint is revealed again and again in the interviews that make up Manuel Gamio's *The Life Story of the Mexican Immigrant* (Chicago, 1931).

The immigrant might have exaggerated ideas about the material riches of the United States, but he did not admire its culture. He fully intended to go back home after he had got his share of the good things to be had in Gringolandia. After all, there was no place like Mexico, and within Mexico there was no place like one's own region and one's own home town. "BONITA ESTA TIERRA" expresses these immigrant attitudes. Gold and silver glitter all around the Big Rock Candy Mountain Land that is the United States. But home is back in Mexico, and that is the place the soul yearns for. "Bonita esta tierra" is an old Mexican song, originally expressing a Mexican mine worker's homesickness. The miner was working within Mexico, but far from his *patria chica.* The migrant in the United States made the song his own, to express an even greater homesickness. In passing to a new environment and acquiring new functions, the song has been somewhat modified. Some singer who came from Mexico was drafted into the American army during World War I and ended up in France with the AEF. He added a new stanza, number 4, which is a variation to stanza 3. The last two stanzas, absent from most Mexican versions, compound the singer's homesickness by putting him in an American jail.

No matter how long he and his ancestors might have lived on the Texas side of the river, when the Border Mexican wanted to criticize American mores and *agringamiento* among his fellows, he was likely to assume the identity of a newcomer from *el interior.* It was tacit acceptance of the Mexican from Mexico as a just critic of Mexican-American customs, something the *mexicotejano* would not consciously admit. This type of criticism—in the form of jokes and comic songs—was old among Mexican-Americans by the time revolutionary intellectuals began to condemn *pochismo.* Things were criticized, however, from a Mexican-American rather than a Mexican point of view, in spite of the convention using a *mexicano del interior* as the "voice."

"DESDE MEXICO HE VENIDO" dates from the 1890s and is still enjoyed on the Border today. It uses as title and initial line a conventional phrase we have met before, in no. 48, "El charamusquero." The things criticized in "Desde México he venido" are more likely to interest the Mexican living in the United States than the casual visitor from Mexico. There is reference to the permissiveness of Anglo husbands, a favorite topic among Mexicans of all classes; Mexican men who allow the same kind of freedom to their wives are called *patos* or cuckolds. But the main interest is on Border politics. During election time, cigar-smoking Anglos mingle with the Mexican-American, flattering him and calling him "my friend." They are helped in electioneering by certain Mexican *vendidos,* who ape the Anglo down to the cigar. Once the election is over, the Mexican no longer hears the Anglo say, "Hello, my friend." There is also a Border proverb that says, "Never trust a Mexican who smokes a cigar, or a *gringo* who calls you *compadre.*"

"LOS MEXICANOS QUE HABLAN INGLES" makes fun of the mixture of English and Spanish characteristic of all Mexican-Americans when they engage in informal conversation among themselves. This song is witness to a very early interest in bilingualism by Mexican-Americans. Present-day specialists in bilingual instruction would agree that Mexican-Americans should work on their Spanish before they tackle the English language (stanza 6). The song also gives us a vivid picture of the *agringada,* the Mexican-American girl who puts on airs and refuses to speak Spanish—a type that has been beautifully portrayed by Amado Muro in his short story "Cecilia Rosas."[1] The final irony is that the critic in the song is guilty of using Anglicisms himself. He tells us he meets the Anglicized doña Inés at the *dipo* (depot). In different versions, "Los mexicanos que hablan inglés" has been known throughout the Southwest.

The selection "FROM A BORDER ZARZUELA" is one of the few lyric songs in Border oral tradition that are easily datable. When Lucio Blanco took Matamoros in 1913, Brownsville was flooded with middle-class *huertista* refugees from its "sister city" across the river. These immigrants against their will found it hard to make ends meet, since few of them had ever worked for a living. Sympathizers in Brownsville gave them food, shelter, and clothing; and the refugees tried to help themselves by organizing theatrical benefits. One such benefit was a local zarzuela or musical comedy, composed and acted by the Matamoros people and including the fragment printed here. What the whole comedy looked like it may be impossible to know, unless copies of the script survived among the descendants of the actors. Ordinary people on the Border took this fragment into their oral repertory because it expressed themes of considerable interest to them: the enormously rich *gringo* (here an English lord), the Anglo's casual interest in Mexican girls, and the question of bilingualism.

In this case, the attitude taken toward the mixture of languages is different from that expressed in songs like "Los mexicanos que hablan inglés." The middle-class speaker in the zarzuela says, "We are in Texas now, so we must learn English in order to get along." He feels himself a transient guest in the United States but is quite willing to adapt while he is here. It is not surprising that *pochismo* should have quickly taken root among the children of the middle-class refugees from the Revolution, who

[1] *New Mexico Quarterly* 34:4 (Winter, 1964), 353-364.

were in the United States for just a short while—or so they thought.

"MUCHO ME GUSTA MI NOVIA" continues on the theme of the *pocho* and the Mexican-American girl who is so *presumida* she will talk only in English; but the tone of overt criticism present in "Los mexicanos que hablan inglés" is not found here. On the contrary, the speaker loves his sweetheart just because she talks to him in English. The satire is a bit more subtle, though it is evident to an audience that disapproves of the *agringada*. If the listener has nothing against Mexican girls who refuse to speak Spanish, though, he may miss the satire altogether and see the song merely as "cute." Such was the reaction of generations of American tourists in the pre-World War II period. They loved to hear "that cute little song" and asked for it again and again from the *guitarreros* who plied their trade in the tourist bars on the Mexican side. Even for the Mexican-American, "Mucho me gusta mi novia" does not have the strong tone of disapproval evident in earlier songs about *pochismo*. The process of acculturation had made the whole problem more acceptable to him by this time.

Like other Americans, the Mexican-American has been profoundly affected by television. TV was important in the complex of factors at work during the 1950s, which effectively severed the umbilical cord connecting the bulk of the Mexican-American population to the Republic of Mexico. In the 1930s, TV's predecessor in mass communication—radio—had worked in exactly the opposite direction, reaffirming *lo mexicano* in the Mexican-American. The 1930s were a decade of powerful radio stations in Mexico, easily heard throughout the Southwest and deep into other parts of the United States. The 1930s were also a golden age in Mexican popular music, which was transmitted throughout the hemisphere by radio and Mexican movies. Mexican songs invaded Anglo-American radio programs; and, though "Jalisco no te rajes" did sound somewhat ridiculous as "Three happy chappies wrapped in their serapes," the Mexican-American could feel pride in his heritage when such attention was given Mexican music by the dominant majority in the United States.

Furthermore, radio and romantic nationalism had combined to produce a musical renaissance in Mexico. *Lo mexicano* in the 1930s was still a major theme in serious music, art, literature, and philosophy; and folklore was considered basic in the definition of *lo mexicano*. Radio programmers scoured the provinces in search of folk and regional musicians, and the best finds ended up as performers in Mexico City's station XEW, from which they broadcast folksongs and folk-inspired compositions to all of Greater Mexico. This was the age of Guty Cárdenas, Agustín Lara, Lorenzo Barcelata, Joaquín Pardavé, Pepe Guízar, and many others, who were as well known in the United States as in Mexico.

By the 1950s, television had changed things in a radical way. The Mexican-American's TV set could reach only local, English-speaking stations. But such was the attraction of the new gadget that everyone who could afford a set bought one, and thousands who could not afford them got their sets on credit. The average Mexican-American—especially if he fell anywhere within the range of the "middle class"—spent considerably more time watching English-language programs on TV than listening to Mexican radio. Eventually, Mexican TV came to the Southwest via cable, but Mexico had also been hit by Anglicizing influences, and its TV programs had nothing to offer the Mexican-American but poor imitations of poor TV programs from the United States. "Mexican music" now meant *roc-en-rol en español*. At the present time, only those Mexicans in the United States who do not understand English spend much time watching Mexican TV.

In this manner, television contributed to the rapid process of acculturation of Mexican-Americans during the 1950s and early 1960s—a process only superficially successful but one bravely embraced by the upward-moving Mexican-American, who had become convinced of the wonders and rewards of the Melting Pot. The impact of television on the *barrio* is portrayed in comic mood in "YA SE VA LA TELEVISION." Everybody must have his TV, even if it is a secondhand set that works only part of the time and is in danger of repossession if one falls behind on the payments. The troubles with the antenna, the poor image, the viewer with his eyeballs glued to the set—all of this is standard American humor. But there is also a parodying of Mexican folklore that is typically Mexican-American of the 1950s. The tune and textual pattern of "Ya se va la televisión" are parodies of an old Mexican lyric song. The *corrido* tradition is also made fun of. In the *corrido* "El hijo desobediente," a dying vaquero wills his possessions to his relatives. In our song, the speaker wills his debts to his brother. The song has a *despedida,* in the manner of the *corrido;* the singer says farewell with the TV set's control knob in his hand—a takeoff on Border *corridos* like "Gregorio Cortez," where the formula "with his pistol in his hand" occurs. Up to the late 1940s, generations of young Borderers had enjoyed the old *corridos*. Now, for the urban Border Mexican of the 1950s, the *corridos* had become objects of ridicule. Few Texas-Mexicans of that younger generation showed interest in their own folksongs, for fear of being considered "country" and out of it.

It was a new generation of Mexican-Americans that had come of age during the Silent Fifties, as we have often been told. The *pachucos* of the early 1940s were now veterans of World War II, and they demanded a share of the good things they had fought to preserve. In the armed forces they had been exposed to new forms of acculturation. During service abroad many had come to think of themselves as Americans for the first time in their lives, when they found that to Europeans and Asians they were just "Yankee soldiers" like all the others wearing the same uniform. They had traveled and seen many new things, and a considerable number of them went to college immediately after the war under the G.I. Bill of Rights. With large numbers of articulate, educated Mexican-Americans, capable of working together and of using Anglo institutions to further their goals, the time seemed ripe for social revolution. The *movimiento*, it would seem, should have occurred in 1950.

But conditions in the majority culture must be taken into account in any attempt to assess the work of the activists of the post-World War II period. Mexican-Americans were ready for change, but the United States was not. Post-World War II attitudes in the United States in many ways resembled those of the late teens and the twenties; the decade of the 1950s was a period of conformity and superpatriotism. We must keep this fact in mind to understand why the Mexican-American activists of the period surrounded their efforts with an aura of super-Americanism surpassing even that of the LULACs in the 1920s. The principle of the Melting Pot was in full force during the fifties, fortified by the anti-Communist fervor of the times. Under such circumstances, Mexican-Americans of this period had to cope with an aggravated problem of identity, and questions of self-identity are expressed in folklore by means of the names we use in reference to ourselves and to others.

Until very recently, the great majority of Mexicans in the United States have referred to themselves as *mexicanos* when speaking in Spanish among themselves; this has been as true in Texas, California, and the Middle West as it has been in New Mexico, where Anglo anthropologists have attempted to establish a separate subculture known as "Spanish American." When it was necessary to distinguish between themselves and the people living in the Republic of Mexico, the *mexicanos* of the United States resorted to ad hoc terms of self-reference: *mexicanos de este lado, mexicanos de Estados Unidos, mexico-tejanos, mexicanos de Nuevo México* or *de California*, and sometimes *mexico-americanos*. *Chicano* was often used as a clipped form of *mexicano*, with familiar or affectionate connotations. It did not refer to any particular class of *mexicano*, immigrant or otherwise. *Pocho*, of course, was a term indicating a condition prevalent among many *mexicanos* in the United States (and some in Mexico) and did not identify any specific subgroup.

It was when the Mexican in the United States learned English and communicated with the Anglo that he had problems with terms of self-reference. To the Anglo, "Mexican" has been a dirty word, indicating an inferior kind of human being and an inferior culture. If a white man in the Southwest wanted to insult one of his peers, he might call him a "Mexican"—or, more subtly, refer to him as "Señor"—just as southern whites used "nigger" to insult each other. Understandably, the semi-acculturated Mexican-American sought to avoid the dirty word "Mexican," and he found a convenient term, "Spanish" already in the vocabulary of his Anglo friends. Since the early days of intercultural conflict, Anglos had been using "Spanish" for individual Mexicans whom they liked or respected. It was a way of telling favored Mexicans that they really were too clean, honest, brave, or civilized to be called "Mexican." "Latin" is a newer term, apparently borrowed from turn-of-the-century writers on hemispheric politics, who had much to say about "Anglo-Saxon" and

"Latin" cultures. It did not become widely used until the 1920s, with the founding of the League of United Latin American Citizens (LULAC).

"Spanish" and "Latin" for the most part were used in conversation, while "Spanish American" and "Latin American" were preferred in writing or formal speech. These latter terms and their Spanish-language versions, *hispanoamericano* and *latinoamericano,* were considered highly preferable to *mexico-americano* and its English equivalent, Mexican-American, since they did not contain the "dirty word." But, though all these labels had "American" in them, they did not satisfy the xenophobia rampant in the United States during the early decades of this century. Advocates of the Melting Pot saw potential spies and traitors in any American citizen whose looks or behavior did not immediately stamp him as an average, middle-class, white Anglo-Saxon Protestant. Highly suspect were those ethnic groups that attempted to preserve their old cultures, or that banded together for political or social action under the rubric of their ethnicity. The Melting Potters thundered out against these "hyphenated Americans" (Irish-Americans, Italian-Americans, German-Americans, Greek-Americans, and, of course, Mexican-Americans). They called on them to be just plain Americans like everybody else or to "go back where they came from." All this must have given our "Latins" and "Spaniards" a case of nerves; they did not want to be included in the general condemnation of "hyphenated Americans." So they took care to write always "Latin American" and "Spanish American." Never with a hyphen.

Strangely enough, many Chicano activists today make it a point to write "Mexican American" without the hyphen, maintaining that they do not want to be identified as "hyphenated Americans"—and thus making common cause on this point with the advocates of the Melting Pot philosophy. This may be due to lack of historical perspective, since some young Chicanos also believe that "Mexican-American" is a term invented by the Gringo to insult the Chicano.

Such was the situation as regards Mexican-American terms of self-reference during the period between the two world wars. When Spanish was spoken, *mexicano* still was the term most commonly used, although *chicano* was gaining currency in varied contexts. But when speaking English, the *mexicano* referred to himself as "Spanish," "Latin," "Spanish American," or "Latin American." Not many had the courage or the self-confidence to identify themselves as "Mexican" or "Mexican-American" when speaking to an Anglo. And no one in the Mexican-American community would have denied some slight discomfort or dissatisfaction in regard to this confused and contradictory question of names.

It was into this state of affairs that the activist generation of the fifties emerged. The need for a common term of self-reference was not lost upon them, but they were unable to come up with an answer to the problem. "Spanish" and "Latin" no longer seemed satisfactory. Individually, more and more of them preferred "Mexican-American" or "American of Mexican descent." But their leaders were sensitive to the super-

Americanism of the period, which still frowned on "hyphenated Americans." So they sought a solution to the problem by denying its existence. Names just are not important, they said. This viewpoint may be illustrated by comparing the names of organizations created by Mexican-Americans during the past century or so. In the very early days, there were leagues and associations of *mexicanos.* Between the two world wars, the leagues and associations were of "Spanish Americans" and "Latin Americans." In the late 1960s and the 1970s, there would be organizations of "Mexican-Americans" and "Chicanos." But the most influential Mexican-American organization of post-World War II was the American G.I. Forum. It was an organization of American veterans who had served their country in World War II. The fact that the members were of Mexican descent was deliberately played down.

This new approach—advanced as a sane and pragmatic one—was epitomized in the popular *dicho,* "I don't care what you call me; just don't call me late for dinner," which became current among Mexican-Americans of the 1950s. It was used as a proverbial expression and found its way into speeches given at banquets and at political rallies. Those who used the expression saw it as a positive statement, a declaration of action that could be translated as "Names are not important, so I don't care what labels you pin on me: Latin, Spanish, Mexican, or whatever. What I demand is a share of the good things in this country."

Implicit in the slogan, of course, was an acceptance of the Melting Pot philosophy; and there were some who took a cynical view of this declaration of one hundred percent Americanism. "To the *gringos,*" they would say, "you will always be a Mexican greaser, no matter what." Others reacted more strongly. "What that *dicho* means," one person told me in 1954, "is that *gringos* can call me all the names they want—even kick me in the ass, perhaps—as long as they give me something to eat. If a dog could talk, that's what he would say." This is an extreme, though typical, indictment of the aims of the Generation of the Fifties by the more traditional-minded Mexican-American. It does point up the basic problem faced by the Mexican-American activist of the period, who was convinced that his goals could be reached by the avenue of total acculturation. Names, after all, do have a great deal of importance. For one thing, they are tied very closely to an individual's sense of identity. The Mexican-American activist of the 1950s found that he could not slough off his Mexican personality as he might a discarded garment. The process, he discovered, could be a traumatic one.

So, as often happens when a person wishes to be rid of something he has loved and perhaps still loves, it was necessary to resort to complete rejection and vilification. "TEX-MEX SERENADE," the last song in our collection, is a vivid expression of the dilemma faced by the type of Mexican-American who yearns for complete acculturation into the WASP society—the "white Mexican," as he calls himself in his more ironic moods. The song builds up to its message (the "don't call me late for dinner" slogan) by means of a series of vignettes ridiculing Mexicans and their customs. In the process, the singer buys all the stereotypes of Mexicans that prejudiced Anglos are likely to use. In attempting to become something else, the Mexican-American has begun by disparaging all that he is. The last stanza reveals what ailed the "all-American" *mexicano* of the 1950s. "Spanish," "Mexican," and "Latin" are ugly names to him, and he knows others that are "meaner." It is hard to believe that he is completely indifferent to ethnic labels; on the contrary, he is afraid of them.

60
Bonita esta tierra

Bonita esta tierra, no puedo negar,
el oro y la plata se miran brillar,
el oro y la plata se miran brillar,
bonita esta tierra, no puedo negar.

Bonitas muchachas que bajan al real,
a gastar dinero de este mineral,
a gastar dinero de este mineral,
bonitas muchachas que bajan al real.

Yo dejé a mis padres por irme a pasear,
por ir a Toluca y a la Capital,
por ir a Toluca y a la Capital,
yo dejé a mis padres por irme a pasear.

Yo dejé a mi patria por irme a pelear,
por cruzar las olas, por cruzar el mar,
por cruzar las olas, por cruzar el mar,
yo dejé a mi patria por irme a pelear.

Qué amarga es la vida de un pobre cautivo
que está en una tumba y se encuentra vivo,
que está en una tumba y se encuentra vivo,
qué amarga es la vida de un pobre cautivo.

Quisiera de un vuelo cruzar esa sierra,
salir de esta cárcel y estar en mi tierra,
salir de esta cárcel y estar en mi tierra,
quisiera de un vuelo cruzar esa sierra.

Beautiful Is This Land

Beautiful is this land, I can not deny it;
gold and silver may be seen shining everywhere.

Beautiful are the girls who come down to the camp
to spend the money from these mines.

I left my parents to go and travel,
to go to Toluca and to Mexico City.

I left my country to go and fight,
to cross the waves, to cross the sea.

How bitter is the life of a poor prisoner,
who is entombed and is yet alive.

I'd like to cross these mountains in one long flight,
to be out of this jail and to be in my land.

61

Desde México he venido

Des - de Me - xí - co he ve - ni - do no - más por ve - nir a ve - er

e - sa ley a - me - ri - ca - na que a - quí man - da   la mu - je - er.

Desde México he venido
nomás por venir a ver
esa ley americana
que aquí manda la mujer.

En México no se ha visto,
ni en la frontera del Norte,
que intimiden a los hombres
llevándolos a la corte.

Yo soy un triste pelado,
guiado por mi cruel fortuna,
he venido a conocer
los patos en la laguna.

Y ¡ay, ay! qué bonito es Texas
en tiempo que hay elección,
verás los yanquis de puro
y a los de nuestra nación.

En tiempo que hay elección
son puro *aló* y *hay mai fren*,
¡ay, navaja, no te amelles!
ya viene llegando el tren.

Ya pasada la elección
ya no hay *mai fren* ni hay *aló*,
pongan cuidado, señores,
que ese tiempo se acabó.

From Mexico Have I Come

From Mexico have I come, just to come and see
this American law that says the woman is boss.

This is never seen in interior Mexico, nor on the northern Border,
that men should be intimidated by taking them to court.

I am just a poor bum, guided by my cruel fortune;
I have come to get acquainted with the ducks in the lagoon.
[I've come to meet the cuckolds in their own surroundings.]

Ay, ay! But Texas is a fine place during election time;
you will see the cigar-smoking Yankees and our own people as well.

During election time they are nothing but "hello" and "hi, my friend."
Razor, don't lose your edge! The train is just coming in.
[Flattery, do your stuff! Success is in sight.]

But once elections are past, there's no more "my friend" or "hello";
better look out, gentlemen, for that time is no more.

62
Los mexicanos que hablan inglés

En Te - xas es te - rri - ble por la re - vol - tu - ra que ha - ay,

no hay quién di - ga "has - ta ma - ña - na," no - más pu - ro *good - bye.*

Yo‿e-na‿-mo-ré‿u-na te‿-ja‿-na,   y de‿e‿-sas de som-bri‿-lla,

le   di - je: ¿Te vas con-mi - go?‿y me di -jo :¡Lu - que jí - a!

En Texas es terrible
por la revoltura que hay,
no hay quién diga "hasta mañana,"
nomás puro *goodbye*.

   Y *jau-dididú mai fren*,
en ayl sí yu tumora,
para decir "diez reales"
dicen *dola yene cuora*.

   Yo enamoré una tejana,
y de esas de sombrilla,
le dije: —¿Te vas conmigo? —
y me dijo: — ¡*Luque jía*! —

   Enamoré otra catrina,
de esas de garsolé,

le dije: —¿Te vas conmigo? —
y me dijo: —¿*Huachu sei*? —

   Luego me fui pa'l dipo
a hablar con doña Inés,
yo le hablaba en castellano
y me contestó en inglés.

   Todos queremos hablar
la lengua americana,
sin poder comprender
la nuestra castellana.

   Y en Texas es terrible
por la revoltura que hay,
no hay quién diga "hasta mañana,"
nomás puro *goodbye*.

The Mexicans Who Speak English

In Texas it is terrible how things are all mixed up;
no one says *"hasta mañana,"* it's nothing but "goodbye."

And "howdy-dee-do, my friend, and I'll see you tomorrow";
when they want to say *"diez reales"* they say "dollar and a quarter."

I made love to a Texas-Mexican girl, one of those with a parasol;
I said to her, "Will you go along with me?" and she told me, "Looky heah!"

I made love to another fashionable lady, one of those with a *garsolé*;
I said to her, "Will you go along with me?" and she told me, "What you say?"

Then I went to the depot to talk to Doña Inés;
I talked to her in Spanish, and she answered me in English.

All of us want to speak the American language,
without understanding our own Spanish tongue.

In Texas it is terrible how things are all mixed up;
no one says *"hasta mañana,"* it's nothing but "goodbye."

63
From a Border Zarzuela

Co - mo es - ta - mos en Te -xas el in - glés hay que a - pren-
der - les cha - ra - mus- cas en la len - gua del Tío

der, pa - ra que con nues -tros pri - mos nos po - da - mos
Sam: Mu - cho bue - no pa - lan - que - tas, pi - lon -

en - ten- der. Y ven - ci - llo *ve - ry fine.* *One cent the* me - ren -gues,

one cent the pas - tel, *one cent the* tu - rro -nes, *and to - do one cent.*

Spoken: "What is it you want, mister?" Oí - ga - me u -na co - pla que voy a can - tar.

a tempo
Ha - ce po - cos dí - as que a-quí vi - no un *lord* que car -

ga - ba las pi - las de *mo - ney* en pu - ro A - me - ri - can *gold.*

Vió a u - na mu - cha-chi - ta y le di - jo a - sí: Mí te

dar to-do es-te di-ne-ri-to si tú quie-res mí.

Al mo-men-to la mu-cha-cha na-da su-po con-tes-tar,

pe-ro vien-do que le da-ban mu-cho *A-me-ri-can gold,*

le di-jo e-lla muy re-suel-ta: *Ve-ry well, all right.*

Como estamos en Texas
el inglés hay que aprender,
para que con nuestros primos
nos podamos entender.

Y venderles charamuscas
en la lengua del Tío Sam:
—Mucho bueno palanquetas,
piloncillo *very fine.*

—*One cent the* merengues,
one cent the pastel,
one cent the turrones,
and todo *one cent.* —

"What is it you want, Mister?"
(SPOKEN)

From a Border Zarzuela

Oígame una copla
que voy a cantar.

Hace pocos días
que aquí vino un *lord*
que cargaba las pilas de *money*
en puro *American gold;*
vio a una muchachita
y le dijo así:
—Mí te dar todo este dinerito
si tú quieres mí. —

Al momento la muchacha
nada supo contestar,
pero viendo que le daban
mucho *American gold,*
le dijo ella muy resuelta:
—*Very well, all right.* —

Since we are in Texas, we must learn the English language,
so that we can make ourselves understood to our cousins.

So we can sell them *charamuscas* in the language of Uncle Sam:
Mucho bueno palanquetas, piloncillo <u>very fine</u>.

<u>One cent the</u> *merengues,*
<u>one cent the</u> pie,
<u>one cent the</u> *turrones*
<u>and</u> everything <u>one cent</u>.

"<u>What is it you want, Mister?</u>" (SPOKEN)

Listen to a little song I am going to sing.

It was a few days ago that a <u>lord</u> came here,
who carried big heaps of <u>money</u> in pure <u>American gold</u>;
he saw a little girl, and he spoke to her like this:
"Me give you all of this nice money if you me like."

For a moment the girl did not know what to say,
but seeing that she was offered much <u>American gold</u>,
she told him quite resolutely, "<u>Very well, all right</u>."

64
Mucho me gusta mi novia

This should be accompanied with the lively rhythm of the *huapango tamaulipeco.*

Y mucho me gusta mi novia,
me gusta nomás porque me habla inglés;
anoche le preguntaba
que si me amaba
y me dice: —*Yes.* —

Oh, my little darling,
please dime que sí,
mamacita linda,
she belong to me.

Much Do I Like My Sweetheart

And much do I like my sweetheart,
I like her especially because she talks English to me;
last night I asked her if she loved me,
and she says to me, "<u>Yes</u>."

Oh, my little darling,
please say "yes" to me,
darling little mamma,
she belong to me.

65
Ya se va la televisión

Ya se va la televisión
porque nunca vimos nada,
fue purita parpadeada,
ya se aleja la estación.

Compraremos una antena,
que de veras sea buena,
abusamos de la ajena,
ya se aleja la estación.

Son difíciles los pagos
aunque sean en abonos,
ya no tengo pa' cerveza
por estar viendo los monos.

Ya con ésta me despido
con el botón en la mano,
las cuentas que yo me eché
se las dejo ahi a mi hermano.

Now the TV Is Departing

Now the TV is departing, and we never saw a thing;
all we saw was lots of blinking, now the channel moves away.

We shall buy us an antenna, one that is a really good one;
we have been imposing on the neighbors, now the channel moves away.

The installments are hard to meet, even on the easy-payment plan;
I no longer have money for beer, just so I can watch the pictures on the screen.

Now with this I say farewell, with the control knob in my hand;
to my brother I will all the debts that I have made.

66
Tex-Mex Serenade

Einstein says he has discovered
All about this "evolution";
He must come to <u>Me-hee-ko</u>,
Where they practice revolution.
He may be a learned man,
He may know a lot of facts;

We've got sleepy Mexico,
Where there ain't no income tax.

Drinking mezcal
And sipping tequila,
Munching tamal
And eating tortilla.

You go to a curio shop,
There you buy much as you can;
When you look at all curios,
They'll be marked "Made in Japan."
Let's go down south of the Border,
Just to buy some souvenirs;
But when you get back to Texas,
They'll be twice as cheap at Sears.

> Ay, ay, ay, ay!
> Unique Mexico.
> Ay, ay, ay, ay!
> You can keep Mexico.

Then you go out to the bullfight,
Just to see the great torero,
But you never see a thing,
You're behind a big sombrero.
Then you ask him to remove it,
Like a courteous caballero,
But he never takes it off
Till you give him some *dinero*.

> Ay, ay, ay, ay! etc.

They don't have no Senate hearings,
That is something you may ponder;
If you start investigating
They will put you six feet under.

All the lovely señoritas
Are as pretty as a picture,
But don't ask them for a date:
She must take her baby sister.

> Ay, ay, ay, ay! etc.

During all the big elections
You'll find plenty of mezcal,
But you never see the Rangers
Till you go up to Duval.
Nothing much about elections,
Only one thing should be noted,
That a man wins by ten thousand
But only four thousand voted.

> Ay, ay, ay, ay! etc.

There are some who call me "Spanish,"
"Mexican" or even "Latin";
I don't see why all the bother,
I was brought up in Manhattan.
I don't mind those ugly names,
And the ones you think are meaner;
I don't care what names you call me—
Just don't call me late for dinner!

> Ay, ay, ay, ay!
> Unique Mexico.
> Ay, ay, ay, ay!
> You can keep Mexico.

EPILOGUE

The Silent Fifties have been succeeded by the Raucous Sixties and the Strenuous Seventies; the philosophy of the Melting Pot has given way to cultural pluralism. The present-day Chicano takes a critical (perhaps a too critical) view of the "white Mexican" achievements of the forties and fifties. He does not want to be left out when the dinner bell is rung, but he also is greatly concerned about his identity and the names he is called. He is very much involved in demanding his rights as an American citizen, but he also exhibits a high regard for Mexican customs and traditions. These concerns are manifest in a revived interest in his folk and popular culture, especially in the folksongs of the past. A Chicano favorite, "De colores se visten las flores," is a Mexican folksong with ultimate origins in Spain. In 1928 Kurt Schindler collected the song from a group of girls in the province of Soria, who sang it as they worked in the fields.[1] The Mexican-American's revived interest in his folksongs includes the composition of what Denisoff in another context has called "songs of persuasion."[2] The preoccupation with identity and terms of self-reference unites with the folksong revival to produce songs such as "Yo soy chicano" and "Yo soy mexico-americano," composed by young musicians in the *movimiento*.

One would expect that the Chicano emphasis on *lo mexicano* would have resulted in close rapport with the still considerable body of tradition-minded Mexican-Americans who never bought the "white Mexican" approach, as well as with the people of Mexico. To a limited extent this goal has been achieved, but it still remains more of a goal than an accomplished reality. For the Chicano activist has become a victim of the Melting Pot in subtle ways. He comes on like an "urban ghetto" type rather than like a *mexicano*. His urban-militant style—picked up from other militant minority groups—turns off the traditional Mexican-American, who is one with the Chicano in his reverence for *lo mexicano* but who is basically old-

---

[1] Kurt Schindler, *Folk Music and Poetry of Spain and Portugal*, ed. and with an intro. by Federico de Onís (New York, 1941), no. 614, p. 30.

[2] R. Serge Denisoff, "Songs of Persuasion," *Journal of American Folklore* 79 (1966), 581-589.

fashioned in his values, whether he lives in the *barrio* or on the farm. Typical reactions to Chicano speakers by traditional-minded Mexican-Americans would include the following: "They look like *gringo* hippies. They have no *respeto*. They don't act like Mexicans."

On the other hand, the people of Mexico are likely to dismiss the Chicano for being too "Mexican" in his outlook. In the Republic of Mexico, the *movimiento chicano* has attracted a great deal of attention, especially among intellectuals and university students. Young Mexican radicals are attracted by the militant stance of the Chicano. But Mexicans in general are mildly amused by the Chicano's interest in *lo mexicano,* and there is more than a trace of condescension in their amusement. To the great majority of Mexicans, such things as *indigenismo, lo mexicano,* the national soul as expressed in folklore, the heroism of Cuauhtémoc, and the perfidy of La Malinche are issues that are very, very dead. The Mexican himself is living in a society shaped more and more by WASP values. For the Chicano, this "new" Mexico has little to offer in a cultural sense. He has taken to his heart the Mexico of the revolutionary period, which the country's cosmopolitan youth has rejected and now derides as a world "behind the cactus curtain."

So, in a very real sense, the Mexican-American still is in search of himself.

NOTES TO THE SONGS

1. "La Pastora"
Mendoza, *Romance y corrido,* p. 106, notes that this song has not been discovered by folklorists in interior Mexico. Well known in the Southwest: Espinosa, "Romancero nuevomejicano," four variants, pp. 467-470; Espinosa, "Los romances en California," four variants, pp. 306-308; Campa, *Spanish Folksong,* one variant, pp. 23-24 (reprinted in Campa, *Spanish Folk-Poetry,* pp. 43-44); Paredes, "Ballads of the Lower Border," two variants, pp. 2-5. All without music.

Recordings: UT Folklore Center F109-4, F131-2.

2. "La ciudad de Jauja"
Campa, *Spanish Folk-Poetry,* pp. 49-50; one text without music. Campa comments that the song "apparently has been found only in New Mexico." Mendoza, *Lírica infantil,* p. 144; one text with music, children's rhyme. Paredes, "Ballads of the Lower Border," p. 8; one text without music.

Recordings: UT Folklore Center F116-6.

3. "El borrego gordo"
Mendoza, *Romance y corrido,* pp. 543-544; one text with music.

Recordings: UT Folklore Center F105-5, F116-5.

4. "El marrano gordo"
Mendoza, *Romance y corrido,* pp. 572-573; one text with music. Santamaría, *Antología folklórica,* pp. 18-24; one text with music. Paredes, "Ballads of the Lower Border," p. 9; one text without music. Compare also Mendoza, *Romance y corrido,* pp. 740-742; also the Anglo-American "Sow Took the Measles"; also Tale Type 621, "The Louse Skin."

Recordings: UT Folklore Center F116-4.

5. "Delgadina"
Espinosa, "Romancero nuevomejicano," pp. 454-461, and "Los romances en California," pp. 308-310; nine texts without music. Campa, *Spanish Folk-Poetry,* pp. 30-33; two texts without music. Campa, *Spanish Folksong,* pp. 25-26; one text without music. Mendoza, *Romance y corrido,* pp. 342-354; twenty-one texts, nine musical examples.

Recordings: UT Folklore Center F108-5, F132-2.

6. "Elena"

Espinosa, "Romancero nuevomejicano," pp. 471-476, 483-484, and "Los romances en California," pp. 304-306; ten texts without music. Campa, *Spanish Folk-Poetry*, pp. 35-41; three texts without music. McNeil, "Corridos de Asuntos Vulgares," pp. 114-117; one text without music. Hansen, pp. 205-207; one text with music. Mendoza, *Romance y corrido*, pp. 336-342; six texts, four musical examples.

Recordings: UT Folklore Center F110-1.

7. "Los inditos"

Campa, *Spanish Folk-Poetry*, p. 220; one text without music. Paredes, "Ballads of the Lower Border, " p. 10; one text without music. Compare Mendoza, *Lírica infantil*, p. 63.

Recordings: UT Folklore Center F91-7.

8. "El general Cortina"

For background on Cortina, see Goldfinch.

Recordings: UT Folklore Center F111-7.

9. "Los franceses"

Compare Mendoza, *La canción mexicana*, pp. 326-328.

Recordings: UT Folklore Center F107-3.

10. "A Zaragoza"

Paredes, "Folklore and History," pp. 56-68; one text with music (reprinted, without music, in Mendoza, "Algunas canciones," pp. 22-23).

Recordings: UT Folklore Center F133-3.

11. "A Grant"

Paredes, "Folklore and History," pp. 64-65; one text with music.

Recordings: UT Folklore Center F133-5.

12. "Kiansis"

Durán, p. 6; one text with music. McNeil, "*Corridos* of the Mexican Border," pp. 10-12; one text with music (same text in McNeil, "Corridos de Asuntos Vulgares," without music). Paredes, "Ballads of the Lower Border," p. 11; one text without music. Mendoza, *Romance y corrido*, p. 487; one text with music.

Recordings: UT Folklore Center F92-2, F103-1, F108-2, F187-1, F313-7, F313-10, F317-13.
Library of Congress AAFS 626A, AAFS 4B, AAFS 731B.

13. "La Pensilvania"

Taylor, *Mexican Labor in the U.S.*, pp. vii-lx; one text with music (ref. to recordings around 1932 on Vocalion #8278 and Okeh #16383). McNeil, "Corridos de Asuntos Vulgares," pp. 88-89; one text without music. Paredes, "Ballads of the Lower Border," p. 35; one text without music. Compare also Taylor, "Songs of the Mexican Migration," pp. 227-228. For background see Taylor, *Mexican Labor in the U.S.*, esp. pp. 3-5.

Recordings: UT Folklore Center F77-2, F94-5, F102-3, F117-2.

14. " Rito García"

McNeil, "Corridos de Asuntos Vulgares," pp. 69-70; one text without music.

Recordings: UT Folklore Center F97-1, F113-4, F186-3.

15. "Los pronunciados" and
16. "El capitán Hall"

McNeil, "*Corridos* of the Mexican Border," pp. 15-22; one text each of "Los pronunciados" and "El capitán Hall," with same musical example for both (texts also in McNeil, "Corridos de Asuntos Vulgares," pp. 110-113, without music). María González, *corrido* no. 3; text without music of "El capitán Hall." Compare also McNeil, "Corridos de Asuntos Vulgares," p. 118. For authentic historical background on Catarino Garza, see Saldívar, *Documentos de la rebelión de Catarino Garza.*

Recordings: UT Folklore Center F133-4 ("Los pronunciados"), F134-2 ("El capitán Hall").

17. "José Mosqueda"

Duran, pp. 2-3; one text with music. Paredes, "El corrido de José Mosqueda," pp. 155-156; one text without music. Paredes, "José Mosqueda and the Folklorization of Actual Events," pp. 2-3; one text with music.

Recordings: UT Folklore Center F318-19.
Library of Congress AAFS 2609A1, mistakenly cataloged as "La batalla de Ojo de Agua."

18. "Gregorio Cortez"

Gamio, pp. 96-99; one text without music. McNeil, "Corridos de Asuntos Vulgares," pp. 3-5; one text without music. Hansen, pp. 297-299; one text with music. Paredes, "Ballads of the Lower Border," pp. 12-14; two texts without music. Paredes, *With His Pistol,* pp. xv, 151-174; one musical example and twelve texts (the book as a whole is a study of this one *corrido*). Compare Vázquez Santa Ana, pp. 173-176.

Recordings: UT Folklore Center F78-8, F94-4, F104-6, F110-5, F121-5, F124-4, F125-3.

19. "Ignacio Treviño"

Paredes, "Ballads of the Lower Border," pp. 17-18; one text without music.

Recordings: UT Folklore Center F94-3.

20. "Jacinto Treviño"

Paredes, "Ballads of the Lower Border," pp. 15-16; one text without music. Paredes, "Corrido de Jacinto Treviño," pp. 483-485; one text with music.

Recordings: UT Folklore Center F110-6, F127-2, F132-1.

21. "Los sediciosos"

Paredes, "Ballads of the Lower Border," pp. 19-20; one text without music. Compare the following variants of a King Ranch *corrido* on the same subject: McNeil, "*Corridos* of the Mexican Border," pp. 26-29; one text with music (same text in McNeil, Corridos de Asuntos Vulgares," pp. 34-35, without music). Dobie, pp. 30-35; one text with music.

Recordings: UT Folklore Center F94-2, F109-3, F305-4.
Library of Congress AAFS 5627.

22. "Pablo González"
Recordings: UT Folklore Center F123-8, F132-5.

23. "Alonso"
McNeil, "Corridos de Asuntos Vulgares," pp. 65-66; one text without music. Paredes "Ballads of the Lower Border, " pp. 23-26; two texts without music.
Recordings: UT Folklore Center F111-5, F121-1, F124-5, F127-1, F186-6.

24. "Arnulfo"
Paredes, "Ballads of the Lower Border," pp. 27-28; one text without music.
Recordings: UT Folklore Center F109-10, F119-1, F128-5.

25. "Alejos Sierra"
Recordings: UT Folklore Center F120-3, F130-6.

26. "Laredo"
McNeil, "Corridos de Asuntos Vulgares," p. 87; one text without music.
Recordings: UT Folklore Center F128-2.

27. "La toma de Ciudad Juárez"
Mendoza, *Cincuenta corridos*, pp. 30-31; one text with music (reprinted in Mendoza, *El corrido mexicano*, pp. 25-27, and *Lírica narrativa*, pp. 68-69).
Recordings: UT Folklore Center F116-8.

28. "La toma de Matamoros"
Recordings: UT Folklore Center F95-1, F95-6.

29. "El Automóvil Gris"
Recordings: UT Folklore Center F128-6.

30. "No decías, Pancho Villa"
Mendoza, *Romance y corrido*, pp. 404, 560; one text, two musical examples. Compare also p. 561.
Recordings: UT Folklore Center F108-11.

31. "La persecución de Villa"
McNeil, "Corridos de Asuntos Vulgares," pp. 143-145; two texts without music. Paredes, "Ballads of the Lower Border," pp. 21-22; one text without music. Mendoza, *Romance y corrido*, pp. 607-608; one text with music (reprinted in Mendoza, *El corrido mexicano*, pp. 60-62, and *Lírica narrativa*, 94-95).
Recordings: UT Folklore Center F94-8, F312-17.
              Library of Congress AAFS 9A.

32. "Benjamín Argumedo"
Paredes, "El concepto de la médula emotiva," pp. 170-175; six texts without music. Mendoza, *El corrido mexicano*, pp. 159-162; one text with music (reprinted in Mendoza, *Lírica narrativa*, pp. 172-173).
Recordings: UT Folklore Center F102-1, F116-1, F131-4.

33. "Felipe Angeles"

McNeil, "Corridos de Asuntos Vulgares," pp. 146-149; one text without music. Hansen, pp. 211-212; one text with music. Campos, *Folklore literario*, pp. 263-266; one text without music. Mendoza, *Cincuenta corridos*, pp. 38-39; one text with music (reprinted in Mendoza, *El corrido mexicano*, pp. 169-171, and *Lírica narrativa*, pp. 177-179).

Recordings: UT Folklore Center F110-8, F111-1.

34. "Mariano Reséndez"

Recordings: UT Folklore Center F91-2, F91-3, F105-4, F127-7, F129-1.

35. "Los tequileros"

McNeil, "Corridos de Asuntos Vulgares," pp. 81-82; one text without music.

Recordings: UT Folklore Center F128-1.

36. "Dionisio Maldonado"

Recordings: UT Folklore Center F123-3.

37. "El contrabando de El Paso"

Campa, *Spanish Folk-Poetry*, pp. 103-104; one text without music. McNeil, "Corridos de Asuntos Vulgares," pp. 75-80; two texts without music. McNeil, "*Corridos* of the Mexican Border," pp. 29-32; one text with music.

Recordings: UT Folklore Center F78-9, F92-3, F98-4, F115-9, F122-2.

38. "Manuel Garza de León"

Paredes, "Ballads of the Lower Border," pp. 38-39; one text without music.

39. "La canción de Carlos Guillén" (El prisionero de San Juan de Ulúa)

Hansen, pp. 309-310; one text with music. Paredes, "Ballads of the Lower Border," pp. 36-37; two texts without music. Mendoza, *Romance y corrido*, pp. 601-603; one text with music (reprinted in Mendoza, *El corrido mexicano*, pp. 225-226, and *Lírica narrativa*, pp. 221-223). Compare also Mendoza, *Romance y corrido*, pp. 275-276, 603-604.

Recordings: UT Folklore Center F91-6, F94-7, F108-10, F121-3.

40. "Las once acaban de dar"

Recordings: UT Folklore Center F105-9.

41. "Las posadas"

Recordings: UT Folklore Center F102-6, F311-5.
             Library of Congress AAFS 528A and B.

42. "Los aguinaldos"

Recordings: UT Folklore Center F102-5.

43. "Señora Santa Ana"

Durán, p. 9; one text with music. Saldívar, *Historia de la música*, p. 204; one text with music. Mendoza, *Lírica infantil*, pp. 21-25; twelve texts, eleven musical examples.

Recordings: UT Folklore Center F91-11, F106-9.

44. "Don Pedrito Jaramillo"

For background on Don Pedrito, see Dodson (1934 and 1951) and Romano.

Recordings: UT Folklore Center F121-8.

45. "La realidad"

Paredes, "Ballads of the Lower Border," p. 40; one text without music. Mendoza, *Romance y corrido*, pp. 674-675; one text with music.

Recordings: UT Folklore Center F101-7, F116-3, F127-5.

46. "El huérfano"

Mendoza, *La décima en México*, pp. 187-192; four texts without music.

Recordings: UT Folklore Center F97-3, F133-1.

47. "La chiva"

Paredes, *Folktales of Mexico*, pp. 185-186, 235; one text with music. Mendoza, *Lírica infantil*, pp. 149-152; two texts with music. See also Schindler, no. 171; one text with music.

Recordings: UT Folklore Center F131-3.

48. "El charamusquero"

Mendoza, *Romance y corrido*, pp. 406-407; three texts, one musical example.

Recordings: UT Folklore Center F134-8.

49. "Trigueña hermosa"

Jovita González, pp. 115-116; one text and first four bars of tune. Mendoza, *La canción mexicana*, pp. 260-261; one text with music, obtained from Manuel M. Ponce.

Recordings: UT Folklore Center F78-2.

50. "La negrita"

Recordings: UT Folklore Center F114-2.

51. "La tísica"

Paredes, "Ballads of the Lower Border," p. 32; one text without music. Mendoza, *La canción mexicana*, p. 448; one text with music. See also Schindler, no. 893; one text with music from Soria, Spain.

Recordings: UT Folklore Center F108-6, F122-3.

52. "A las tres de la mañana"

Paredes, "Ballads of the Lower Border," p. 31; one text without music.

53. "Andándome yo paseando"

Vázquez Santa Ana, pp. 121-122; one text without music. Mendoza, *Romance y corrido*, pp. 333-334; one text without music.

Recordings: UT Folklore Center F106-3.

54. "El colúmpico"

Campos, *El folklore y la música*, pp. 120, 283; one text with music.

Recordings: UT Folklore Center F103-2.

55. "La borrega prieta"
Recordings: UT Folklore Center F109-1.

56. "Malhaya la cocina"
Campa, *Spanish Folk-Poetry*, pp. 186-187; one stanza without music. Campa notes versions in Spain, Puerto Rico, Argentina, and Chile.
Recordings: UT Folklore Center F107-6.

57. "Dime sí, sí, sí"
Recordings: UT Folklore Center F93-7.

58. "Carta escrita sobre un cajón"
Recordings: UT Folklore Center F106-8, F116-7.

59. "El crudo"
Moncada García, pp. 26-27; one text with music. Personal communication from Professor Moncada, June 16, 1972: "Was sung in Jalisco around 1901."
Recordings: UT Folklore Center F100-1.

60. "Bonita esta tierra"
Recordings: UT Folklore Center F106-10.

61. "Desde México he venido"
Recordings: UT Folklore Center F133-2.

62. "Los mexicanos que hablan inglés"
Campa, *Spanish Folk-Poetry*, p. 214; two texts without music. Compare also p. 215. Hiester, p. 27; one stanza without music.
Recordings: UT Folklore Center F103-4.

64. "Mucho me gusta mi novia"
Compare García Cubas, p. 439, "Las margaritas," from U.S. occupation of Mexico City, 1847.

65. "Ya se va la televisión"
Recordings: UT Folklore Center F134-7.

66. "Tex-Mex Serenade"
Recordings: UT Folklore Center F134-5.

GLOSSARY

acordada A special body of armed men, authorized from time to time in some localities of rural Mexico in past generations. These bodies had extraordinary police and judicial powers to capture and execute highwaymen, thieves, or smugglers. Their popular label, *acordada*, stems from the institution of such a body in 1710, authorized by a viceregal order or *carta acordada*. (No. 34.)

agarrón A fight; any violent encounter, verbal or physical. Also may refer to the act of seizing violently on something. A play on these two meanings is intended in "El capitán Hall," when the Ranger captain is depicted as involved in an *agarrón* with a side of beef. (No. 16.)

albur y tecolote Names of Mexican card games of the nineteenth century. Metaphorically, to know how to deal *albur* and *tecolote* is to be an expert. (No. 9.)

alburuzero Noisy boaster, braggart. Variation of *alborotero*, a regional form of *alborotador*, probably influenced by *alburero*, one addicted to *albures* or verbal dueling. (No. 34.)

allá, al mismo precio de At U.S. prices, *allá* (over there) being the American side of the Border. People in Mexico paid extremely high duties for imported textiles. (No. 34.)

ancón A remote part of the countryside; usual dictionary definition is "bay" or "corner." (No. 23.)

anisado Any drink flavored with anise; in Border usage, however, usually refers to anise-flavored tequila, said to be particularly potent and therefore a preferred item in the smuggling trade during Prohibition times. (Nos. 26, 35.)

arrastrado Derogatory term in Mexican Spanish, similar to "low-down" or "no-account" in American English. (No. 1.)

arroba Old Spanish weight, equivalent to twenty-five pounds. (Nos. 3, 4.)

atole Gruel made of boiled corn meal, often flavored or mixed with milk; was a staple in the poor Mexican's diet. (No. 2.)

azúcar cande From the Arabic *as-sukkar* and *qand;* crystallized or rock sugar, rock candy. Cf. English "candy" and the American song "Big Rock Candy Mountain." (No. 3.)

Belén An infamous jail in Mexico City, torn down after the Revolution. (No. 29.)

bola A great number of persons, animals, or things. To live in the midst of excitement: *vivir entre la bola*. To have a gay, boisterous time: *andar la bola*. (Nos. 12, 53.)

Bola de Oro A dry-goods store in Matamoros, Tamps., widely known for several generations. (No. 34.)

bolón   A very great number; augmentative of *bola*. (No. 16.)

bragado   Said of an animal with brisket and forelegs of a color different from the rest of its body. Also "brave, aggressive" of a person; "mean, vicious" of animals. (No. 12.)

bueyes al nopal   *Buey* (ox) is one of the many variants of *cabrón* (cuckold, bastard). Cattle were often fed nopal cactus that had been scorched to burn off the thorns. (No. 16.)

cabeza de puerco   Hypocrite, double-crosser. (No. 37.)

camandulero   Sly, cunning, treacherous. (No. 27.)

caporal   Boss of a group of cowboys. (No. 12.)

cargo   In context, a job in the Díaz government. Alludes to practice during the Porfirio Díaz regime of offering government employment to celebrated guerrillas or bandits in order to bring them under control. (No. 34.)

carquís, baile de   No commentator on Mexican Spanish known to me has been able to etymologize this term, but Border people are definite as to its meaning. They define it as *baile de categoría*, a formal or elegant ball. *Carquís* could be a corruption of *cariz* (aspect), or it may be a Hispanicized form of some foreign term, like *garsolé*, which see. (No. 31.)

carrillera   Cartridge belt. (No. 23.)

Carrizales   Popular rendering of El Carrizal, where a battle between Carranza troops and elements of Pershing's punitive force occurred in 1916. (No. 31.)

catear   To conduct a search in someone's house after forcible and unauthorized entry. (No. 14.)

cauteloso (a)   Used in the sense of "artful" or "cunning," rather than "cautious." (No. 6.)

cazar   To hunt, and by extension to ambush an enemy. May be used without modifier, as in *lo cazó*, but most often found as *cazar como a un venado*, from the practice of still-hunting deer. (No. 35.)

Chaguito   Double diminutive of Santiago (Santiago→Chago→Chaguito). (No. 23.)

charamusca   Mexican candy much like hard caramel, in the form of chewy little bars. (Nos. 48, 63.)

cherife mayor   The sheriff of a county, in Border Spanish; sheriff's deputies are known as *cherifes*. (No. 18.)

chimal   From Náhuatl *chimalli*, a round shield; applied by frontier Mexicans to the round shields of the Comanches and other Plains Indians. (No. 7.)

coba, dar la   To trick or swindle by means of smooth talking. (No. 29.)

coche coche chino   Phrase used to call hogs at feeding time. (No. 4.)

colar   In general Mexican usage, a synonym of *andar* or *moverse*, to go or to move (intransitive). *¡Cuela!* is equivalent to "Move!" or "Scram!" (No. 24.)

colateral(es)   The altars on either side of the main altar; in popular Mexican usage, any altar. (No. 2.)

cometa   Refers to Halley's comet, which had appeared with unusual brilliance in 1910, the year before the taking of Ciudad Juárez and the crumbling of Don Porfirio's power. To many the world over, the comet's appearance had presaged wars, social upheavals, and the fall of governments. Europeans had to wait until 1914 to see such prophecies come true, but Mexicans saw their fulfillment in the fall of Porfirio Díaz's thirty-year dictatorship. (No. 27.)

comisión   *Posse comitatus*. Cf. *andar en comisión*, used in reference to a police officer when he is on duty. (No. 14.)

como era un americano   The meaning of *como* seems to be "even though," instead of "because." (No. 20.)

compadre, comadre A form of ritual brotherhood existing between the parents of a baptized child and the child's sponsors or *padrinos*. In Mexico, the *compadrazgo* relationship may be achieved through other forms of ritual. (No. 58.)

conducieron Dialectal form of *condujeron*, third person plural of the preterite of *conducir*. (No. 4.)

cuadro Cadre or squad; in present context, a firing squad. (Nos. 29, 40.)

cuanto-cuanto, darse un To have it out, to settle things by fighting. (No. 15.)

cuera Rawhide or leather jacket worn by frontier cavalry in colonial times and retained by vaqueros as a protection against Indian arrows. (No. 12.)

cuerda Line of prisoners tied to each other, as in the North American chain gang. To be *en cuerda* is to be a prisoner. (No. 46.)

dipo Railroad station; from the English "depot." (Nos. 21, 37, 62.)

Duval Reference is to Duval County, in Texas. In the 1950s the political machine in Duval was under fire from the state government, and Texas Rangers were involved in the investigations. (No. 66.)

embalar Literally, to tie up into a bale or package. In present context, to round up cattle into a compact bunch. (No. 12.)

enchivarrado Said of a vaquero wearing chaps *(chaparreras)*, also known as *chivarras* because they often were made from goat hide. (No. 12.)

enganche, enganchista *Enganchar* means to hook; by extension, to recruit soldiers or to contract laborers. The labor contracts entered into by migrant workers, and the group of contracted laborers as well, are called *enganches*. The *enganchista* is the labor contractor. Incidentally, the down payment on an installment purchase is also called an *enganche*. (No. 13.)

esp'rimentar Variant of *experimentar*; in present context, to be a learner or a greenhorn. (No. 12.)

estarjado (a) Bruised, injured. Variant of *estragado?* (No. 58.)

fiscales In present context, officers of the law; contrasted with peaceful civilians, *pacíficos*. (No. 24.)

flete Freight charges; freighted goods. *Como flete:* like a bundle of merchandise. (No. 32.)

For(o) West Fort Worth, Texas. (No. 13.)

frontino Animal with a blazed face. (No. 12.)

garsolé No dictionary that I have consulted contains this word, which is quite common among Border Mexicans and Mexican-Americans throughout the Southwest. A sunbonnet or sunshade, used in former times by stylish women and still in use by women working in the fields. Apparently from the French *garde-soleil*. (No. 62.)

guayabas en los magueyes, buscando Looking for figs among thistles. (No. 55.)

hilacha, darle vuelo a la To live it up, paint the town red, have a ball. (No. 53.)

horma de su zapato, hallar la To meet one's match. (No. 19.)

huelga, hacer To have a good time, to make merry. (No. 8.)

indiana Calico, a printed cotton cloth. (No. 34.)

insortar Action taken by the law when it declares a man wanted and puts up a reward for his capture. Professor Ramón Martínez-López has suggested that *insortar* derives from *exhortar*, used in Spanish legal terminology under the same circumstances (see Paredes, *With His Pistol in His Hand*, pp. 222-223). This word has been reported only on the Texas-Mexican Border. *Insortar* and the Martínez-López etymology are also found in Mendoza, *Lírica narrativa*, p. 205, along with a Border variant of "Gregorio Cortez"; but this is an obvious though unacknowledged borrowing from *With His Pistol in His Hand*. (Nos. 14, 18.)

juíscle Whisky. (No. 19.)

Lerinbor Leavenworth Federal Penitentiary. (No. 37.)

liacho A bundle, of clothes or such; by extension a bedroll or one's personal possessions, especially when used in the plural: *mis liachos.* (No. 15.)

maletero In present context, a small-time smuggler; perhaps from the ordinary meaning of *maletero*, a porter or carrier of luggage, influenced by *maleta*, in the sense of "bungler." (No. 34.)

medio Short for *medio real;* half a *real* or about six centavos. (No. 48.)

melado Honey-colored, applied to horses; *corrido* heroes often ride horses of this color. (Nos. 12, 17.)

menudo Tripe; also the rich, spicy stew made from tripe, hominy, red chile, and herbs, supposed to be the best cure for a hangover. (No. 3.)

merengue In Mexican popular usage a kind of candy, a meringue tart topped with nuts, fruit, or jelly. (No. 63.)

metralla For *ametralladora*, machine gun. (No. 27.)

mono(s) Pictures, in the colloquial sense. Cartoons, movies, images on TV. (No. 65.)

muina Variant of *mohina;* anger, displeasure. (No. 5.)

navaja, no te amelles Proverbial expression used in response to a crude or obvious attempt at flattery. A metaphorical extension of better-known Mexican terms such as *hacer la barba*, to flatter, and *barbero*, a flatterer. (No. 61.)

nublinazo A heavy mist. (No. 18.)

oportuno Apparently used here for *inoportuno*, untimely, inopportune. (No. 28.)

pabellón, manchar el To besmirch one's colors, to do a base or cowardly deed. Among Border rancheros used as a tongue-in-cheek euphemism for *manchar el pantalón*, to soil one's trousers out of fear. Also found as *manchar la garra*. (Nos. 21, 22.)

palanqueta Candy bar made of a paste of *piloncillo* and *pinole*. (No. 63.)

Parián Name of the main marketplace in Mexico City, 1696-1829. In northern Mexico and the southwestern United States, the main marketplace in any town. (No. 28.)

parpadeada A blinking; refers to the flutter or blinking of the image on a TV set. (No. 65.)

pato Fool, patsy, fall guy, cuckold. Used as an insulting term in general, especially in the phrase *Eres pato y te apesta el buche.* (No. 61.)

patón Bigfoot, from *pata*, an animal's foot or paw; one of the many Mexican terms applied to the Anglo-American. (No. 31.)

peineta Ornamental comb traditionally worn by Spanish and Spanish-American women as part of their hairdo. (No. 3.)

perfilar To do *perfilado*, a lacelike decoration on the borders of linen handkerchiefs, napkins, tablecloths, and the like, resembling cutwork. The pattern is sketched out by cutting away certain threads in the cloth, one thread at a time. The remaining threads are tied together to finish the pattern. (No. 1.)

perros jaunes Bloodhounds, literally "hound dogs." (No. 18.)

picota In the sense of "gibbet" or "pillory." (No. 9.)

piloncillo Brown sugar loaf in the form of a truncated cone. Formerly used both as a candy and to sweeten coffee. (No. 63.)

pinole Toasted corn ground to a fine powder and mixed with brown sugar. May be dissolved in water to make a beverage, but it is eaten dry just as often. Hence the saying *El que tiene más saliva traga más pinole.* (No. 2.)

plantación Agricultural lands in general, not "plantation" in usual U.S. sense. (No. 13.)

platiada Variant of *plateada*, used as a noun; a large quantity of silver. (No. 17.)

poleo Mexican herb (*Clinopodium laevigatum*, according to Santamaría, *Mejicanismos*) used in folk medicine for ailments such as fright sickness or soul loss; pennyroyal tea. (No. 34.)

posesionado Wealthy, possessing an abundance of worldly goods. (No. 45.)

primo(s) Cousin(s); one of the many names for the North American. "Cousins" because they are the children of Uncle Sam. But since *primo* may also mean "fool" or "simpleton," there is a double edge to the term. Usually *los primos* (the cousins) rather than *nuestros primos* (our cousins). (No. 63.)

rabón Bob-tailed. Here applied to the soldiers of Porfirio Díaz, perhaps because they wore their hair cut very short. A more common name for the Díaz soldier was *pelón*, hairless or close-cropped. (No. 15.)

raza, la As in common Mexican usage both north and south of the Border, the meaning is simply "the people" or "our people." (No. 31.)

real Formerly a coin worth one-eighth of a peso or 12½ centavos, hence pesos were "pieces of eight" in the buccaneer's vocabulary. The coin no longer exists, but the *real* still is used as a unit of monetary value in some parts of Mexico and the southwestern United States. Cf. the American "bit." (Nos. 47, 48, 62.) Short for *real de minas*, a town or settlement where gold or silver is being mined. (No. 60.)

remuda A string of saddle horses, as in the southwestern United States, usually kept together by an old mare, often belled. (No. 58.)

rinche A Texas Ranger and by extension any Anglo armed and empowered by the law to kill Mexicans: posseman, vigilante, border patrolman, and in one ballad members of Pershing's punitive force chasing Villa. (Nos. 18-21, 26, 31, 35, 36, 38.)

San Diego afamado San Diego, Texas, rather than the better-known port city in California; "famed" because of the Plan de San Diego, the manifesto issued in connection with the Pizaña-De la Rosa uprising of 1915. (No. 35.)

Senate hearings Reference to the Red-hunting activities of Senator Joseph R. McCarthy during the early 1950s. (No. 66.)

sesteadero Place where cattle or sheep rest during the heat of noon. In the Border country, usually a stand of mesquite or huisache. (No. 1.)

sobremano, andar To be without adequate support or preparation. (No. 23.)

suaderos Variant of *sudaderos*, saddle blankets. (No. 16.)

suidad Common variant of *ciudad*, city. (No. 13.)

tamal turco Along the Border, a fat *tamal* without meat filling but with raisins, almonds, and other ingredients mixed into the dough. Differs from the *tamal borracho*, also fat and without meat filling but without raisins or almonds. *Turcos* and *borrachos* are made from *tamal* dough left over after all the meat has been used for filling in other kinds of *tamales*. (No. 2.)

tirano Cruel, unjust. (Nos. 14, 32.)

tlaco Coin used in colonial Mexico, valued at one-eighth of a *real*, or about 1½ centavos; in current usage, a penny. (No. 3.)

toro, éntrenle al Phrase used to encourage or deride those who hesitate before a difficult or dangerous enterprise. Literally, "face up to the bull." (No. 34.)

torrija Bread dipped in batter and fried; resembles French toast. Also *torreja*. (No. 3.)

torzón Diarrhea in livestock; figuratively, gripes caused by extreme fright. (No. 16.)

tragedia Synonym for *corrido*, a ballad. (No. 28.)

trifulca A brawl. (No. 21.)

turrón A kind of nougat, made of almonds, nuts, and honey. (No. 63.)

vacilar To have a good time; to joke or banter. (No. 17.)

venduta   Auction. (No. 17.)

ventajoso (a)   Superior, therefore giving one an advantage; *arma ventajosa,* a superior firearm. (No. 14.)

West Kentockle   West Kentucky, conceived of as a separate state, like West Virginia. (No. 13.)

yanqui   North American in general. (No. 61.)

zuavos   The crack French infantry regiments wearing colorful uniforms that were part of the French forces invading Mexico; by extension, French soldiers in general. (No. 10.)

BIBLIOGRAPHY

Campa, Arthur L. *Spanish Folk-Poetry in New Mexico.* Albuquerque: University of New Mexico Press, 1946.

_____. *The Spanish Folksong in the Southwest,* University of New Mexico Bulletin, vol. 4, no. 1. Albuquerque: University of New Mexico Press, 1933.

Campos, Rubén M. *El folklore literario de México.* Mexico: Talleres Gráficos de la Nación, 1929.

_____. *El folklore y la música mexicana.* Mexico: Talleres Gráficos de la Nación, 1929.

Denisoff, R. Serge. "Songs of Persuasion," *Journal of American Folklore* 79 (1966), 581-589.

Dobie, J. Frank. "Versos of the Texas Vaqueros," in *Texas Folklore Society Publication no. 4* (Austin: the Society, 1925); reprinted as *Happy Hunting Ground* (Hatboro, Pa.: Folklore Associates, 1964), 30-43.

Dodson, Ruth. *Don Pedrito Jaramillo: Curandero.* San Antonio: Casa Editorial Lozano, 1934.

_____. "Don Pedrito Jaramillo: The Curandero of Los Olmos," in *The Healer of Los Olmos and Other Mexican Lore,* ed. Wilson M. Hudson, Texas Folklore Society Publication no. 24 (Dallas: the Society, 1951), 9-70.

Durán, Gustavo. *14 Traditional Spanish Songs from Texas,* transcribed from recordings made by John A. Lomax and others. Washington, D.C.: Pan American Union, 1942.

Espinosa, Aurelio M. "Romancero nuevomejicano," *Revue Hispanique* 33:84 (April, 1915), 446-560; 40:97 (June, 1917), 215-227; 41:100 (December, 1917), 678-680.

_____. "Los romances tradicionales en California," in *Homenaje ofrecido a Menéndez Pidal* (Madrid: Casa Editorial Hernando, 1925), vol. 1, pp. 299-313.

Gamio, Manuel. *Mexican Immigration to the United States: A Study of Human Migration and Adjustment.* Chicago: University of Chicago Press, 1930.

García Cubas, Antonio. *El libro de mis recuerdos.* Mexico: Arturo García Cubas, Hermanos Sucesores, 1905.

Goldfinch, Charles W. "Juan N. Cortina, 1824-1892: A Reappraisal." M.A. Thesis, University of Chicago, 1949.

González, Jovita. "Tales and Songs of the Texas-Mexicans," in *Man, Bird, and Beast,* ed. J. Frank Dobie, Texas Folklore Society Publication no. 8 (Austin: the Society, 1930), 86-116.

González, María del Refugio. "The Spanish Folklore of Webb and Zapata Counties." M.A. Thesis, University of Texas, 1952.

Hansen, Terrence L. "*Corridos* in Southern California," *Western Folklore* 18 (July, 1959), 203-232; (October, 1959), 295-315.

Hiester, Miriam Webb. "Los Paisanos: Folklore of the Texas-Mexicans of the Lower Rio Grande Valley." M.A. Thesis, University of Texas, 1954.

Limón, José E. "El Primer Congreso Mexicanista de 1911: A Precursor to Contemporary Chicanismo," *Aztlán: Chicano Journal of the Social Sciences and the Arts* 5:1 and 2 (1974), 85-117.

McNeil, Norman Laird. "*Corridos de Asuntos Vulgares:* Corresponding to the *Romances Vulgares* of the Spanish." M.A. Thesis, University of Texas, 1944.

———. "*Corridos* of the Mexican Border," in *Mexican Border Ballads and Other Lore,* ed. Mody C. Boatright, Texas Folklore Society Publication no. 21 (Austin: the Society, 1946), 1-34.

McWilliams, Carey. *North from Mexico: The Spanish-Speaking People of the United States* (Philadelphia: J.B. Lippincott, 1949; reprinted, New York: Greenwood Press, 1968).

Mendoza, Vicente T. "Algunas canciones y sátiras durante la Intervención y el Imperio," in *Temas y figuras de la Intervención* (Mexico: Editorial Libros de México, 1963), 17-30.

———. *La canción mexicana: Ensayo de clasificación y antología.* Mexico: UNAM Instituto de Investigaciones Estéticas, 1961.

———. *Cincuenta corridos mexicanos.* Mexico: Secretaría de Educación Pública, 1944.

———. *El corrido mexicano: Antología.* Mexico: Fondo de Cultura Económica, 1954.

———. *La décima en México.* Buenos Aires: Instituto Nacional de la Tradición, 1947.

———. *Lírica infantil de México.* Mexico: El Colegio de México, 1951.

———. *Lírica narrativa de México: El corrido.* Mexico: UNAM Instituto de Investigaciones Estéticas, 1964.

———. *El romance español y el corrido mexicano: Estudio comparativo.* Mexico: UNAM Instituto de Investigaciones Estéticas, 1939.

Moncada García, Francisco. *Estudio analítico de la canción "Los magueyes."* Mexico: Ediciones Framong, 1971.

Muro, Amado. "Cecilia Rosas," *New Mexico Quarterly* 34:4 (Winter, 1964), 353-364.

Paredes, Américo. "Ballads of the Lower Border." M.A. Thesis, University of Texas, 1953.

———. "El concepto de la médula emotiva aplicado al corrido mexicano: Benjamín Argumedo," *Folklore Americano* 19-20 (1971-72), 139-176.

———. "Corrido de Jacinto Treviño," in *Buying the Wind,* ed. Richard M. Dorson (Chicago: University of Chicago Press, 1964), 483-485.

———. "*El corrido de José Mosqueda* as an Example of Pattern in the Ballad," *Western Folklore* 17 (1958), 154-162.

———. "Folklore and History," in *Singers and Storytellers,* ed. Mody C. Boatright (Austin: Southern Methodist University Press, 1961), 56-68.

———. *Folktales of Mexico.* Chicago: University of Chicago Press, 1970.

———. "José Mosqueda and the Folklorization of Actual Events," *Aztlán: Chicano Journal of the Social Sciences and the Arts* 4:1 (Spring, 1972), 1-30.

———. "*With His Pistol in His Hand":* A Border Ballad and Its Hero. Austin: University of Texas Press, 1958.

———, and George Foss. "The *Décima Cantada* on the Texas-Mexican Border: Four Examples," *Journal of the Folklore Institute* 3:2 (August, 1966), 91-115.

Pierce, Frank Cushman. *A Brief History of the Lower Rio Grande Valley.* Menasha, Wis.: George Banta, 1917.

Romano, Octavio Ignacio. "Charismatic Medicine, Folk Healing, and Sainthood," *American Anthropologist* 67 (1965), 1151-1173.

Saldívar, Gabriel. *Documentos de la rebelión de Catarino E. Garza.* Mexico: Secretaría de Agricultura y Fomento, 1943.

_____. *Historia de la música en México: Epocas precortesiana y colonial,* colaboración de Elisa Osorio Bolio. Mexico: Secretaría de Educación Pública, 1934.

Santamaría, Francisco J. *Antología folklórica y musical de Tabasco,* arreglo y estudio musical de Gerónimo Baqueiro Foster. Villahermosa, Tabasco: Publicaciones del Estado, 1952.

_____. *Diccionario de mejicanismos.* Mexico: Editorial Porrúa, 1959.

Schindler, Kurt. *Folk Music and Poetry of Spain and Portugal,* ed. and with an intro. by Federico de Onís. New York: Hispanic Institute, 1941.

Simmen, Edward, ed. *The Chicano: From Caricature to Self-Portrait.* New York: New American Library, 1971.

Suplemento de Navidad, *Revista de Revistas,* December 21, 1912.

Sydow, C.W. von. "Folktale Studies and Philology," in *Selected Papers on Folklore,* ed. Laurits Bødker (Copenhagen: Rosenkilde og Baggers Forlag, 1948), 189-219; reprinted in *The Study of Folklore,* ed. Alan Dundes (Englewood Cliffs, N.J.: Prentice-Hall, 1965), 221-242.

Taylor, Paul S. *Mexican Labor in the United States,* vol. 2: *Bethlehem, Chicago, and the Calumet Area,* University of California Publications in Economics, vol. 7. Berkeley: University of California Press, 1932.

_____. "Songs of the Mexican Migration," in *Puro Mexicano,* ed. J. Frank Dobie, Texas Folklore Society Publication no. 12 (Austin: the Society, 1935), 221-245.

Vázquez Santa Ana, Higinio. *Canciones, cantares y corridos mexicanos,* prólogo de Luis González Obregón. Mexico: Imprenta M. León Sánchez, 1925.

INDEX